Matchbook

THE DIARY OF A MODERN-DAY MATCHMAKER

Samantha Daniels

Simon & Schuster
NEW YORK LONDON TORONTO SYDNEY

SIMON & SCHUSTER
Rockefeller Center
1230 Avenue of the Americas
New York, NY 10020

For information regarding special discounts for bulk purchases,
please contact Simon & Schuster Special Sales at 1-800-456-6798
or business@simonandschuster.com.

Designed by Ruth Lee-Mui

Manufactured in the United States of America

10 9 8 7 6 5 4 3 2 1

Library of Congress Cataloging-in-Publication data is available.

ISBN 0-7432-6953-5

In memory of my mother,

Donna Daniels,

whose strength, creativity, and love

inspires me daily

"You get invited, you go.
You never know . . ."

—Edith Kessler, My Grandmother, 1983

Contents

Disclaimer	*xi*
Introduction	*1*
September	11
October	39
November	65
December	93
January	117
February	143
March	167
April	193
May	217
June	239
101 Dating Thoughts	*269*
Acknowledgments	*279*

Disclaimer

Dear Readers,

Please keep in mind that this book is written from a place of love—love of my clients (platonic, of course) and love of Matchmaking. In the book, I try to find the humorous side of my life, my clients, and myself because my business is hard and draining, so without humor I would never survive in it. Matchmaking has a huge burnout rate. As a matter of fact, when I first went to start my business and I was doing research, I spoke to three retired Matchmakers and they all told me the same thing: don't go into the business. They felt that it was too difficult and too heart-wrenching to listen to people's personal problems and heartbreak, hour after hour, day after day. I took the plunge anyway, but some days, I have to admit, it's hard to be in the biz. It's hard to be the person so many people are counting on for their happiness for the rest of their lives. I know, cry me a river, but without the ability to make fun of myself, my life, and my clients, I would have been just another retired Matchmaker by now.

In some way, I love each and every one of my clients. In the book, I call them "Desperados" and give them funny nicknames only to make light of my world and the craziness of it, not because they are in fact desperate or undesirable. In reality, my clients are actually the cream of the singles crop. I am contacted by hundreds of people every week who want to become one of my Desperados and have me help them find a husband or a wife. I'm now somewhat like a talent agent, picking through and choosing among all the people who contact me, trying to decide who to "represent." Believe you me, these people are anything but desperate. They are handsome and beautiful, wildly successful in their careers, accomplished in a variety of hobbies, and have very interesting personalities; the only thing they don't have is a significant other, and they are tired of looking, too busy to look, or no longer know where to look, which is why they contact me. The really desperate ones I leave to one of the Maries. You will meet the Maries in the book—they are the other Matchmakers.

At the end of the day, I work really hard to help all my clients achieve their ultimate personal goal: love and marriage. So I spruce them up, coach them, pick at them, criticize them, and give them a hard time, all because I want them to be the best daters they can be so that they can meet that perfect person . . . and fall in love . . . and get married . . . and live happily ever after.

Also, keep in mind that in some ways, although I hate to admit it, one could say that I am the biggest Desperado of them all. As a Matchmaker, I probably meet as many, if not more, men than any other single woman in existence (or at least in New York or Los Angeles), but I have yet to settle down. I don't have a special pass to the "Marriage Promised Land," unfortunately, and I personally screw up dates and relationships just like everybody else, sometimes even more so, though, given my profession, I really should be the perfect dater. However, I'm not a perfect dater, but I keep trying because I am a firm believer in love and marriage. And I remain very effective at helping other people with their dating issues because I can remain objective and impart to others the knowledge I have acquired over the past many years in this business.

To sum up (so that you can get to reading the juicy stuff): five years and forty-seven marriages later, I am very good at my job. I am moderately okay at my own dating. I am very good at being brutally honest with my clients. And I continue to poke fun at my life and my clients on a daily basis so that I can continue to do what I love best, Matchmaking. The characters I have created for you in these pages are composites inspired by a variety of my best and brightest and most colorful clients and friends. Nobody in the book is real. I have gone to great lengths to maintain everyone's anonymity because, at the end of the day, I take my business very seriously.

I hope you will appreciate my humor, my candor, and my life. Happy reading.

Samantha Daniels,

DESPERADO #1

Matchbook

Introduction

Yesterday I was a divorce attorney. Today I am a Matchmaker. Crazy, I know, but that's my life.

I went to law school and decided to pursue a career in divorce law basically because my mom suggested it and it seemed like a good idea at the time. I didn't put all that much thought into it. My mom said that maybe divorce law would be the most people-oriented, and I agreed.

I practiced divorce law for a while, and it was in fact very people-oriented, but in an unpleasant way: divorce lawyers do help people, but at a time when they are at the lowest point in their lives and depressed all the time, which in turn makes them depressed all the time. I soon discovered that most divorce attorneys burn out quickly.

To ward off potential burnout, I began throwing parties. I took over swanky clubs early in the evening, before their regular patrons showed up. I gave the management a small cut of the door. I charged $20, collected by one of my "bouncers" (my brother Sean or my brother Christopher), and I had several scantily clad "playmates" (younger sisters of my brothers' friends) stand by the door and collect business cards so I could invite the attendees to the next shindig. Each evening would end with me lying on my bed surrounded by hundreds of $20 bills and hundreds of business cards from all of my new friends.

I loved throwing the parties, I loved meeting the new people, and I found that I was really good at remembering little factoids about people and at introducing couples. Sometimes I couldn't help myself. I would see a guy on one side of the room and a girl on the other, and I would grab them by their hair and pull them toward each other, make the introduction, and walk away. Time and time again, I heard through the grapevine that these couples were dating, had gotten engaged, or had even gotten married. Soon, according to the Jewish faith, I earned a place in heaven, since more than three couples had ended up getting married through my introductions.

For years I continued to start up all sorts of singles businesses—group-share vacation homes, coed back-to-summer-camp weekends, more and more singles parties, singles newsletters—all the while subconsciously wanting to be a Matchmaker but refusing to step up to the plate and officially declare my Matchmakerhood. I remember with particular fondness my idea for a coed back-to-summer-camp weekend: I envisioned three hundred or so single people traveling to a sleep-away camp in upstate New York to relive their camping days. Originally, the fantasy was that I would sell so many tickets that I would have to put people on a waiting list, but the reality was that I dragged myself and my very patient boyfriend at the time up and down the beaches of Southampton, approaching strangers and trying to convince them to purchase tickets so I wouldn't have to cancel the weekend. Though a near disaster with no profit whatsoever, the weekend wound up being a lot of fun, and I walked away with a few thousand new friends whom I had met combing the beaches.

I also recall with fondness my newsletter, called "In the Loop," which I decided to mail out to all my new friends. In it, I pontificated about being single in New York, suggested great places to go as a single person, and wrote a Dear Samantha column in which I responded to people who wrote in with serious dating dilemmas (I made up more than a few for the purpose of the first column). I promised that the newsletter would come out monthly, but it never came out again, and in retrospect I'm not sure all that many people missed it.

In the beginning, some of my singles ventures were harebrained, to say the least, but through it all I built up a pretty kick-ass mailing list of the best and the brightest young singles in the New York tristate area. I probably could have handled being a divorce lawyer for a few more years, but what was the point? I always wanted to have my own business, to be something, someone a little different, even unique. And I definitely had a following in the singles world, so I decided to become, as far as I knew, the world's youngest Matchmaker.

Becoming a full-fledged Matchmaker didn't just happen to me overnight. It took me quite some time to get comfortable with the notion that people were going to be thinking of me as a yenta. In my mind's eye, a yenta was that ugly, loud woman in *Fiddler on the Roof,* complete with a hair growing out of her chin, or one of the real-life Matchmakers—let's call them the Maries. There were a bunch of Maries, based in New York, who had cornered the Matchmaking market. The Maries were the kind of Matchmakers I didn't want to be. They just had a way about them that I didn't like: they seemed pushy and aggressive and seemed like they would never take no for an answer. I never really understood why anyone would put one of them in charge of their personal life, but I guess when there's only one game in town, beggars can't be choosers. The thought of being equated with a Fiddler Matchmaker or one of the real-life Maries was a little more than I could handle for a really long time.

Meanwhile, several of the Maries got wind of me. One called me trying to convince me to hire her to find me a husband. That was just plain comical because at the time I was 26, had dates up the wazoo, and the last thing I was looking for was a husband. Another Marie found me some time later and invited me to a singles party she was having, and she suggested that I come and pay $150 so I could check out her roster of eligibles. I told her I would think about it, and that seemed to satisfy her enough to let me off the phone. I immediately called my mom to laugh about the phone call, but my mom became serious and said I should go to the party and do some research.

I guess my mother knew I was destined for this business. Back when I was in law school, a friend of mine moved to Houston and signed up at a local synagogue for a dating service that charged $100 as an initiation fee and then $2 per introduction; she met a man who ultimately became her husband that way, and that got me thinking. I soon developed a preoccupation with starting a dating service. Of course I wanted to charge a little more than $2 a date, and I wanted to add another dimension and make the dates be only over drinks, but I liked the overall concept of it. So I came home one day and told my mom that I wasn't going to be a lawyer, I was going to be a business-woman and I was going to open a dating service. My mother laughed and said that I was in law school and naturally I would be a lawyer. *Of course that's what a Jewish parent would say!* At any rate, a few months after my mother instructed me that I would be a lawyer, she saw an advertisement for a dating service that introduced people over drinks and over lunch. She cut out the article, handed it to me, and said with a smile that maybe I was on to something, but that something should be after law school was over. The article fueled my interest, but I was already in law school, so I figured I should listen to my mother this time and put aside my entrepreneurial aspirations temporarily.

Getting back to my many Maries story, when I called my mom and told her about Marie's invitation to her party, my mom said that since I had always had a preoccupation with dating services, I might as well swing by the event and see what was what. So I went to the party alone because I didn't think it was fair to ask one of my friends to fork over $150 for what might be a terrible party. And for me, it was a terrible party—for starters, the youngest man there probably could have been my father, and the people were just not my speed. I learned a lot about this Marie, her clients, and her business. Later she apologized profusely for the age discrepancy and swore on a stack of Bibles that it wasn't always like this. *Right, Marie.*

Time went on and I kept matching people up at all my crazy singles events, but I hesitated about opening a real Matchmaking service because of my preoccupation with becoming a Marie. I actually spent time in therapy obsessing over this. My therapist finally convinced me that I didn't have to be a Marie at all. I guess that's why therapists get paid the big bucks; finally the lightbulb went on in my head and I realized that I would never be a Marie because that just wasn't me, and that I would succeed by offering New York singles an alternative.

Soon I set out to come up with a *brand* of Matchmaking that would be cool. I decided right then and there that if I started a service and the only people who called were unattractive and awkward and hadn't had a date in years, I would go out of business immediately and that would be that. I had no interest in becoming the Queen of the Undatables in New York. I determined that the only way I would stay in business and make my service work would be to find people who were socially adept and desirable and to convince them that they truly *wanted* and *needed* my help. Ultimately, I wanted a service that would not just be successful but even fashionable and hip.

First step, allow people to think that mine was not a dating service, even when it was one. I know it sounds crazy, but it worked. I decided that I would offer one-on-one dates, but I would also offer introductions over small group dinners. This way, people who weren't comfortable admitting that they joined a dating service could gloss over the truth by saying they joined an eating club or a dining club in which a small group of people would get together every so often to eat in a trendy restaurant. They could leave out the part about the real objective of the group being to sit with single people looking to meet a mate. *Good idea, right?* I thought so. And that's what I did. I came up with a corny name, Table for Two (or More), which basically meant that you could sit at a table for two (a date) or a table for more than two (a group dinner). Then I put together a very classy brochure that explained the idea, and I mailed it out to seven thousand of my closest friends. These seven thousand friends had been enjoying free introductions over the years simply by attending my events, so they knew that I knew a lot of people, and this was the key to starting and succeeding in the Matchmaking business. So I hooked up a business phone line and I sat and waited and waited and waited for the phone to ring.

The phone did ring every once in a while. Mostly the callers were telemarketers, along with a few lonely hearts and one Marie saying that she thought it strange that I would mail my brochure to her (I didn't, of course), but she would love to talk to me about my business. *Sure, Marie. I've got some calls coming in right now. Let me ring you back.* In other words, buzz off. I'm the competition now.

Eventually a few of the people seemed a little less undatable than the rest of the callers, so I started meeting with them. I figured at the very least it would be good practice for when the heavy hitters got around to calling—*after all, they were very busy people.* The first girl I met with was Jennifer, 29, cute, and worked in advertising. Of course I didn't tell her that she was my first. But she was my first, and I asked whatever questions I thought I needed to ask her. When she told me that she was surprised that I didn't ask her certain things during our meeting, I immediately added them to my repertoire. I met with her for two hours, for free, and she never signed up. *Oh well, her loss.*

The next guinea pig was a girl with curly blond hair, petite, probably not over five feet tall. She was an opera singer who had an unusually high-pitched voice. She wasn't bad-looking, but I remember thinking that her voice would probably drive the guys crazy, because it was definitely going to drive me a little nutty. I wondered if it was worth it to take her money. But then she offered it, my first $1,000 check, and guess what? You got it—her voice became a little less irritating. As I continued to putter along, a phone call here, a lonely heart there, I would alternate between thinking I was the world's biggest idiot for trying to start my own Matchmaking business and optimistically telling myself that the business would take off any day, I just had to be patient.

Then came my big break. About six months into my entrepreneurial venture, I met a reporter for a major magazine. She asked what I did and I told her. As a matter of fact, I talked her ear off about how fabulous my business was and how successful I had been, how my phone was ringing off the hook and how I had the hippest people in New York as clients—although I was unable to name names. The fabulous business part was true. The cool client list was maybe a bit of an exaggeration; I kind of left out the part that the clients weren't all that cool *yet*. Well, guess what? She bought it. A few days later, she called me and said she wanted to write a story about me and my booming business, complete with a photograph and everything.

And she did just that. Not only did she write an article, but she wrote a glowing, positively enviable article. She made my business sound unbelievable, sought after by only the most desirable singles in New York, with waiting lists and unpublished business lines. Once the article came out, I realized that now I might just have the opportunity to be the stellar Matchmaker that I knew I could be. I could help a lot of people who needed my help, and they would want it once they knew I existed.

The day that the magazine hit the newsstands I was very nervous. It was do-or-die now. If the datable people called—*no, when they called*—I needed to be able to put my money where my mouth was or I would be out of business very quickly.

My anxiety was well founded because I was besieged with fifty-seven phone calls before noon! Every person who called wanted to meet with me in person. The writer of the article became my favorite person on the planet! The power of the press was truly remarkable! When I woke up that Tuesday morning, I had a whole bunch of clients, but not all of them were that set-uppable. By lunchtime, I had fifty-seven A-list "Desperados" who wanted to meet with me and pay $1,000 each for my expertise and services!

Up until that point, I had been meeting with everyone for free, but all of a sudden my time was becoming valuable. I panicked and called my "business adviser," a guy I had dated who went to Harvard Business School. I asked him what to do. Harvard boy told me that when I called back the next five people to schedule appointments, I needed to tell them that there was a $200 consultation fee to meet with me. And then I needed to see what happened: the less serious callers would balk and, for those who didn't, I would have myself a consultation fee.

I did just that for the rest of the afternoon, and guess what? No one batted an eyelash. So *much for that plan.* By the end of day one, ninety-six people had called and I was truly panicking. It would take me two months to meet with ninety-six people. So I called back Harvard boy and asked for some new advice. He said, tomorrow morning tell the first five people I called back that I had a $400 consultation fee and see what happened. He said that some people would think that number was way too steep—*I don't know, buddy, they were supposed to think that of the $200 fee; I am becoming quite desirable, you know*—and then I would have a manageable number of people to meet with for $400 each. So the next morning, I started asking $400 to meet with me, little old me. And just as Harvard boy predicted, some people said buzz off, and the more committed people said fine. And so the kookiness began. . . .

September

September is an interesting month for Matchmaking. I guess every month is, but September is especially interesting because many peeps come my way. First of all, summer has ended. Why is this significant? Because a lot of single people were expecting to meet the person of their dreams over the summer—when people are tan and look better, healthier, and thinner; when women wear sexier clothing and show more bare skin, which attracts the hombres; when there are a lot more people out and about, happy and interacting; and when people take vacations to try to meet other people. Moreover, in New York, a lot of people buy shares in vacation houses in the Hamptons and these houses are hookup central. There we have tons of single men and women all looking to meet and be met. Unfortunately for many single New Yorkers, they meet a lot of people, have a lot of flings, but at the end of August they're still alone. That's where I come in. They gave it the summer, four months and still nothing, so they come to me, hat in hand. Yes, I might be sloppy seconds in this situation, but I am okay with that.

DESPERADO #1

Yours truly, Me

I am definitely "Desperado #1." I should be in a great relationship, but I am not. I should be married, but I am not. I guess there are no "should be's" in dating land, but there are. I really haven't wanted to be married until recently, but now, well, now I think I am ready. My guy of the moment: Jerkoff. My guy of the past three years, on and off: Jerkoff. The guy of my future: probably not Jerkoff, but I just can't get him out of my system. I am such a Desperado.

Tuesday, September 6

I took a table at the Regency hotel's Library Bar and held court all day. I chose one in the corner, off to the side. I wanted to try to establish it as my regular table so that the waiters would get used to me and would know where to send my peeps. I chose to sit there because it was private but also because it gave me a full-on view to the door, so I could see each Desperado walk in. I scheduled three back-to-back consultations. Twelve hundred bucks in five hours seemed like a very doable number before the day started, but let's just say after the third Desperado of the day, I needed a big break or a big drink.

DESPERADO #2

Mr. Gazillionaire

The hundred-million-dollar man with nine houses—my first gazil-lionaire and a real blue-blooded WASP to boot. He sat down at the table and the first thing out of his mouth was, "I am worth in excess of a hundred million dollars." Period. Then he took a sip of his drink. I wasn't quite certain what to say to that. My left eye started twitching a bit because he was my first gazillionaire. I looked at him more closely. He was very tall, about six feet four, with light brown hair, deep brown eyes, little horn-rimmed glasses, in a preppy country-club getup. He went on to explain that it was important for me to know just how wealthy he is so that I would introduce him only to women who would be comfortable with a man so affluent. *I could probably think of a few.* He described the nine homes he had around the world. There was one in Palm Beach for winters. There was one in Park City for all his skiing needs. There was one in Connecticut, a big-ass country house. An apartment in Paris, for when he goes shopping. Two apartments in Manhattan, one on Fifth Avenue to impress the ladies and the other on Central Park South, for when he's slumming. One apartment in Vegas for when he goes gambling. One Tuscan villa in Italy for when he wants a dose of romance. And one more in Southampton so he can go to Southampton Bath and Tennis. What kind of girls did he ask me for? Supermodels, of course, but WASPy ones!

DESPERADO #3

Brad Pitt Guy

Brad Pitt Guy. He sat down at the table decked out in stylish New York garb—Gucci loafers, a blue blazer, a Façonnable shirt, and a Rolex white-gold Daytona watch. He was medium height, maybe five feet ten, balding, and claimed to be very wealthy. *He clearly didn't know about my hundred-million-dollar man or he wouldn't have been bragging.* We went through the consultation, and when I started describing the women I wanted to introduce him to, after every description he would say, "She sounds good, but would you introduce her to Brad Pitt?" I kept looking at him more closely to see if somehow I was missing the resemblance or relationship to Brad Pitt himself. Finally, I had to say what had been dancing around my head for quite some time: "Buddy, first of all, Brad Pitt is not available right now. He's with Jennifer Aniston. Second, I don't know Brad Pitt so I have no idea who I would introduce him to, and third, hate to break it to you, but you are *not* Brad Pitt!" He chuckled and said, "Well, there's no reason why I can't date like he does." *There isn't?*

DESPERADO #4

Miss 39

The "I'm a 39-year-old female corporate exec and I don't know where the time has gone but I need to meet a man immediately" woman was my first freaking-out female. She was near tears through the whole meeting. She showed up in her very corporate, very expensive-looking black Armani pantsuit with a silk blouse underneath and an Hermès scarf tied around her neck. She clutched her sleek black Chanel handbag throughout our entire meeting, as if letting it go would make her lose her composure completely. She was very pretty, about five feet two, with straight red hair, pretty skin. She was very smart, went to Mount Holyoke for undergrad and Wharton for her MBA, owned her own corporate recruiting firm, and was making a boatload of money, but she was all alone and she was sad, really sad. She went on and on, rationalizing to me (or maybe to herself) how she got to be thirty-nine and alone. I wish she had come to see me or somebody like me when she was twenty-nine, not thirty-nine, and she probably wishes that, too. I want her to become my poster child to help convince women in their late twenties and early thirties that they are not too young to focus on their personal lives; they are not too young to hire me. I liked her and I wanted to help.

BACK TO
High-Pitched Opera Girl

I decided to offer Opera girl her money back. I had accepted her as a client out of fear way back when, but in actuality she doesn't really rise to my Desperado standards. In addition to her earsplitting voice, she turned out to be neurotic and impossible to satisfy. She would grill me on the men's horoscopes and whether their moon signs corresponded with her sun sign. She'd insist that I find out how many women each man had slept with in the past two years because she had this crazy notion that if he had slept with more than six or less than two women, he was undatable, and she wouldn't meet him. She seemed to want to be difficult just for difficulty's sake. I thought it was better that we part ways. I sent her money back in full, even though I had provided her with three dates. I've come to the conclusion recently that I only want to work with people I really think I can help and who are actually open to being helped. She was not. She seemed okay with the termination, probably because working with me had cost her virtually nothing.

Miss Fantasy

This Desperado came in through a friend of a friend. She was a striking girl, about five feet five, with jet black hair, wispy bangs, and piercing green eyes. She had a lot that she wanted to talk to me about. She came armed with a lot of preconceived notions about the person she was "supposed" to be with. I explained that there were no "supposed to's" at my Table. And she retorted that she didn't know about the way things were at my table, but there were plenty of "supposed to's" in her life. I asked her what some of them were. Well, she is supposed to be with a tall guy, a Jewish guy, a guy who wants to live in Westchester and not any other New York suburb, a guy who likes warm-weather vacations (not cold ones), a guy who can play golf with her dad and ski with her brother, who makes at least $500,000 a year, who wants her to have only two kids, a boy and a girl, the girl first.

And then she took a breath. "Is that all?" I teased with a grin on my face. She was looking for the waiter so she didn't catch my sarcasm. "Well, actually . . ." I interrupted her, waved my hand in front of her face to get her to look at me, and said, "Miss Fantasy, that's enough for right now. I need to explain to you that I don't have a button on my computer that allows me to manufacture men, as much as I wish I did. So we are going to go through all of your 'supposed to's' and figure out which ones are really deal breakers for you and which ones are things that you would *like* in a guy but you could *deal* with if they didn't exist. Okay?" "No," she said. "No?" I was surprised at her nerve. She explained, "All of these things are important. In my mind, this is the guy I see myself with." I said, "Exactly, Miss Fantasy, this is in your mind, in fantasyland, but here we deal in reality, not fantasy, and if you would like to work with me and actually get married to a mortal human being instead of an imaginary friend, you will let us do this my way. You might see that not every single thing you mentioned is really a 'supposed to.' Is that okay with you?" I stared at her intently. "Do I have a choice?" she asked. I said no.

So we began. Why does he have to be tall? "Well, I don't know. Ever since I was younger, I liked tall guys." "Well, Miss Fantasy, what would happen if he were five feet eight but terrific in every other way?" "I guess that would be okay." "Great, then tall is no longer a 'supposed to.'" "But wait," she stammered. "I like tall." "I know you like tall and I will try to make them tall, but if I come across a shorter guy, not a midget but a shorter guy, and I think he is good for you, I need some leeway, okay?" Still doubtful, she said okay.

I looked down at the notes I had scribbled while she had been talking. "Next, religion as a must-have is okay. A lot of people feel that way, but I want it to be an absolute only if it means something to you personally, not just to your great-great-great-grandmother." "It means something to me personally as well," she said. "Okay, then we will keep only Jewish on the list." And I put a checkmark next to religion on my notepad. I moved on. "Wanting to live in the New York suburbs and only in Westchester, not any other one," I read from my notes. "I understand why you would want to live in Westchester—it's a very nice place—but what would happen if I found you a great guy and he wanted to live in, say, Connecticut. Could you handle that?" She tilted her head sideways and tentatively said, "Maybe. But I prefer

Westchester. My parents live there, and I grew up there." I tilted my head the opposite direction and said, "How about this? I will put down that you prefer a guy who would be open to living in Westchester but that I shouldn't rule out a great guy who would prefer another New York suburb for his own reasons. Can you live with that?" She tilted her head back and forth, weighing what I said, and agreed. *We were getting somewhere.*

I took a sip of my Diet Coke. "Next, let's deal with warm-weather vacations, golfing, and skiing all at once. Yes, I agree all of those things would be nice, but don't you think you could compromise, maybe alternate on the warm and cold vacations? After all, where will he ski if you always go to warm weather? And don't you think that if you love someone, your dad and brother would be okay with him not playing certain sports?" She looked dejected. "But, Samantha, I always imagined that my husband would go golfing at the country club with my dad and go skiing with my brother. It's where they will bond." I looked at her again. "Look, Miss Fantasy, you are not getting any younger, I am sorry to point out, and you really can't afford to keep waiting to find all these things in one person, because you may never find them, and then years will pass and you will still be alone and your family won't bond with anyone about anything." She started tearing up. "Look, don't get upset. There is hope yet, but let's try to live in reality for a while. What do you say?"

She ran out of steam and said she would be flexible about the rest of the things, just please get her married. I said I would try; and as I said it I fervently hoped that she could live in the real world like she said she wanted to. In the meantime, while she is adjusting, I know just the guy for her. Brad Pitt Guy clearly does a lot of fantasizing himself, and he's Jewish, makes a lot of money, and he plays golf and skis. *Hmm, a match?*

Saturday, September 10

The weekend—I'm tired. It's hard work to sit for five days straight and listen to people's stories of heartbreak and difficulties. They look at me like I am God. *Don't know yet if I should tell them I'm not, or just play along for a while.*

BACK TO

Mr. Gazillionaire

Got a phone call from Mr. Gazillionaire—he really enjoyed meeting me and thinks I will be able to find him his wife. *I hope so.* He asked if I thought I might be able to introduce him to his first woman quickly because at the beginning of October he has to go to a black-tie fundraiser for the Princess Grace Foundation—$10,000 a plate—and he would like to have a date for it. I laughed and said that I didn't see why not. *I guess I could always suffer through as his date in a pinch.* He said thanks, he would appreciate that.

BACK TO

Miss 39

Now that I had taken all this money, I needed to start setting up the peeps. I began with Miss 39. She was at the top of my list for the moment because time was of the essence for her. I thumbed through my database of 35- to 50-year-old RFM (Ready for Marriage) guys:

What about Bill, 39, the architect with a big nose? No. Robert, 46, divorced with two kids? No, probably won't want more kids. Phil, 40, investment banker? A little too boring. Alan, hmm. Alan could be interesting. . . .

Alan, 44, has never been married. He is successful but not setting the world on fire, and cute enough (meaning I would be okay with his looks if he came to my door). Alan e-mailed me back and told me he thought Miss 39 was too old for him. He had a lot of nerve—he should only be so lucky to get Miss 39. *Who does this guy think he is?*

So I picked up the phone and called Alan. I told him that he needed to trust me, that he had nothing to lose, and that he was getting a highly coveted, expensive service, mine, for free by going out with Miss 39, so he might as well go. He whined that she was too old. I couldn't resist telling him that he "played closer to 50 than to 40, and that a 39-year-old woman would be exactly the right age to really appreciate him." Nothing doing, he continued to refuse. I wasn't going to beg, so I hung up the phone and scratched him off my list. *Database down to 6,999.*

Continued my crusade to set some of my ducklings up on some dates. I pulled up my SJF (Single Jewish Female) list for Brad Pitt Guy.

Hmm, for Brad Pitt Guy, I need a hottie but a little spoiled and not an intense intellectual. Hmm . . . What about Jennifer, 32, blond, in advertising? No, too cutesy. Maybe Brooke, 29, investment banker? No, she's a workaholic. What about Joanne, 26, mature for her age? No, too outdoorsy for him. Julia, 28, PR girl from Long Island? Yes, she's a good one. But maybe Miss Fantasy is better for him. Let me call Miss Fantasy and see if she wants to meet Brad Pitt Guy. Otherwise I will go with Julia.

Miss Fantasy

I called Miss Fantasy to tell her about Brad Pitt Guy. I had a feeling that these two would really hit it off. I could just *see* them together. She answered and was all chitchatty, treating me like I was her best friend. I started telling her about Brad Pitt Guy but she interrupted, "Samantha, I think I am going to hold off on your service for a little while. I want to put it on hold." *What?* "Oh-kay, any reason why?" I asked a little apprehensively. I guess I was nervous that she was changing her mind. She must have realized what I was thinking, so she said, "Oh no, it has nothing to do with you. I love you and I want you to keep my money, but just put the membership on hold. You see . . ." Her voice got lower as she started confiding to me, "You see, I decided it's time to explore the possibility of being intimate with my best guy friend. He and I have been friends forever and I guess I have always wondered if we could be more than that, but I have always been afraid to cross the line because I was afraid of ruining our friendship—but at the end of the day, maybe it will be worth it and it won't ruin it at all." She paused to take a breath, and then continued. "Recently, we have been spending a lot of time together, he just broke up with someone, and for the first time in a very long time we are both single. I want to go for it, I have to, I think he could be 'the One.' I think he has all of my 'supposed-to's.'"

I chuckled in relief. *Phew, I didn't want one of my first A-list clients to back out before I even set her up!* "What do you think?" she asked. "Well, I say go for it. Let's face it, once he marries another girl, she will probably think that the two of you are too close and will put the kibosh on your friendship." *Been there, done that.* She snorted. I continued, "My suggestion, go with the obvious choice, have him over for dinner, drink a lot of wine, cozy up on the couch to watch your favorite movie, and then go in for the make-out kill." "You really think that's the best way to handle it? I was thinking maybe I should invite him out for a drink and just discuss it with him." *Bad idea!* I shook my head, "No, I don't think you should discuss it. Guys hate discussions, and it could get really awkward. Go with the getting-drunk thing, and go for it. If it works, then great, and if he resists you can always blame it on the vino, laugh it off, and go back to being best friends." She hesitated and then said, "I guess you're right. Do you have a best guy friend who you wonder about sometimes?" I laughed and said, "Don't we all! Hey, good luck, and keep me posted."

BACK TO
Brad Pitt Guy

Since it wasn't going to happen with Miss Fantasy, at least not right now, I called Julia, my second choice, and pitched Brad Pitt Guy to her. She got all excited and agreed to go out with him. I told her (and giggled while I said it) that he was sort of like the Brad Pitt of the Long

Island Jewish set *or at least he wanted to be!* She told me that Brad Pitt was her favorite actor of all time. *Perfecto!*

BACK TO

Miss 39

After a while, I went back to Miss 39. This time, I pulled up 45- to 50-year-old men on the DM (divorced men) list and picked Mr. 50. Miss 39 said she didn't really want 50 or divorced unless I thought he was exceptional. Well, this one was exceptional because he wanted to meet Miss 39, and that was just exceptionally good news for the moment!

Friday, September 16

Afternoon. I think the staff at the Regency hotel is starting to wonder what I do for a living. Every day I sit at my table in the corner, facing the door, and I interview a variety of good-looking people for hours at a time. Definitely don't want them to think that I am a madam. One waiter, a very nice guy, seems to be observing me. He puts extra cashews in the nut portion of the snack tray, I guess because I only eat those. And yesterday when I arrived, he immediately asked me if I wanted cranberry juice with no ice or a hot chocolate with whipped cream on the side. I laughed and said that I must seem awfully high maintenance if he actually remembers the drinks I order. He laughed with me and said that sometimes I'll order a Diet Coke, but he knows that I like it in the bottle with a straw. *Okay, I am crazy!* I'm pretty sure that if I left the magazine open to my article, this waiter would probably notice it and then everyone would be clear about what I do and what I *definitely* don't do for a living.

DESPERADO #6

Mr. Bonus with the Pinkie Ring

"I want to pay you a big bonus if you get me married" were the first words out of this Desperado's mouth. *What's a girl to do?* I came to the consultation expecting the guy to pay me my $400 fee and maybe agree to sign up as a client, paying the standard $1,000 for twelve dates. But this man said that he wanted to give me an incentive to find him his wife, so he wanted to pay me my usual fees but he also wanted to pay me a bonus bigger than any bonus anyone else had ever offered. Little did he know that he was the first one to offer, but I know how to play poker, so I said with a confidence that I was not feeling, "Well, the highest bonus I have ever been offered was pretty high." He countered with, "Well, how about $50,000? Is that higher than anyone else?" "Fifty-one thousand would be," I said boldly, figuring this was a reasonable exaggeration of the truth. He came back with, "Well, I will pay you $60,000 to be safe." *Okay, that sounds safe to me, too.*

Turns out this guy is a real character. He comes from a very wealthy family, has a male relative who is a big political figure, has been to the White House many a time, and hobnobs with the highest of ritzy political sets. And of course, he too wanted a gorgeous girl, tall, with very large boobs, was what he "ordered." However, he himself would not quite make it into the gorgeous category. He looked more like a penguin: dark hair, and a little oval in his physique. He dressed the penguin part as well, in a shiny black suit, an oxford white shirt, and a narrow black tie. He looked like he was stuck in the eighties. And to top it off, there was his pinkie ring and his slight New York accent. I wanted to whip him into shape, but I wasn't really sure how to broach the subject. *I am not sure I am equipped to be so brutally honest with my Desperados, but that will come in time. . . .*

Note to self: Learn to critique people to their face!

MAYBE FOR ME GUY

Jerkoff

Jerkoff has been in and out of my life for the past three years. I met him through a mutual friend. We have a lot of the same friends, we enjoy the same things, and we look good together. He is five feet eleven, with light brown hair, green twinkly eyes, and the cutest sexy smile that just makes me melt. His clothes just seem to work on him without his really trying. We are perfect on paper, and we should be right together, but we aren't. We fight all the time because I want more and he can't give it. He owns three companies and spends so much time working that he doesn't have time for us.

Well, I finally did it once and for all. I broke it off with him, and even when he flashed his pearly whites, I didn't cave. I have told him it is over, a million times, but this time I mean it. He and I are through, finito, kaput. He is never going to change, he is never going to focus less on work and more on me. He is never going to deal with his issues, stop drinking, and stop being an egocentric commitmentphobe. It's time to start practicing what I preach, or at least trying to. *Wow, a single*

Matchmaker—is that weird? But what's a girl to do? I don't want to be a single matchmaker forever. I'd like to be a married matchmaker, so being a dating Matchmaker in a crappy relationship is not going to get me down the aisle. For better or for worse, I need to move on.

BACK TO

Mr. Bonus with the Pinkie Ring

Made some calls today for Mr. Bonus with the Pinkie Ring—I pulled up my VHW (Very Hot Women) file:

> *I could try Diana, 33, five feet nine, graphic designer? No, maybe for his second date. Jeannie, 29, five feet eight, with big boobs? No, she's too country-bumpkin. Melanie, 32, five feet ten, with a bit of an accent? Yes, her. No, wait, what about Miss Gold Digger, five feet ten, very attractive, part-time model, full-time sales rep, likes a man with cash? Perfect.*

I called Miss Gold Digger. I figured Mr. $60,000 Bonus would get his beauty queen, and in order to get her rich guy, Miss Gold Digger might overlook the cheese factor a bit. *Perfect match.*

TABLE CHANGE

Effective immediately, I have a website. I heard today that a few of the Maries have created websites for their businesses. I decided that I needed to get busy if I want to keep up with the Joneses.

Note to self: Hire a Web designer and get the site up immediately.

Monday, September 19

I took a break yesterday and today from meeting with new people. Matchmaking is draining. Got an e-mail from Brad Pitt Guy and he told me that he's having his date tonight. He's very excited. Of course, he asked me if Brad Pitt would like her. I told him that I wasn't even going to entertain that question. Miss 39 called me yesterday. She didn't like the way Mr. Divorced 50 sounded on the phone. "I don't want to go," she wailed. "You have to go," I ordered. "You need to trust me. I'm sure that he was just preoccupied at work." Finally she conceded. "Okay, I'll go, but I just want it on the record, I am nervous and I don't think he is good for me." I reassured her, realizing that I'm not just a Matchmaker—I'm now both a therapist and a cheerleader! Mr. Bonus with the Pinkie Ring also complained about how Ms. Gold Digger sounded on the phone, so I told him that she was truly gorgeous and he should cut her some slack. When he heard she was five feet ten, weighed 120 pounds, and had a D cup, he stopped complaining and said he would deal with her voice.

Tuesday, September 20

Tonight I am supposed to have my first date since I embarked upon my newfound singlehood. I met him at a party over the weekend. We only talked for a few minutes and then our mutual friend called to say he was interested, so I figured I should accept a date with him. He doesn't know what I do for a living, and it's probably better that way. He did ask me at the party, but I played coy and said I never talk about work after 10 P.M. at night; he bought it. So now we have a date. I am a little scared to go—I haven't dated in a while and especially not since I became a "famed" Matchmaker. I wonder if I can avoid talking about what I do for a living all night. Probably not. *How should I say it? Will it freak him out?*

Note to self: Figure out my rap.

BACK TO
Brad Pitt Guy

Got a phone call first thing from Brad Pitt Guy. "I hated the girl!" he shrieked. I took a bite of my Pop-Tart and asked him calmly, "Was she pretty?" (Yes.) "Was she smart?" (Yes.) "Did you have things in common?" (Yes again.) "So what was the problem?" "She was too ordinary!" he said, sighing with exasperation. "Brad Pitt would never give her the time of day." *Okay, I'm ready to slit my wrists now. This guy is truly starting to frighten me. Why the preoccupation with Brad Pitt?* "Don't you worry," I said, trying to cajole him. "I have many more women for you to meet, and we will find you a great one, someone Brad would be into as well, okay?"

Note to self: Find a therapist in New York to align with and make Brad Pitt Guy her first client.

DESPERADO #7
Mr. Her

Had a noon meeting with a new client. He sat down at the table and right away I was uneasy. Something just felt off. I couldn't put my finger on it. First of all, his looks were odd. He wasn't fat or bald or grotesque or anything, he was just unattractive, not pleasant to look at. And he looked much older than the 30 years that he was. This didn't concern me, though, because there are plenty, I repeat plenty, of women in New York City who will date Frankenstein if he has a few bucks (*although it probably wouldn't be a bad idea to see photos before I meet with the peeps, just in case*).

As the meeting went on, I started noticing a lot of things that weren't adding up. He was a painter but hated museums. He was a big exec at a prestigious investment bank but he hated wearing a suit and he hated authority. He lived on the Upper East Side yet he hated his conservative, well-bred neighbors. He had a strange vibe. So toward the end of the meeting I just said, "I'm not sure why, but I am sensing a lot of contradictions in your life." And then I paused and took a sip of my hot chocolate to give him a chance to respond. He hesitated with an almost tortured expression on his face, as if trying to make up his mind about something. But then he seemed to grow calmer. "Well, there is one more thing, and I have been debating whether or not to tell you." I thought he was going to tell me that he was trying to figure out if he was gay.

Wish that had been his issue. No such luck. With that, he took a crumpled photo out of his battered brown leather wallet. He wrote something under the picture and handed it over to me. The photo was of an atrocious-looking woman, and under it he had written the words *hetero* and *TS. Okay, a puzzle and this guy was expecting me to solve it and quickly.* I am a fairly conservative Upper East Side gal, but all of a sudden it dawned on me what and who I was looking at. *Hetero* obviously meant heterosexual, and *TS* meant transsexual, and the photo of the awful woman was my guy as he used to be—an ugly woman! My eyes started blinking rapidly and I felt a little light-headed as I slowly said, "So you are transsexual who is heterosexual?" If you knew me even a little bit, you would understand the comedy in my sitting across from this guy—*I mean girl, I mean guy.*

I started sweating. I felt a little out of my league. *I wasn't even sure I understood what that meant. Did it mean that he was a man who used to be a woman who is now attracted to women, making his heterosexuality connected to who he is today, or vice versa?* Clearly, whatever the circumstances, I knew that I would not be able to work with this person, but I knew I wanted to be—I had to be—professional. Who would I possibly set him up with? What was I supposed to do, send around an e-mail to my conservative, mainstream crowd in New York and ask if anyone was interested in going out with a guy who used to be a girl, used to have a vagina, and now has a penis and wants to have sex with women? The waiter came by, and I ordered a chardonnay. Though I never drink liquor during my meetings, suddenly I needed alcohol, a lot of it. The thing of it was, the guy was nice, and I felt sorry for him. He spent about fifteen minutes explaining to me what it meant to be a hetero TS and what type of people he dated, thereby answering all the questions floating around in my head. Of course, I barely heard any of the explanation. I was too focused on steadying my pulse.

Then almost to himself, he said, "So what do you think?" *What I thought was I needed to screen people better so I would never be sitting across from a hetero TS again without being prepared!*

I told him that I needed to think about it, but I wasn't sure that I would be able to help him. I explained to him that the thing about taking someone on as a client was that I needed to have people to set the client up with, and unfortunately I didn't think I knew anyone with his same orientation. He looked sad. He asked me what I thought he should do. I didn't know. I said I would give it some thought and we could be back in touch.

He left. I canceled my date and took a Valium. I needed one. And then I went to Jerkoff's apartment and spent the night. I know I broke up with him, but sometimes drastic situations require drastic measures.

Friday, September 23

When I got home from Jerkoff's apartment, I already had a ten-page fax from Mr. Her with all sorts of different information on transsexuality. My head started pounding. It was only 10 A.M. I looked it over briefly and then I did what any conservative Upper East Side girl would do: I called his voice mail at the office and left him a message saying that there was no way I could do this and that I was sorry. And I wished him well. I felt uneasy most of the day, icky actually. I felt bad that I couldn't help him, a little lame that he frightened me, but mostly relieved.

Note to self: Do not meet with anyone in person unless and until they forward a photograph. If the person does not look set-uppable, don't meet with them. It's easier to turn someone down in advance than to have to say no after the fact.

BACK TO

Mr. Gazillionaire

I pulled up my SCF (Single Christian Female) list, 25- to 35-year-olds for Mr. Gazillionaire.

> *Maybe Devon, 32, from Darien, Connecticut? No, she's a little too horsey, I mean, too into her horses. Kim, 34, from Palm Beach, in equity research? No, too negative. Leila, 29, from Arlington, Virginia? No, wait, what about that Goldman Sachs WASP girl? Perfect!*

Miss Goldman Sachs WASP is the typical blond, blue-eyed WASP. (You know the type, perky-looking, with sensible Ferragamo pumps, a Ralph Lauren navy blue suit, and delicate pearls.) I called Miss Goldman Sachs WASP and I sold my gazillionaire to her. It wasn't very difficult. What girl is going to turn down nine houses? I did spend some time explaining to her that his lifestyle was a little high profile, and making sure that she would feel comfortable at $100,000 table charity events and dinners at the White House. She assured me that all that was old hat to her; she had dated a very influential, moneyed congressman for two years, and she knew the drill. Perfect!

BACK TO

Miss 39

Got a phone call from Miss 39 reprimanding me. "Samantha, Mr. 50 is 50!" she yelled. I said calmly, "I know that, Miss 39, but thanks for pointing it out." She didn't think I was funny. "He's too old for me," she wailed. "Did you have fun together?" (Yes.) "Did you laugh?" (Yes.) "Did you have things in common?" (Yes again.) "So what was the problem?" I asked. "He was just too old. How can I go out with a 50-year-old? It feels so depressing. Where did the years go? I should be with a guy who is 39, not 50." "No, Miss 39, what you *should* do is give him another date if he asks for it. And in the meantime, I will look for your next guy in the late thirties / early forties pool. But you need to keep in mind that 50 is the new 40, and you need to get comfortable with that somehow because if you continue to discriminate this way, soon we will be discussing 60 as the new 50 for you!"

BACK TO

Mr. Bonus with the Pinkie Ring

Got a call from Mr. Bonus. He liked Miss Gold Digger a lot. "She was smokin' hot," he said. *Oh goody.* I started fantasizing about the new apartment I would buy with his bonus. But then I got an e-mail from Miss Gold Digger; she needed to talk to me on the phone immediately. *Oh no, it's only 11 A.M.* I waited until about one to call her. We chitchatted at first and then she launched in, "He tried to have phone sex with me. Mr. Bonus called me from the taxi on his way home and started talking dirty to me." "What!" I said. *There's no phone sex allowed on my company's first dates. Didn't he read the manual?* I was shocked. *Mr. Bonus, a little kinky, I had no idea!*

"Gosh, I am so sorry, Miss Gold Digger, this is completely unexpected," I said. She agreed and said, "Yes, it shocked me. I can't figure out what would make him think it was okay, and right after he dropped me off, too. I was really surprised." Then she confided that they did talk about sex a lot during the date. *Why, if you didn't want to encourage him?* She also inquired if Mr. Bonus's relative was really Mr. Famous Senator. When I confirmed his political connections, she paused and said, "Well, maybe I would give him one more chance. Maybe he didn't mean to offend me." *Hmm, maybe or maybe not, go figure the rationalization from Miss Gold Digger.* Whatever. Clearly they should go out again, or have phone sex, whichever works.

Note to self: Before setting up Mr. Bonus with the Pinkie Ring again, have the phone-sex conversation with him. Not every girl might be so understanding.

NOT FOR ME GUY
Mr. Sweet Nothings

Rescheduled my date from the other night. This guy seemed fine at first. He was nice-looking, not all that tall, about five feet eight, and he had a good build, brown wavy hair, and a lopsided grin that was appealing. But he was all about the sweet nothings—"Hey, *babe,* how are you? *Honey,* where do you want to go for dinner? *Baby,* I'll call you back. *Sweets,* have a good day." How could I not have noticed this at the party where we met? I probably could have dealt with one sweet nothing, maybe two, but fifteen of them was just over the top. I asked him straight out why he used so many endearments and he said, "I didn't even notice. It's just me, *babe,* chill out." "Do you say these sweet nothings to everyone?" I asked. He chuckled. "No, just to girls I like and my really good female friends." I wanted to believe him, but I didn't. He seemed so used-car salesman or Hollywood talent agent. I love endearments if they mean something, but not from a near stranger. Call me crazy, but I want to feel special and I want my own sweet nothing when the time is right.

Still . . . he was funny, and fun to be around. His laugh was infectious and I'm feeling like quite the Desperado right now. So I went out with him, twice actually, and I was just about to accept date three when the waitress walked by and my guy said, "Hey, *honey,* can we get the check?" Then I asked him, "Is that waitress a good female friend of yours or just a girl you like?" He didn't get my joke, which annoyed me because it wasn't that hard to get. I started thinking he was stupid, but then I realized he was just not my type. "Later, my *little cream puff,*" I said.

Tuesday, September 27

I forgot all about it, but I agreed to speak about dating tonight at the Learning Annex. After the week I was having, I wish I hadn't agreed, but my business adviser, Harvard boy, told me that it would be good for my career, so I said yes. It's crazy: women actually signed up to hear me speak about the do's and don'ts of dating. *Do I really have any words of wisdom on this subject?* Well, fifty women thought I did, so I had better come up with something. All the Maries speak at the Learning Annex, so I guess I need to do it to keep up with the Joneses again.

I was a little bit nervous because I remembered one unforgettable *Sex and the City* episode in which Carrie agreed to give a relationship seminar at the Learning Annex. Some pushy New York broad interrupted her and asked if Carrie was in a relationship herself. When Carrie said no, the broad asked, "Well, then, what authority do you have to advise us on our sex lives?" And then one by one the women left the classroom. After the break, Carrie came back to speak and there were only two women left. Yikes! *What if that happens to me? Damn the fact that I'm single. Maybe I should just lie and say I'm in a relationship. I did have ex-sex yesterday, does that count?* Oh God, a headache was developing quickly.

But I committed, so I went anyway and, sure enough, there was a colorful cast of fifty women sitting there, waiting to hear what I had to say. There were women of all shapes and sizes: a beaky woman who looked like a hungry bird, a woman who was wearing a straw hat that I was certain had something growing in it, a woman who looked like she was fifteen years old but turned out to be a Swedish nanny, even a senior citizen who walked with a cane and wore bifocals and who somehow thought my lecture could help her dating life. It was strange that all these women were gathered in one room, but it was even stranger that they had actually paid to hear me speak. *Were they on drugs?*

I started to feel guilty. I needed to teach them something; it wouldn't be fair otherwise. So I started speaking and instead of sticking to my planned lecture, I started talking about that *Sex and the City* episode. I put it right out there and told them that I was just like Carrie; I didn't have a boyfriend, my own dating life sucked, and anybody who wanted to give me a hard time about it could leave. Nobody made a move. Okay, good. Then I told them that the information I was presenting did not come from my own life because God knows that I personally have just as much trouble dating as everyone else does. I explained that *my expertise* came from all the things I had seen and heard while Matchmaking and, as a result, I had an insider's view on what works for men and what works for women.

They bought this explanation and so I continued. I covered a variety of dating do's and don'ts and gave them what I considered a lot of sound advice, things that perhaps they had never thought of before. First, I told them they need to be strategic in their dating. Then I told them that they always need to let the people in their lives know that they are single and open to being set up. I explained that a lot of times people won't even think to set someone up, so it is imperative to communicate one's willingness and interest to those around them. Then I told them that they need to ask themselves with whom they spend most of their time. Are these people the best people to surround yourself with? I explained that you can have friends who are good to confide in and go to the movies with but they aren't necessarily the best women with whom to go out manhunting. I asked them questions such as: Do your friends enhance your socializing abilities or detract from them? Are all of your friends prettier than you are and, as a result, do they always get the male attention and you go home alone? Are your friends unattractive physically and as a result no men approach the group? Do you hang out with women who resemble you physically and as a result there is constant competition for the men? I looked up midway through and saw a lot of women nodding their heads in comprehension and a few were even taking notes. I realized that these women were actually taking me seriously. I think I was good, really good. I guess I do have something to say, or at the very least I am a good bullshitter.

October

October, another interesting month for Matchmaking. There are the people who gave it September to see if any of their contacts from the summer would turn into something romantic. There are the people who gave themselves September to get over their summer breakup and now they're ready to hit the dating ground running. And there are the Jews who waited until after the Jewish High Holidays, thinking that they might see an old flame sitting in the service or that the real yenta in their life, their mother, might actually fixate on an interesting friend of the family (instead of the nightmare friend she always fixates on) while she's supposed to be fixating on the prayer book.

DESPERADO #8

The Girl I Always Thought Hated Me

This girl went to my college. I always thought she hated me and now she was sitting in front of me, wanting to pay me money to find her a husband. *Very strange.* Now she's a successful lawyer, doing antitrust litigation. She's pretty in a cute-as-a-button way, about five feet two, petite, with light brown kinky hair, and a sweet but maybe a little reserved manner. I realized fairly quickly that she probably didn't hate me in college—she was probably just nervous around people in general. I began to notice that she had trouble looking me in the eye. She kept looking away and she giggled a lot.

As we got into the consultation, she came right out and admitted, "I was shy in college but everyone thought I was snobby. I know that was the case. It's been my problem my whole life." Her eyes met mine briefly and gave me a more serious look. "What did you think of me in college?" *Here we go again.* It was a little early in the morning for the whole brutally honest thing. Oh, what the hell. This was part of my job now, so I told her, "I guess I thought you hated me. I think you're right that a lot of people felt the same way. I was actually pretty surprised when you called." There, I did it; I was proud of myself until she started to cry, and then I wished I hadn't even started. *Oh God, my first real crier. Miss 39 almost cried and so did Miss Excuse, but they kept their composure, thank God. This one, no such luck.*

I am so not good with tears. They scare me. (I had a friend in college who always cried. I couldn't take it so I finally told her that we could continue to be friends only if she promised never to cry to me again. She cried but said okay.) *Perhaps I should make a decree that there will be no crying at my Table or you will lose your seat.* I could probably decree no phone sex after the first date for Mr. Bonus with the Pinkie Ring, but I don't know about the crying edict. The Girl I Always Thought Hated Me finally wiped her face and rolled her eyes, clearly embarrassed that she was crying. To my surprise, I told her crying was good and cathartic, and she should feel free to cry to me anytime. *What was I saying?*

DESPERADO #9

Looks Good from Afar Guy

Back to the trenches. My consultation schedule is filling up. People are coming out of the woodwork. Today I have Looks Good from Afar Guy—he's the guy that my friends and I have been seeing around forever, and he looks soooo good from afar because he's tall, lean, and a great dresser. But then when you get up close, he's so boring that his looks don't help him. When he greeted me, he seemed very nervous. Immediately he asked if we could switch seats so he could have a view of the door. Throughout the consultation his eyes kept darting to the door as if he were expecting someone he knew, or someone who knew him, to walk in at any second. It turned out that he was hypersensitive about people knowing that he was working with me. He started off by saying, "I assume that our business relationship will stay within these four walls." "Don't worry, Looks Good from Afar Guy. I am like a steel trap, nothing gets out." Once I said that, we got up close and personal. Wouldn't my friends laugh if they knew?

BACK TO

Mr. Gazillionaire

Got an e-mail from Miss Goldman Sachs WASP. She had a great time with Mr. Gazillionaire. He took her for drinks and to the Princess Grace Foundation dinner. *Yay!* Then he invited her to Palm Beach for the weekend. Do I think she should go? *Wow! He works fast.* She asked me if I had heard from him. I e-mailed back that I had not and that I would be in touch when I did.

I called Mr. Gazillionaire and was all ready for him to thank me profusely, but instead he told me he was disappointed. *What!* Miss WASP was not pretty enough for him. I scolded him, "But didn't you invite her to spend the weekend with you?" He said he did because he had to. He has a function to attend and he needed a woman by his side who could chitchat finance, and clearly she could, but he had no interest in her other than that.

Oh boy, that sucks for Miss Goldman Sachs WASP. She likes him and thinks he likes her big-time. I tried to convince Mr. Gazillionaire that it wasn't really right to lead her on like that and that she really liked him, but he got annoyed and said, "Look, Samantha, butt out. Your job is to make the setups. After that everyone is an adult and can make their own decisions." I was stumped for a moment. He was right, of course, but inconsiderate, and I felt guilty having information that this woman deserved to know and not telling her. I wondered if there was some sort of Matchmaker oath, Matchmaker/client privilege. *Do I owe him this allegiance? Probably.* I promise the utmost discretion. Lying I don't promise, but I guess, for the moment, I should just let things play out between them; after all, they *are* both consenting adults. *That sucks!*

Mr. Priority

This guy came to the consultation and immediately said, "I don't want the usual deal. I want to pay you $5,000 to be a priority client." *Okay, no problem. I can prioritize you.* It became clear very quickly that this guy was used to being prioritized. His whole demeanor commanded respect, from his posture in his chair to the slow and deliberate way he spoke. He told me that he wanted to be at the top of my A-list, and when I met an amazing girl he wanted to be the first guy that I introduced her to. Sounded easy enough. I mean, call me crazy, but there is probably more than just one amazing girl out there, so I can probably spread the wealth and at the same time make him feel like he's my number one priority. No *problema*.

BACK TO
Looks Good from Afar Guy

Got a freak-out phone call from Looks Good from Afar Guy. He called his first date: she *sounded* awful, and he wasn't going out with her. "She was boring *(I couldn't believe the irony),* she didn't laugh at my jokes *(maybe they weren't funny),* and there is no way we were going to get along." I felt frustrated and defensive, so I said, "Now look here, Looks Good from Afar Guy. Who's the Matchmaker? I am. And I spent a lot of time picking this girl for you—she is pretty, she is smart, and she is funny. You will like her and she will like you. So you are going out with her and that's an order." He refused. I might be the Matchmaker, but he was the client and he paid me a lot of money and he didn't want to meet this girl, period. Fine, you win. I will come up with a new girl and get back to you.

TABLE CHANGE

Time to change the rules at the Table. Effective immediately, the clients are no longer allowed to speak to one another on the phone.

That's it—they are being punished. I don't want any more complaining phone calls like the one from Looks Good from Afar Guy. From now on, I will set up all the dates, and they will just show up and meet each other. This way, I no longer have to hear that they hate each other's voices or they are not bright and bubbly enough on the phone. I don't want to waste any more time coming up with dates for people just for them to call me and refuse to go. *So there!*

BACK TO

Mr. Priority

If I am going to prioritize Mr. Priority, I had better get cooking on his dates. I pulled out the VHW (Very Hot Women) list again . . .

> *What about Melinda, 33, bathing suit model? Maybe Betty, the radio announcer? No, too loud. Chrissie, 36, lawyer with big boobs? No, not interesting enough. Wendy, 35, blond with killer blue eyes? No, not impressive enough. Hmm, what about Miss TV Reporter . . . ?*

Most men in New York are hot for Miss TV Reporter. She has come-hither eyes and a sexy, flirtatious laugh. Everywhere she goes people recognize her. I figure with Miss TV Reporter, Mr. Priority would feel prioritized.

I left Miss TV Reporter a message on her voice mail, introducing myself and telling her that I wanted to introduce her to a great guy. I bragged on and on about my guy so as to whet her appetite, and I told her that if she was comfortable, she should call me back. I also told her that I wasn't going to barrage her (that was the Maries' style, not mine). I was going to leave it to her to call me back if she wanted to hear about my guy. And then after hearing about him, she could choose whether or not she wanted to meet him. No pressure, it was up to her.

Good message, huh? What single girl, no matter how self-absorbed or famous, is not going to call me back after a message like that, just for the sake of curiosity alone? If it were me, I would start to think that if I didn't call back, somehow this particular guy, whom I didn't even know, would end up being "Him," my intended, and somehow because I hadn't called back, I would be destined to be alone forever. *I am a little superstitious.*

Anyway, it took a few days but Miss TV Reporter did call me back. When I saw her station's name come up on my caller ID, I clapped my hands. *I knew she'd call!* She admitted that curiosity had gotten the best of her, so here she was, but she wanted to make sure that everything was completely between us. I said, "Of course it is, and as a matter of fact [a lightbulb went off here] I don't even have the clients speak to each other beforehand, to keep everything hush-hush. I set up the whole thing, and I only give the two people general descriptions of each other and each other's first names and cell phone numbers. Once they get there, they can decide between themselves whether or not to share any more info." And with that, she said she was game.

Then I called Mr. Priority all excited and bragged to him about Miss TV Reporter. He said she sounded great. Where was her phone number? I told him that I would set up the whole thing, that clients don't talk beforehand—they just show up. He complained that I never told him that and he didn't like it. I responded in my no-nonsense voice, "Oh yes, that's my policy and everyone loves it. It's so much easier for my busy clients. You will love it, trust me." He finally accepted my explanation, and my table change became official.

NOT FOR ME GUY

Good on Paper Guy

This one was a setup. I obviously need to be open to blind dates since my livelihood depends on them. But the truth is, most blind dates are just too blind—single guy, single girl, both nice people, both . . . single, let's introduce them. *Thanks for the forethought!* I spend a lot of time thinking about who should be set up with whom, but my friends' blind dates are not so strategic, to say the least. I guess beggars can't be choosers. And everyone does keep offering, so I bit the bullet and said yes to this one.

I guess you could call him Good on Paper Guy. You know the type: the guy's well educated, has a good job, comes from a good family, is friends with your friends, is the same religion, the whole nine yards. He has the perfect résumé for you. Unfortunately for me, the Good on Paper guys always end up being only that, good on paper. Well, this guy didn't prove me wrong. Yes, he was smart and well educated and made good money and came from a good family, but he was sooooooo boring. He didn't say one funny thing during our whole date, though somehow I made him laugh the whole time. If only he had attempted a joke, or something, anything. . . .

Database Girl

This girl only wanted to be in the database. She said she didn't want to hire me, she just wanted to have a consultation, pay the $400, and have me keep her in mind for my men. That seemed reasonable to me as long as she was clear that there were no guarantees. She asked me a lot of questions about how the database worked. Did I have a computer program that I used to figure out who went well with whom? *No. Sorry, Database Girl, no fancy program. It's just little ole me who decides who goes well with whom.*

She asked me how people got into the database. I didn't know if I should tell her that my database was really just my e-mail list of all the single people I had ever met in New York over the past many years. I take those people and group them into different classifications—by looks, by age, by religion, by hobbies, by personality, by disposition, etc., and then those groups are "subgrouped" and on and on. I also write a short summary about each person, something to jog my memory and help me determine if they would be appropriate for one of the Desperados. There are the people I know really well—friends of mine, men one of my friends or I used to date (*we tried them out, so to speak*). There are all the people I met in the Hamptons and at the hundreds of expensive charity parties I have attended. There are the friends of friends who attended one of the many parties I had thrown in the past. And there are the randoms who wound up in it, well, just because. And now with this new girl there will be a new group: the paying database peeps. My database is truly a perfect imperfect system that could be so much more modern, but I like it this way.

How do I use the database? Well, each time I take on a new Desperado, I thumb through each and every grouping and look at each and every name and description. Then I make a list of possibilities for the new peep. After that, I go through that short list and decide who to start with. Sometimes I'll contact a person in the database and find out they're in a relationship or have even gotten married, so they're obviously not available. But most of the time when I contact people they are very appreciative and thankful and excited to give the date a try.

TABLE CHANGE

Effective immediately, people can pay just to be in the database and be kept in mind for the Desperados, as long as they know that there are no guarantees. If the paying database person winds up getting set up with a Desperado and marrying that Desperado, he or she will pay a backend fee.

NOT FOR ME GUY
Dr. Touchy

I made this week a doubleheader. I figured that if I wanted to meet "Him," I needed to date a lot, whether I felt like it or not. So when someone else offered to set me up, I reluctantly said yes. This guy should have been a good date, but I keep forgetting that there are no "should be's" in dating. He was a doctor, an anesthesiologist. He was handsome, with a chiseled face, pretty eyes that crinkled at the corners when he smiled, and very nice long fingers. He was also very successful and interesting, but *(why is there always a but?)* he was too touchy. We sat down at the table and within fifteen minutes he was holding my hand. It freaked me out—I barely knew him. I didn't know what to do. I am not a big fan of strangers touching me in the first place; the whole "handshake with everyone you meet" thing seems unnecessary.

I got up to use the bathroom and called my best friend, who was rooting for this date to work. My best friend and I had moved to New York together right after I graduated from college. We were partners in crime on the dating front from the very first day. In the beginning, it never seemed as if we liked the same guys, but then I realized that that was because every time we would walk into a party, my friend would point out the men she was attracted to, reserving them so that I would know they were off-limits. At first I played along, but then I realized that she was reserving all the best-looking guys wherever we went, which was patently unfair. So we had a little chat and I suggested that, since our looks (I am a brunette, she is a blonde) and our personalities were so different, we should let the guy do the choosing. After that, New York for us couldn't have been more fun. We gallivanted around and had the time of our lives. I even helped her find her husband, which I was happy to do, although it meant losing my wingwoman. Still, she's the one person with whom I can obsess about all my personal dating issues without feeling stupid. She knew Dr. Touchy personally and had had visions of Saturday night couples' dinners and Sunday afternoon doubles tennis tournaments. I dialed her number from the bathroom stall and told her I was freaked about this touchy-feely situation. She suggested that I sit on my hands through most of dinner so he wouldn't have the opportunity to grab them. *Not a bad idea.*

I did just that, and it worked. He really didn't have an opportunity to grab my hands at all. But then just when I thought I was home free, Dr. Touchy got frustrated with my hands being out of reach and he asked me outright for one of my hands so he could hold it. I wanted to say that I really wasn't comfortable with the hand holding, but somehow it didn't come out of my mouth. So reluctantly I gave my hand back and tried to focus on whether I had any real interest in this guy. Aside from the hand holding, he seemed okay, and eventually there might come a time when I would like it if he held my hand. I couldn't believe that I was having this internal battle on the first date. He asked me for a second date, and even though I was waffling, I said yes. After all, to say no just because of a little hand holding might be classified as truly, insane, *right?*

BACK TO

Miss 39

She called me in a panic this morning. She saw Mr. 50 again and she slept with him and now she thinks everything is ruined. *What? It was only a second date!* "Why did you do that?" I asked. She started to cry, and I put my head in my hands. *It is too early in the morning for a crier.* "I am so bad at relationships! I truly have never had a real relationship and I never know what to do and what not to do. He really wanted to sleep with me and I just didn't know how to say no." *Try just saying it: "No."* Oh God, this one needs some major dating coaching. I think it's time to add that to my repertoire. I told her to stop crying and tell me what happened slowly; perhaps she hadn't ruined everything. I massaged the back of my neck as I felt the stress setting in.

"He invited me to his house in the Hamptons for the day. He sent a car into the city to pick me up and bring me to Westhampton, and we spent the day together." "Sounds good so far," I commented. "We played tennis and went swimming in his pool and then he invited me into the hot tub, naked." "Naked?" I said, surprised. *What is it with these people? The dates from my company are supposed to be PG.*

She continued, "I was reluctant at first, but when he got in naked, I thought that I would seem like a prude if I balked, so I got in naked, too." She gave a nervous laugh and asked me if I really wanted to hear all this. I urged her on. "Uh-huh, it's fine. I'm your Matchmaker. This is what I am here for. What happened next?" "We kissed a little in the hot tub and cuddled but he was relatively polite. Then things started getting heated so he asked me to come in the house in front of the fire. At this point, he asked me if I wanted to go home or spend the night." She paused, lost in thought. And then she continued, "Samantha, it had been so long since I spent the night with anyone that even though I knew I should say that I would go home, I didn't. I said that taking me home sounded like too much trouble and that I would stay over, and he seemed happy that I said that.

"Then we were fooling around again and cuddling naked in bed." Her voice started shaking a little. "And then he started trying to have sex with me and I balked and he got upset. We got into this whole argument, and we argued and argued and even though I didn't really want to, somehow the no turned into yes, and we had sex but barely, and he turned away and went to sleep angry." *Oh boy.* Then she asked me in a way that indicated what answer she was looking for, "Do you think I did something so wrong? Isn't it a woman's prerogative to say no? Why did I have to have sex with him? It was only our second date. What would give him the idea that I would have sex on a second date?"

I pushed my hair off my face and went from rubbing the back of my neck to pushing on the pressure points on my forehead. *Hello, Miss 39, of course he got upset, of course he got pissed off. You were at his house, naked in the hot tub, naked in his bed, and you said you wanted to spend the night. What signals did you think you were sending him?* She asked me again, "Do you think I did anything so wrong?" I answered patiently, although I was marveling that she could be so successful in business and such a ding-a-ling in male-female interaction. "Unfortunately, you might have given Mr. 50 the wrong signals." "What do you mean?" She was incredulous. "Well," I said slowly, deliberately, "let's look at it from his point of view for a moment. You were naked in his hot tub, you were naked and cuddling in his bed, and you turned down his offer to go home. He's a man and men have sex on the brain, so to him you were giving him the impression that you were interested in a sexual evening. He had no reason to believe that this was not the case."

"Well, what should I have done?" she asked as her voice rose. "I got naked in the hot tub because he was naked in the hot tub and I didn't want to seem like a prude, and then once we were both naked and cuddling in the hot tub, it didn't seem like such a big deal to be naked and cuddling in the bed under the covers. And then when he offered to take me home, I felt like I was just being polite and trying to be easygoing by saying that I would stay over, considering that it was 11:30 at night and we had been drinking and his home was over an hour away from the city. None of these actions were my way of saying that I wanted to have sex. See, I told you. Mr. 50 was too old for me!"

I shook my head in astonishment as I responded to her comment. "Honey, unfortunately, this situation had nothing to do with his age. A twenty-year-old would have tried to have sex with you." But somehow she didn't get it, so I decided it was best to drop it and move on. I told her not to worry, to remember that she didn't even like Mr. 50 to begin with. I had tons of other guys. And next time, we would talk about how and when she would get intimate with the guy so there wouldn't be so many mixed signals. She seemed satisfied with that.

DESPERADO #12

Soft Talker Guy

My nerves were a little shot when I showed up for this meeting after my conversation with Miss 39. I grew testy after I had to ask this Desperado to speak up for the fourth time. He asked me if I was always so irritable, and I found myself apologizing and explaining that unfortunately I did have a bit of a hearing issue (a lie, my ears are my best sense) and if he couldn't speak up, I wasn't going to be able to work with him. When he heard this, he actually made an effort to speak up, but I could already tell that he was going to annoy me.

Thursday, October 20

Somebody asked me today how would I describe my ideal guy. I figured that was a fair question, considering I ask it of all my Desperados on a daily basis. Hmm, My Guy . . . He's confident and take-charge (I need a man, not a mouse), he's family-oriented (family is important to me, especially since I have such a small one and such a close one), he smells good (I have a smell thing), he wants and loves children (I love kids and know I'll be a good mom), he likes dogs, but only big ones (I only want a big doggie, preferably a Bouvier but I would have another big dog, just no little, yapping spoiled dogs), he's quick, witty and funny (gives good banter), he's a great kisser (I love to kiss), he's patient (I am a huge pain in the ass), he's very honest (I dated a pathological liar once; that really screwed me up big-time), he's a good communicator (I dated a guy once who would never say when he was upset, and this was very frustrating and unhealthy), he's the person I will be able to laugh with and who just *gets* me, and I, him for the rest of our lives (this is the underlying premise of how I make my matches), he also thinks that my gift of gab and socializing is the greatest thing ever (I once dated a guy who hated how social I am and hated that I knew everyone; he was a bad guy for me and *an idiot, of course!*), and he loves me for who I am *and* for who I am not (my mother taught me that).

Am I asking for too much? I didn't even mention looks—I don't care, as long as I find him sexy, and sexy to me is an intangible, not a physical, thing. So, am I asking for too much? *Right now, I would probably settle for a guy who I just wanted to have a second date with, whose name is not Jerkoff. . . .*

BACK TO

Mr. Bonus with the Pinkie Ring and Miss Gold Digger

Miss Gold Digger called me. Mr. Bonus with the Pinkie Ring is a pig. Not only did he try to have phone sex on date one, but on date two, he cursed nonstop and was shockingly crude. I was beginning to suspect that Mr. Bonus with the Pinkie Ring was a complete dating disaster. "I am over him. I don't care who his uncle is!" she complained. I sat nodding my head in agreement as I told her that I didn't blame her, no more Mr. Bonus with the Pinkie Ring for her. Then she paused and asked me if I had other men like Mr. Bonus, absent the phone sex and the crudeness. I smiled as I realized that I might just have a new client. "I know many men like him, but they aren't all necessarily paying me. Are you interested in hiring me to find you those kinds of men?" I ventured. She hesitated at first but then said she thought she was and scheduled a consultation for the following week.

Note to self: After one freebie, always ask if the person wants to transition to a paying client. You never know.

Monday, October 24

Went to dinner with a group of people tonight. It's funny how, whenever I'm out with a group of single people, the conversation invariably turns to dating and guy/girl interaction. I wonder if it's because of my business, or do single people always talk about dating? One of the less attractive women asked me if men only care about looks. *Yes!* But I am good at politically correct answers, so I said no, not all men. The shallow ones care only about looks, but a lot of others care about good personalities.

Then one of the shallow guys at the table, one who had been drinking heavily, challenged my answer and said that he and all his buddies only liked hot chicks. I quickly changed the subject to bust his balls a bit and told him that what girls really don't like are heavy guys who rationalize that they are big guys, not fat guys. My heckler had definitely kept the freshman fifteen and then some for the past ten years. He blushed and changed the subject to sports.

BACK TO

Brad Pitt Guy

I set him up with a real hottie last night. There is no way he can ask me if Brad Pitt would like her. *If Brad Pitt didn't like her, I think that at least some other celebrity would.* She was 27 and gorgeous, but no rocket scientist. I e-mailed him first thing, looking for some praise so I could start my day off right. He said he wanted to talk on the phone. I happily dialed his number, figuring he wanted to thank me in person. His first words were, "You were right, even Brad Pitt would think she was hot." *Yippee!* "But . . ." *Oh no!* "But . . . Brad Pitt would not be able to hold a conversation with her because she was a total ditz." *Yo, guy, you only asked for looks. Brains cost extra!* I reminded him that he said that he only cared about looks, and that's what I gave him. "I changed my mind. Brad Pitt would need to find her hot *and* be able to have an intelligent conversation with her." *Mon dieu!*

BACK TO

Soft Talker Guy

Got a call today from the Soft Talker, and he whispered into the phone that he was going to take a pass on the service. He felt that I was a little too preoccupied and he didn't feel comfortable hiring me. I didn't even try pleading my case.

BACK TO

Mr. Bonus with the Pinkie Ring

He called and gushed on that he really liked Miss Gold Digger, but he had called her several times with no return phone call. Did I know anything? *Yes, I do. Oh boy, do I tell him I know?* I guessed now was as a good a time as ever to have the phone-sex conversation with him.

I took a breath and began: "Mr. Bonus with the Pinkie Ring, I spoke with Miss Gold Digger and I want you to know that I say this to you with no judgment at all (ahem!), but she told me that she was a little put off by your interest in having phone sex with her after the date." I waited a beat to see if he would chime in and try to explain or apologize. Nothing. So I continued. "Now it's not my business, and maybe she asked for it—I have no idea—but all I can tell you is that she was a little put off and she said something to me about it." Finally, he interrupted, "But that was after the first date, and she went on a second date anyway. It couldn't have bothered her that much."

Dude, she told me about it. Clearly it bugged her. How about an expla-nation, how about being embarrassed, how about denying it to me? Wow! "Well," I huffed, "she *was* put off by it after date one, but I *encouraged* her to give you another chance and she did." I paused again, waiting for him to say thank you. Again nothing. So I continued. "Then she called me again after date two and she told me you were crude and cursed a lot during the date." He half chuckled and said, "So I used the f-word once or twice. What's the big deal? And I told a few off-color jokes. I thought she was cool." I shook my head in amazement. "Look," I said patiently, "again I am not judging you, but when you go on dates, the women are judging you and you probably need to think before you act and save some of your off-color jokes, cursing, and phone sex for later in the relationship. I don't want women to not give you a chance because of little stupid things like this."

Then I made my joke about my Table being strictly PG. He didn't laugh. I don't think he even understood what I was saying. "Phone sex, why is that so bad?" he asked again with that same half chuckle. You could tell he was actually amused, rather than embarrassed, by his behavior. He clearly did not understand, so I simply said, "Let's move on, but with the next woman let's try to keep it a little tame at least until date four. . . ."

BACK TO

The Girl I Always Thought Hated Me

Once I realized that this Desperado didn't hate me, I wanted to find her a good man. A good man for her, I thought, would be someone who wouldn't instantly decide that she was either too shy or too snobby for him. Might be difficult in Manhattan—men are so apt to make snap judgments and move on to the next if they don't immediately deem someone perfect. *Men, we can't live with them, we can't live without them.*

I started thumbing through the database. I pulled up two lists for her: the 30–40 MNBM (Male Never Been Married) list and 35–45 DM (Divorced Male) list. I figured I should be able to find a few good guys for her here.

What about Jim, 42, divorced, plastic surgeon? No, a little too full of himself for the Girl. There's Henry, 40, never married, an ophthalmologist. Noo, he's not ready to settle down yet. Bob, 43, divorced lawyer with that annoying laugh? No. Hmm, what about Robert, 35, single, successful, a little reserved as well, hmm. . . .

I sent a short and sweet e-mail to Robert. I figured he would empathize with The Girl I Always Thought Hated Me's plight and that he would definitely be excited to meet her. I thought wrong. He e-mailed me back and said he didn't think she sounded right for him. He wrote that he didn't care for women who were reserved; he preferred really outgoing ones—they were more fun. I grew determined and typed back that The Girl was outgoing once she warmed up to someone. I cut off the e-mail exchange and said that I was going to call him to discuss. So we got on the phone and first he fixated on her demeanor, but then he slipped and said, "Besides, women who are 33 are always plotting and end up putting pressure." I rolled my eyes as I realized where this was heading. He continued, "The shy demeanor is always an act." *Okay, this man has issues!* This guy now earned his own nickname: Mr. Generalizer. I got annoyed and told him that he was making a huge generalization and that my client was just a little reserved at first. It had nothing to do with trying to trick him or anyone else. But he refused to meet her. *Here we go again, database decreasing. . . .*

Came back to The Girl I Always Thought Hated Me later that night and e-mailed another guy who I thought was a good possibility: Steven, 40, never married, a management consultant and easygoing. I didn't think he would have the nerve to reject The Girl out of hand, as

Robert had. I tried a new tactic. This time I just sang her praises so I could rope him in. And he got roped. Then I told him to call me so I could tell him more. On the phone, I told him about her looks, and since she's cute, that was easy. As an aside at the end of the conversation, I said, "Oh, you should know that occasionally she's a little reserved when she first meets people, but once you get to know her, she's great and very outgoing." He told me that his sister was like that and he totally understood. *Thank God. For the moment, we're on track.*

BACK TO

Mr. Gazillionaire

It turns out that Mr. Gazilllionare has developed feelings for Miss Goldman Sachs WASP despite having used her only to fill a chair at his charity table. He has been out with her a number of times, and this morning he e-mailed me and said that he had left a few messages for her that have gone unanswered, and did I know anything? *Am I starting to be everyone's confessor?* So I called Miss Goldman Sachs WASP and asked her what was up. She sounded annoyed. She told me that she liked Mr. Gazillionaire a lot at first but now she is over him. Why? I asked. He didn't call me, she said. I confided to her that he had mentioned to me that he had left a few messages for her that went unanswered; maybe he had the wrong number or maybe she didn't check her messages.

"No." I heard her tapping her nails on her desk as she said definitively, "He had the right number and I got his messages but they were ten days after our last date and ten days after the first time we had sex!" *Oops!* She told me that she was just plain over him. She said that he was 38 years old and it was unacceptable that he didn't call sooner, regardless of how busy and how wealthy he is. She was looking for a husband and someone respectful, not self-absorbed. I told her that I couldn't agree with her more, but was she certain that she didn't want to give him another chance? She was certain. Even though it meant that I had to go back to the drawing board for Mr. Gazillionaire, I applauded her resolve.

I called Mr. Gazillionaire. It was time to teach this Desperado a few manners. I told him that I had spoken to Miss Goldman Sachs WASP and that she didn't want to go out with him again because he waited so long to call her after their last date. "That's crazy," he nearly yelled. "How long was it exactly? . . . Ten days, was it really that long? So what if it really was ten days? Once I called, I called three times on the same day. That should count for something, right?" *It counts for nothing, especially if it was ten days after the first night of sex—that's a biggie.*

I said, "Let me explain to you how a woman works. She goes out on a date with you, and if she has fun, she goes home excited to see you again. She goes home fantasizing about what your future kids are going to look like and how fancy your wedding is going to be." "Uh-huh," he said in rapt attention. "Then the next day she brags to a few friends about how great the date was because she feels pretty confident that she is going to hear from you again and see you again. She hopes you will call the very next day but understands that if you wait one day you are 'playing the game' properly. So, day one goes by, and she still feels confident because cool guys wait until day two to make the call. Day two rolls around and she is looking forward to your call all day and then it doesn't come. Then she starts rationalizing: well, maybe you are trying to be really cool, so you are waiting an extra day; she stays calm still. Day three comes and goes, no phone call, now she starts panicking. Maybe something happened to you. Maybe— God forbid—you were in a terrible accident that prevented you from calling. She hopes this isn't really true, but at the same time she hopes it is true so it will explain why you haven't called. She waits until the end of day four. When there has been no phone call, and she calls your office anonymously to make sure you are there, and when the secretary says you're on another call, she knows you are alive and well, and she hangs up." He snorted. "Then she starts backpedaling for survival—she rationalizes that you weren't that great anyway. You weren't so cute, not so smart, and not really her type. She is upset, but she rationalizes and rationalizes until she is over you and gets you out of her mind and then she moves on and stops thinking about you at about one week. Then all of a sudden you call her on day ten. She doesn't want to hear from you then. She has already rationalized you away. She has already expended time and energy liking you and hating you and moving on from you, and she doesn't want to go backwards. You are out at that point. So . . . don't wait until day ten!"

I finished my whole explanation slightly out of breath and waited for his response. Suddenly he was remorseful. "But I was really busy. I liked her all along. I was planning to call her all along. I was just busy, that's all." *Well, how was she supposed to know that? Through osmosis?*

Monday, October 31

I had a Halloween party tonight. Halloween is my favorite holiday, but don't tell anybody because on the record Valentine's Day is supposed to be my favorite holiday. Whatever, I do love Halloween. I think a lot of people love the holiday because it gives them the excuse to hide behind their costumes and be something or someone that they aren't. Halloween takes away a lot of inhibitions. The party was swarming with new couples, and love was in the air. The costumes were terrific: there was Superman, of course, actually several of those; there was the sexy Got Milk? girl; there was a guy dressed up as a fish in a fish tank; there were Sonny and Cher, a bunch of sexy black cats, a few hookers, and a few devil-and-angel combos. I met the Lone Ranger. He was sexy and brooding and very mysterious. We dirty-danced and flirted all night long. I could have galloped off on his horse with Tonto behind us if only he didn't live in Hong Kong. The super-far long-distance thing. I've been there, done that, and I will never do it again. Oh well, it's always nice to have a little random excitement.

November

November is another busy month for me because people are starting to think about New Year's Eve. Nobody wants to be dateless for the big night. So in November, all the strategic planners come to me to find Mr. or Ms. Right, or at least Mr. or Ms. Right for New Year's Eve.

DESPERADO #13

The Married Single

This guy showed up at the meeting with a wad of cash. I asked him why he couldn't pay me by check like everybody else, and he said that he had just been at the casino and had won a lot of money and he had it lying around so he brought it. *Okay.* Then he filled out my form but neglected to give his home phone number. I gave him a perplexed look and I asked him why. He said he has his cell phone and his office number, no home phone. *Hmm.* He had a very strange schedule too: he could only have dates between 5 and 6 P.M., and when I asked him why, he said that that was just what he preferred. I thought he was an odd bird, but he was also very successful, a Columbia grad, an entrepreneur, very smart and nice-looking in an absentminded-professor-with-his-shirt-hanging-out kind of way. I figured that maybe he was just too smart for his own good and that made him an eccentric. I decided that he should not be too difficult of a sell, so I might as well take him as a client. It never dawned on me to suspect duplicity. I took his money and had him sign the contract.

About a week later, I set him up on a date. He liked her, and she liked him. But I began to feel uneasy about this mystery man so I secretly started doing a little digging. I spoke to an old friend at the law firm where he used to work and, in an indirect way, I asked about him. My friend reported, "Very smart guy, odd guy, crappy husband." I closed my eyes in disbelief. Crappy husband? I asked; how long ago did he get divorced? "Oh, he's not divorced. He brought his wife to a fundraiser last week, but I hear he cheats on her all the time. Some woman I know started dating him over the Internet. They dated for four months, but she never had his home phone number and then she found out from me, by accident, that he was still married. . . . Samantha, please tell me that you are not dating him. He's bad news." *Oh!*

I was stunned. *What a scumbag! I should have checked him out before I set him up.* I was upset. Mine is definitely not a service for married men who want to cheat on their wives. I won't even take separated people; I want them to be fully divorced before they start working with me. I called him immediately and told him forcefully that I had found out about his wife, that I didn't work with married people, that our contract was officially terminated and as per the terms of our contract I was keeping the $1,400 he paid me. I never wanted to hear from him again. I then picked up the phone, tail between my legs, and told the truth to the woman I had set him up with. She seemed to like rich guys, so I immediately offered to set her up with Mr. Gazillionaire. I knew that he would definitely like her. She got over The Married Single very quickly when she heard Mr. Gazillionaire had nine houses!

Note to self: Trust your instincts, they're good. If you sense something amiss, pass.

Wednesday, November 2

Went to a restaurant opening tonight with my brother Sean. We hang out a lot because we're close in age and have a lot of mutual friends. This was the first time we had been out together since the story on my Matchmaking business broke. A lot of people at the party were curious about what it was like to be single and to be my brother. They kept asking Sean variations of "Dude, does she set you up all the time? Does she let you test-drive the women for her?" Each time someone said something like that, Sean would look at me and I would look at him with that what-a-doofus look we both understood so well. The truth is that we made a pact when I first started my business that I would not set him up with any of the paying Desperados unless I was absolutely convinced that she was wife material for him. I wanted to keep my personal life separate from my business—although I can't help but keep a close lookout for women for him as I do my hunting.

Another guy said enviously, "You must be set, dude, all those women. All you need to do is say, 'Hey sis, slide me over one.'" Again another look passed between my brother and me. Then Sean gave a coy grin and said, "Dude, I get a few perks now and again, and you could get them too if you ponied up the cash." Everyone laughed, and the doofus flushed in embarrassment and walked off. Sean continued now that he had an audience. "She actually started hooking me up when we were teenagers. She helped me get my first girlfriend." He chuckled. I smiled, remembering how I had distracted his camp counselor so he could sneak over to girls' camp for a make-out session with the girl he was interested in. I rolled my eyes and said, "I think I had pigtails then, and didn't you have braces?" "Those were the days," he said as we left the party.

TABLE CHANGE

Effective immediately, I am going to change the name of my company. Table for Two (or More) was never a catchy name. In fact, I did very few of those group dinners and I don't do them at all now, so there is no point in keeping that name, especially when I don't like it. Now I have to figure out a new name. I could call it Table for Two, but that name is too ordinary, and I think there are some tableware companies already using it. Hmm, it seems like most people just know of me and the company by my first name, Samantha. What about the people who know the current company name? How will they find me? I had it: *What about Samantha's Table? It's my name plus a little bit of the current company name. Perfect.*

DESPERADO #14

The Self-Proclaimed Metrosexual

I should start by clarifying that a metrosexual is different from an effeminate guy. An effeminate guy has female interests and even mannerisms; he's the guy who makes people wonder whether he's gay. The metrosexual is different: he loves getting manicures and spending thousands on designer clothes and definitely isn't the most macho guy in the world, but he also actually loves football and other sports and he's definitely attracted to women.

My Mr. Metrosexual is all too aware that he is a metrosexual. He loves the term. When he sat down with me, he immediately asked, "Do you know what the term *metrosexual* means?" And before I could reply, he answered for me: "I heard the term on *Sex and the City,* and all of a sudden it became clear that I am a metrosexual. When I was younger, people called me Jappy, which was silly because I'm not even Jewish, although all my friends are and I do prefer Jewish women." He scoffed, "Then people called me high-maintenance, girly, and a homo, but none of those terms really fit me." *I couldn't think of many people who would like to be called a girly homo, either.* "Then I heard the term *metrosexual* and it became clear!" He leaned in. "So, Samantha, when you describe me to women, you should definitely let them know that I am a metrosexual so they know what they are getting themselves into. I need a woman who will be fine with my need for all my creature comforts but who isn't necessarily obsessed with them herself." I looked at him more closely, trying to get a handle on him. He seemed very together: his bright striped shirt was starched, his jeans were the latest trendy brand, his nails had been recently buffed, and his shoes were polished to a high-gloss finish. I wondered what woman would want to be with such a high-maintenance guy unless she herself was incredibly high maintenance and thought that such a trait would be something for them to bond over? I said, "I don't get it." He said with a laugh, "There's room for only one high-maintenance person in every relationship and I've definitely taken that spot." *Okay, now I get it. Not.* I asked him if it was okay if the woman was moderately high maintenance and liked nice things, and he said that was fine. We got up to leave, he took out his Louis Vuitton wallet to pay for our drinks with crisp new bills and surprised me by saying, "Oh, and if you do find me Mrs. Metrosexual, there is a Mercedes in it for you!" I smiled and told him that I'd put that in the contract.

TABLE CHANGE

Effective immediately, there is a "bonus line" in my contract. It's funny—my service is expensive, but client after client has come in and offered me a bonus if I get them married, so I might as well have a line for it in my contract. They seem to think if they offer me extra and above what everyone else offers, I will give them extra-and-above service. I don't—at least I try to treat all my Desperados equally. But I have to admit a new car or $60,000 lump sum does sound appealing.

BACK TO
Brad Pitt Guy

I got a phone call from Brad Pitt Guy this morning. Could I log onto JDate and check out a woman for him? What was this new little request? *Hey, Brad Pitt Guy, in case you forgot, I run a Matchmaking service, and you signed up to be a client here. Why are you sending me to an Internet dating site?* For some reason, even though I am convinced Brad Pitt

Guy is nuts, I like him because he always makes me laugh. So fine, I went online. He gave me his password and I checked out his girl. A real stunner. "Okay, I see her. Now what?" "Well, this is a woman who would be up to Brad Pitt's standards. Can you get me a date with her?" Now I was confused. "You want me to go onto an Internet dating site that you subscribe to and poach a girl for you? Why don't you just e-mail her? Isn't that how this whole thing works?" "Well, I did e-mail her but she is not e-mailing me back and I really want to meet her so I thought you could help. And besides, that's what I am paying you for." I wondered if he told her about his strong connection to Brad Pitt— maybe that would have helped. *Not.* I got indignant. "Look, Brad Pitt Guy, I think it's fine for you to use Internet dating in addition to my service—it increases your odds—but I am not going to poach women from JDate for you. I will keep her looks and her description in mind as I am out there looking for women for you, but that is the best I am going to do." My voice got softer. "Okay?" "Okay, I guess so," he said, sounding disappointed.

I hung up with Brad Pitt Guy but stayed connected to this JDate service of his. First I checked out Brad Pitt Guy's profile: "Good-looking Brad Pitt look-alike with shiny new black Porsche looking for his very own Jennifer Aniston." *Oh God, he sounds so cocky. No wonder his hottie didn't e-mail him back. Maybe I should subtly suggest that he soften that up.* Then I checked out the rest of the site. Wow, it's like a candy store, so many men, so many women, all single, and all appear pretty interesting. *Maybe I should start poaching.* No, that would be wrong. Maybe I should start JDating instead. Hmm . . . *Where does a barber go for a haircut?*

Nowhere Man

Another blinder for yours truly. This guy is a friend of my best friend's husband's friend. I know, I probably shouldn't have agreed to go. This guy is too far removed, and he will probably have three eyes. But there's no one else on my plate right now except Dr. Touchy, and I keep putting off date two with him because I don't really want to go.

My date called me on a Wednesday to ask me out for the following Tuesday. Good advance planning, I liked that. He knew I was a Matchmaker and thought it was cool; another gold star for him. He sounded pretty funny on the phone, so I actually was looking forward to the date. But—and there's always a *but*—when I came downstairs to meet him, he had no plan, nowhere for us to go. This was a shame because, up until that point, he had seemed promising and was actually kind of cute. He was about five feet nine, with dirty blond hair, blue eyes, and a big nose—not one that would offend but one that added character. He asked me where I wanted to go and I said it didn't matter, we could go anywhere. He said that he hadn't picked anything because he thought I would have a suggestion, since it was my neighborhood. My heart started to sink, but instead of making a big deal, I just picked a restaurant around the corner from my house. On our walk over, I thought about making a pit stop to buy him a Zagat's restaurant guide to help him on his next date outside of his own neighborhood!

When we reached the restaurant, he paused at the door to scan the menu, then announced that he didn't want to eat there. "Why not?" I demanded. "I don't like the way it looks," he said. "Okay, Nowhere Man, where would you like to go?" "Let's stroll a little bit," he suggested as he tried unsuccessfully to reach for my hand, "and we can see what we can find." So we strolled a little bit, but I was getting discouraged. I had pretty much decided that I had no interest in the guy, I just wanted to eat so I could go home. I didn't understand why it mattered where we went. We passed several restaurants that I pointed out and suggested we try, but he kept saying no, let's keep going. Finally my patience wore thin and I said, "Nowhere Man, we have been strolling for forty-five minutes, looking for a place that will satisfy you. Did you ever think that if you are this finicky about restaurants, you might want to choose one before you pick up your date?" He told me that he actually was testing me to see if the only thing I cared about was going to a nice restaurant and getting a free meal! I stopped in my tracks. *The only thing I care about right now is getting away from you, you crazy guy!* I didn't even want to eat with him anymore. I should have insisted on drinks, as I do with all the clients. I told him that perhaps it was time for me to go home—*immediately.*

Note to self: To avoid meeting freaks, don't accept blind dates if they are more than once removed. And make sure to tell male clients to always show up for their dates with a plan.

DESPERADO #15

Miss Manhunt

I have never met a woman who was so intense about meeting her husband and, believe you me, I have met a few uptight and focused ones in my day. She is a committed manhunter, and she wants me to be the lion tamer. She has a spreadsheet to record her dates. She has run ads, tried out for dating reality shows, and even hired a private investigator to help with her plight—and she's only 34! She showed up at our meeting in an understated I'm-in-charge suit with a short skirt and a plunging neckline. I couldn't help noticing her perfectly manicured fire-engine red nails because she kept tapping them on the table for emphasis. She had a Filofax full of men she had already met and rejected, and she gave me a Xeroxed copy of her list. *She scared me, a lot.* "What do you need a private investigator for?" I asked. She tapped a finger. "I won't date a guy if his net worth is under two million dollars, and I need a private investigator to verify that. Just because a guy claims he is wealthy does not mean that his net worth is all that high." She went on to explain that a lot of men lie or just dress the part, and she wanted to make sure that they were actually able to live as large as they were living. "I want to make sure that his Mercedes 500 SL is brand-new and bought outright and that he hasn't leased it just to impress people." She tapped again. I stared at her in bewilderment. I started to wonder if even my wealthy guys would meet her requirements: I do ask about their salaries, but not their net worth. Maybe some of my guys' cars are in fact leased or second-hand. *Who knew that would be important?*

Hmm. She was so mercenary about the whole thing that I asked her straight out if she considered herself a gold digger. I couldn't resist. She sat back in her chair, shook out her hair confidently, and told me she had owned an Internet company, sold it, had two million dollars net worth herself, and just wanted to make sure that the guy didn't want to live off her wealth. Now that she explained her reasoning, she no longer seemed like a first-class gold digger, but I still thought she was taking all the romance out of love. I was waffling about taking her on as a Desperado. I sensed she was going to be very demanding. But then she told me that she wanted to be a priority client and for my troubles she wanted to pay me $10,000. *Hmm, another priority client. I am starting to like her better already.* I took the money and wondered if that made me a gold digger or just a good businesswoman. . . .

BACK TO

Mr. Priority

Mr. Priority called me this morning. He and Miss TV Reporter are dating. His only issue is that she's a TV reporter. I wasn't sure what to say to that since she's always been a TV reporter. "She's always interviewing everyone, including me, always asking question after question after question, probing, and it gets really annoying," he complained. "Hmm, I can see how that would be annoying. Have you discussed it with her?" "No, I'm not sure how to bring it up without offending her." I was starting to think that maybe Mr. Priority might be a nice guy. I suggested that he start teasing her about it, in a playful way, so she would get the point. "Maybe when she goes into TV reporter mode you can call her 'Miss TV Reporter' and ask where her cameraman is. Maybe she doesn't even know she does that, and once she realizes it, she probably will want to stop." "Smart idea," he said. *I know. That is why I get paid the big bucks.*

Note to self: Tell the clients to leave their jobs at the office.

Soho House Guy

I went to a party tonight at the Soho House, an exclusive club in New York. It's private in the sense that you can't get in unless you belong, or you know someone who belongs, or you are a hot girl, or a VIP; in other words, most people can figure out a way to get in. Anyway, almost immediately upon arriving, I met a guy. I wasn't expecting to meet someone and I wasn't really thinking about meeting someone, which was probably why I did. I noticed him from across the room. He winked at me and raised his martini glass in salute. I tentatively raised my wineglass back at him. Then he approached. He was handsome, almost six feet one, with curly longish brown hair, little glasses. He was definitely a downtown guy from what I could see of his outfit. I'm usually not attracted to that look, but there was something sexy about him. Right away he made a joke about knowing me from somewhere and I laughed, mostly in relief that we didn't know each other at all. I decided not to tell him what I did for a living, at least for the moment. I didn't want to have to talk about my business, and I didn't want him to focus on all the women he might be able to meet through me instead of focusing on me directly.

We got into a flirtatious, fun conversation, and the topic of What Do You Do didn't even come up. Then about thirty minutes later, a girl came scampering over and gave him a big kiss on the cheek. You know this type of girl—who's all over the guy and doesn't even notice or care that he was in the middle of a conversation. I couldn't even see who she was because she had fallen into his arms so quickly. Eventually he turned to introduce us, and it didn't surprise me that she was one of those girls in New York whom I've known forever and who is simply not a girl's girl. Then she noticed me for the first time and said, "Oh my God, Samantha, I didn't even see you standing there. *(Shocking!)* How are you? I hear you are this superfamous Matchmaker now." Then she turned to the guy and linked her arm in his and said, "Do you know about this girl's business? She sets people up for a living and she has had something like five thousand marriages come out of her setups." Soho Guy looked like he didn't know what to say. I couldn't tell if he felt awkward talking to me, if he felt stupid because he didn't know who I was, or if he was just impressed. I quickly corrected her. "Oh, stop. It's not five thousand, but, yes, there have been a bunch." She laughed, planted a kiss on his cheek, very close to his mouth, and then saw someone else who needed to be fawned over and scampered off.

The guy and I were left there in awkward silence. He started playing with the rim of his martini glass, then looked up and said a little tentatively, "Wow, so you are a Matchmaker. Are you only talking to me to try to get me to sign up for your service?" He looked uncomfortable. "Because I'm not interested in your service. I don't think I'd ever do that." A part of me wanted to defend my service, but I didn't. I said a little shyly, "No, that was not it at all. I was talking to you because you seemed nice. And, well . . . I'm single and I would like to meet someone, too. Can you handle that?" He smiled and said he could.

Sunday, November 6

I know it sounds ridiculous, but I just can't talk to every Desperado on the phone before they sign up for the service. Most people don't follow through and schedule a consultation, and I wind up having random, long, and wasteful conversations with people I never hear from again. I am getting too busy to do this job all by myself. Sometimes potential peeps will keep me on the phone for twenty minutes or more, grilling me with questions; I just don't have time. I must find an assistant.

BACK TO
Mr. Bonus with the Pinkie Ring

I called Mr. Bonus to set him up with his next date, and he told me that he was dating someone. What? Where did you meet her? He met her on his own. *No! You can't meet someone on your own. It's not fair. What about the new apartment that I want to buy with your bonus? Why did you have to go and meet someone on your own? I feel sick. I want my chance to earn my money! You just ruined my day!* But instead I sucked it up and said, "Oh, that's so great, Mr. Bonus, I really hope it works out for you; keep me posted and know that I am here for you." *Waaaaaaa!*

Sunday, November 13

I started thumbing through my database haphazardly for some of the peeps. It probably wouldn't hurt to replenish the crop a bit. I had been invited to another charity party tonight, so I decided to go and do a little *shopping.*

The charity party, in a penthouse in Midtown, was to benefit the Wildlife Preservation Society. There was a safari theme, with life-sized giraffes, zebras, and lions everywhere, and drinks with names like Gorillatini and Jungle Fever. The people looked the part as well. There was a woman dressed as Jane in a grass skirt, a guy who was wearing a bear mask, and a whole lot of scantily clad girls in safari-print outfits.

I met a bunch of new people: a 31-year-old woman who grew up in New York and Paris, my friend's boss, a hot 42-year-old CEO of an apparel company, a 27-year-old Pamela Anderson look-alike who, once she met me, wouldn't leave my side. I ran into a woman who worked at *Vogue*—I'd known her my first year in New York and then she had disappeared, but now I guess she's back. I ran into a guy with whom I had three good dates before I decided to get back together with Jerkoff for the umpteenth time. Everyone seemed fascinated by what I do, and loads of people wanted to get set up.

I've also noticed how some women act differently around me these days. A bunch of them weren't always so nice to me in the past. But now that they know that I have a substantial list of available men, they've become all friendly, hoping that I'll set them up. And then there are all the other women who are not so friendly—it's like they are scared of me. They must think that if someone sees them talking to me, the implication is that they are a client. *Who am I, the second-grade teacher that students can't say hello to outside the classroom? The fact is, I don't matchmake 24/7 and I don't have leprosy. One day they will come a-crawling and beg me to set them up and I will remember. I always remember. . . .*

BACK TO

Soho House Guy

I never heard from him even though he took my number and said he would call. I was disappointed. Maybe he couldn't handle the fact that I was a Matchmaker. *An occupational hazard, I suppose.*

Jerkoff Again

Jerkoff sent me four dozen tulips today, purple ones. I love purple tulips. In the tulips was a first-class ticket to Paris. I love Paris. The note said, "Paris this weekend? I need you." I love Jerkoff, but I hate him, too. *Oh God, here we go again.* I can't go, but I want to go. Jerkoff sucks, but all these other guys suck worse. I can't even find a guy to go on a second date with. Is Jerkoff really so bad? I mean, it's one week-end and it's Paris and the Champs-Elysées is calling my name. What's a girl to do? Help! *Isn't there someone to tell me I can't go, someone to tell me I have to be strong, someone to tell me that I hate Paris?*

I am not strong. I'm weak and bored, and I will never, ever hate Paris. *Oh God, I'm caving.* Then the phone rang. It was Jerkoff. He purred into the phone, "You have to come to Paris. It's an emergency. I need to see you. It will be so romantic and it will be different this time, I promise." *I'm a sucker. It's Paris. I'm going.*

Thursday, November 17

Somebody asked me today if I have a formula for my setups. A for-mula? I am dealing with people's lives here. It is not about charts and fractions and formulas! I guess most of the time I work on intuition, the vibe I get when I meet a person. I listen to what clients say to me, and what they don't say. I ask a lot of questions and I think to myself, With whom do I see this person walking down the street in fifteen or twenty years, happy and content together? And then I make the intro-duction. That's *my formula.*

DESPERADO #16

Miss Gold Digger

Miss Gold Digger came to see me today. She immediately gave me a difficult time about filling out the questionnaire. "You know me already, you know what I like: men who are successful. You know what I don't like: men who are crude and classless and try to get me to have phone sex. So let's get started!" I gave her a hard stare and told her that I had a lot of successful men who were not into first-date phone sex but I wanted to get to know her a little better so I could determine which ones to introduce her to. She accepted that explanation and filled out the form. It turns out that Miss Gold Digger is actually from a wealthy family, which surprised me. I asked her why she only wanted wealthy men if she didn't need the money. She laid it on the table for me. Money turns her on, ostentation turns her on, and extravagance turns her on. She tossed her blond hair as she explained that her dad has tons of money but is a miser. He might leave it all to charity, and she needed to protect herself. She wanted someone who was going to let her spend and spend and spend, no limits, no comments. She didn't care what he looked like; she was willing to give him all the blow jobs he wanted as long as she could spend the money. She was sick of Daddy. Did I understand the full picture? *Yup, loud and clear.* Miss Gold Digger gets the ugly rich guys who will be so grateful to have her that they will let her spend to her heart's content.

I felt a little slimy agreeing to help her dig for gold, but I liked her candor. And the fact is that the men I'm going to set her up with are digging also. They're digging for boobs and hot bodies, isn't that the same? *It's a transaction of sorts and I am just the broker, I think. . . .*

NOT FOR ME GUY
Mr. Fingers

I went back to the personal dating trenches reluctantly. I met a new guy on my own at a charity party—I have decided to stay clear of the blind date for a while. He seemed promising. He collected modern art, brewed his own beer, and was obsessed with the Houston Oilers football team. He seemed like an interesting mix of culture and athletics. And he was nice-looking, a sexy bald man I would call him. I happily gave him my number. When a mutual friend asked what I thought, I gave her the keep-your-fingers-crossed sign.

He called me right away and asked me out. We had a good conversation. (I know I scold the Desperados for judging people on the phone, but of course I don't play by my own rules.) He took me to a cute restaurant on the Upper East Side, nothing fancy but fine nonetheless.

Of course, I gave him what they call in Yiddish a *kayne horeh* (pat on the back) too quickly. This guy had eating problems. He was a pig. His manners were so atrocious that I honestly thought I was imagining it. He ordered steak tartare for his appetizer and picked up every single piece of it, without exaggeration, with his fingers, completely ignoring that *little thing called a fork*. I starting thinking that maybe in some remote region in France it was proper etiquette to eat steak tartare with your hands and I just never knew about it. I convinced myself to give him the benefit of the doubt about this until the next day when I could get the skinny from one of my French friends. But then his main course came, a Cobb salad. Apparently there is another foreign region where it is proper etiquette to eat salad with your fingers because yet again no fork was used. The spectacle was so disgusting, I wanted to vomit or cry. Even the waiter noticed.

In retrospect, I should have said something. How does someone go through life eating with his hands like an animal and no one says anything? This guy went to Princeton, grew up on the Upper East Side of Manhattan, works at a large, prestigious investment bank. I didn't get it. Was I dreaming? I called my best friend when I got home. She wasn't home. I felt like crying. *When is this cycle of dating disasters going to end? What should I do?* And then I saw the computer and remembered that supermarket of Jewish men. Maybe I needed to go for a little shopping spree. How could it hurt?

So I logged onto JDate and started checking it out. There was Brian and Adam and John and Philip and Peter and Henry and . . . so many guys I know, so many guys I have been on a dates with or kissed over the years, so many guys I have set up with the Desperados. Wow, so this is what it's all about now, online dating. Thousands and thousands of single people, so many wanting to meet Mr. or Ms. Right. I think this is a good indicator that my business is here to stay for a long time.

Wow, that guy is cute, and so is that one, and that one seems really funny. Okay, so how do you do it? Should I do it? *How can I do it? But everyone does it. Why should I be penalized for being a Matchmaker? If I help everyone else, can't someone or something help me? Isn't that only fair?* Maybe I could just dabble a little. I don't have to meet anyone. Maybe I can just create a profile and see what happens. No photo, no mention of the Matchmaking. Just see what happens. *It can't hurt, can it?*

Note to self: Create an online profile.

BACK TO

Dr. Touchy

I have round two with Dr. Touchy tonight. I've been having the heebie-jeebies all day. I think I might be developing a rash in anticipation of his paws all over me. But I have made a decision. If he touches me within the first fifteen minutes of the date, I am going to slap him across the face. *Or maybe not.* I am just going to politely tell him that his touching me is making me a little uncomfortable and I would appreciate it if he just didn't do it. It's easy. Honesty is the best policy, right?

So I went on the date. I had a glass of wine in my apartment before he came to get me, just to calm my nerves a little. He was more handsome than I had remembered, and my spirits started to lift. Maybe the night wouldn't be so bad. But then we got into the cab and right away he started holding my hand. Not even fifteen seconds had gone by, never mind my fifteen minutes. *Oh God, this was going to be a long evening!* I started composing what I was going to say in my head, but then I stopped myself. I might seem too high maintenance if I scolded him right away. I would tell any of my clients to suck it up and wait until they had been together for at least a half hour or so. Sometimes I have to practice what I preach, so I tried pretending that I was elsewhere, almost levitating outside the cab, until we got to the restaurant.

When we arrived, he asked if we could sit next to each other, on the same side of the table, like they do in Europe. Before I could stop myself, I blurted out, "Why?" He looked longingly into my eyes and said he thought it would be nice. I said with a plastic smile that I thought I would be more comfortable if we faced each other—we would be able to have a better conversation that way. He seemed surprised but said okay. Right then I decided I couldn't do it, I couldn't go out with him again. Clearly if I am this uptight about his touching me, I shouldn't be with him.

Note to self: Tell my male clients that it is bad, very bad, to be so touchy so early on.

Friday, November 25

Maybe my best bet would be to cultivate my own guys, grow them in a petri dish of sorts. I am starting to realize that I am never going to find Him as a single-bodied individual. No *one* guy seems to work for me. If only I could combine a dash of one guy with a sprinkle of another, then some of a third, and see what happens. I could ask for a cell or some blood from all the good ones. Wonder if it would work? I'm not really sure why meeting Him is so hard. I don't know if I am just pickier than other girls, or if I just know too much, but no *one* guy is working for me, not even a little bit.

BACK TO
The Girl I Always Thought Hated Me

I got a phone call from The Girl I Always Thought Hated Me. I was excited to hear how her first Samantha's Table date went. She seemed dejected. She said she liked him but didn't think he liked her. I was disappointed. Why? I asked. He just seemed like he wasn't all that interested in what she was saying. He kept looking at his watch, and got up several times, supposedly to go to the bathroom, but she thought he was getting up to use the phone. "I think I am a terrible dater. Would you sit down with me and go over dating etiquette?" *Hmm, I guess it's time to start actually doing dating coaching instead of just saying that I do it. Now, the question is, Do I charge money for it? No, not for the paying Desperados, maybe for the others.*

Note to self: Figure out how much money I should charge for dating coaching.

Sunday, November 27

My little brother Christopher called me tonight. He asked me how *things* were going. *Things* is his code word for asking me about my love life. He's my younger brother, is already married, and has a very caring wife, Amy. Why was it so easy for him? Why is he giving me dating advice? When did the tables turn? *Aren't I supposed to be the older, wiser one? Aren't I supposed to be the expert?* "How's Jerkoff?" he asked in a voice that hinted of dislike. "We aren't speaking at the moment," I said. "No loss there," he said under his breath, but I heard him. My brother never liked the way Jerkoff treated me. In Jerkoff's defense *(why am I always defending him?),* my brother heard a lot of the bad and very little of the good, so it's not surprising that he would hate him for me. "Amy's mom might have a blind date for you. Should I find out more?" I perked up a bit. "Sure, find out. I'm game to meet anyone once, I guess."

BACK TO
Miss Manhunt

She called today, all excited because she had just bought a fixer-upper house in upstate New York. She couldn't wait to start fixing it up, and she wanted to tell me about it. I flew into a panic. "Miss Manhunt, you paid me $10,000 to introduce you to men as quickly as possible so you could get married as quickly as possible, so why would you buy a house more than four hours outside New York that needs your time and your attention? How can you focus on dating in New York City if you just committed to taking yourself away from New York City every weekend?"

Silence on the other end. She said tentatively, "Well . . . I didn't think of it like that. This is a great house. I can afford it and I have a lot of friends who have houses there. I actually thought you would be impressed that I bought it because it shows that I made a commitment to something when you say I am so commitmentphobic." I shook my head in frustration. "What kind of friends, Miss Manhunt? All married ones, I am sure. And, yes, I want you to make a commitment, but not to a house in upstate New York—to a man, a man, Miss Manhunt. How are you going to find that man if you are hanging out with married people a million miles away?" Silence again. "Well, my plans are to have a date in New York on Friday night, get up very early on Saturday morning to make the drive so it only takes two and a half hours, work on the house all day, and be back in time for a Saturday night date. What's so bad about that?"

I was getting exasperated. "Oh right, Miss Manhunt. Every weekend you are going to drive five hours minimum on one day back and forth. Give me a break. You will do that a few times, and you will realize it's easier to make the drive at night, and then the contractor will run late at the end of the day Saturday a bunch of times, and you won't make it back for your Saturday night date, and then eventually you will just wind up spending the full weekend there *alone* in your fixer-upper house." She started to cry. "Did I make a mistake?" she sniffled. I felt bad then. Maybe I was being too harsh with her, although I do think that what she did was a very stupid, commitment-phobic thing to do. But I told her not to fret; we will just have to find her a man as quickly as possible so he could accompany her on the weekends!

TABLE CHANGE

Effective immediately, I hired an assistant. Her name is Vanessa. I found her through a friend of a friend. She is the perfect person to work for me. She is 27, with a perky personality, easy to get along with, and flexible. She's comfortable talking to or approaching any-one. She screens all the would-be Desperados, answers all of their questions, goes out to parties and hunts for new people, and helps me with my events. *Mission accomplished.*

NOT FOR ME GUY
Mr. Teeth

I went to another charity benefit last week and met a guy, Mr. Teeth. He was a nice-enough guy, fine-looking, very well educated, a little boring, but it seemed like once he got more comfortable he might come out of his shell, but *(there is always a but),* he had bad teeth. I found myself wondering if a little teeth-whitening session could do the trick. I decided that maybe I should try him out for yours truly first before I flipped him into Desperadoland. So I minimized talk about the biz, maximized talk about me, and he asked me out. I decided to keep it more friendly than flirtatious, so I would have the luxury of deciding what I thought and what I wanted to do with this guy. We decided on a day date, a safe date in my opinion, so I could see if I could stomach him.

Well, I stomached him, but the kissing thing was just not going to happen, ever, for me, with those teeth. It's funny, the teeth became a chicken and the egg situation. Which should come first—being able to tell the guy to go get his teeth whitened so you can kiss him and you can then decide if you want to go to the next level with him or going to the next level with him so you can tell him to get his teeth fixed?! If he were my client I would just tell him to get his teeth whitened and I would lie a little bit and say that I don't really care but a lot of girls do. However, in our own personal arena, it's trickier.

I probably shouldn't have said anything, but I felt I had to. I figured if he became my guy or one of my girl's guys, it would do him well to go the whitening route. I did chicken out a bit by telling him a funny little anecdote about one of *my clients,* a fictitious one. I told him that I was trying to figure out how to help one of my clients. I told him that I had sent the clients on a bunch of dates and the girls kept saying that he had such terrible teeth that they had no interest in kissing him or going out with him again. I asked Mr. Teeth if he thought I should tell my client. Mr. Teeth did exactly as I had hoped. He said, "Well, I don't have such great teeth and I guess I never knew that it would bother a woman so much; you should tell him." I said, "Oh, really, I didn't even notice that your teeth are bad, let me see." With that, he showed me his teeth and I said, "You are right, your teeth aren't great, you should really go get them whitened, it's such an easy thing these days and it's not expensive." I figured fait accompli, but then I got stuck—he asked, "Well, would *you* not kiss me with my teeth like this?" *Oh boy, the time of truth.* I decided to be honest, so I told him that I probably would prefer kissing him if his teeth weren't like that. He said, "Very interesting, you are very picky." *Yes, I guess I am.*

Then he proceeded to tell me how he hadn't dated very much, he was embarrassed to admit, and what did I think of that. Again I went with bluntness and said, "Well, if you were to hire me I would hand-pick girls for you who are nice and sweet and would give you a chance even though you aren't a very experienced dater. I would be your agent of sorts, selling you to all these great women. Trust me, my service would be the greatest thing you ever did for yourself." He said he was confused, he thought we were on a date. I said, "We were *trying each other out,* but to be honest there is no way that we would work as a dating couple, but as Matchmaker/client, there we would make a great couple!" "Do you test out people often before you take them as clients or before you date them?" he asked. I guess what I said sounded funny, so I laughed and I said I was just being cute but seriously he should think about hiring me. He said he would and sheepishly he asked for a teeth-whitening recommendation.

Note to self: Find a teeth-whitening dentist and give the information to Mr. Teeth.

I have a funny job. I can go out on a date and if the guy isn't for me, I can either flip him into the database and use him as fodder for my Desperados or I can try to get him to become a full-fledged Desperado himself. And I can go to a party and if and when I get bored and decide that there really isn't anyone I want to speak to for me personally, I can immediately go into work mode and just meet the peeps for biz. Isn't life grand? Well, it's financially grand, *but it would be better if there was one guy who I didn't want to flip at all. I guess a girl can dream a little. . . .*

December

Matchmaking in December. A lot of clients freak out because they can't believe they are about to go through another New Year's Eve without a date. A lot of new callers make preliminary appointments with me, saying that if they get to January first and they haven't met "the One," they want to sign up. Other people beg and plead to sign up immediately on the off chance that they might be able to meet someone, *like yesterday.* My general feeling about December: I would rather push most of the new Desperados to January so I can relax a little, take in a whole bunch of holiday parties, and go on a much-needed vacation.

BACK TO
Miss Manhunt

I think I must have panicked Miss Manhunt a little about her purchase of the fixer-upper house because she insisted I go double time on the dating front. She wanted me to introduce her to two men at a time so that she didn't waste any time at all. This was unnecessary. I tried to convince her that if she's always so focused on meeting the next guy down the pike, she might not notice a great guy right in front of her. She said not to worry, she could handle the volume, I just needed to line them up.

I pulled out the 35- to 50-year-old HI (High Income) list:

First I considered Danny, 35, youngest ever MD (managing director), at his investment bank. No. What about Peter, II (Institutional Investor) rated research analyst? Might be too full of himself. Phillip 47, divorced with two kids, took his company public? Maybe, but not as her first date. What about the Troll? No, she would eat him for breakfast. I know, Mr. Gazillionaire. Why didn't I think of him immediately? He's perfect and I can kill two birds with one stone. And for a second guy, what about Dot-Com Guy, 38, very wealthy, not that good-looking but a really good guy, seems ready to get married pronto. Perfect.

I called Mr. Gazillionaire and told him about Miss Manhunt. I teased him that if he liked her, he needed to be very proactive about the follow-up phone calls. He said, "Aye, aye, skipper!" Soon afterward, I called Dot-Com Guy and he, too, was game. And last I called Miss Manhunt and gave her her roster for the week. She was pleased.

BACK TO

Miss Gold Digger

As long as I had the 35- to 50-year-old HI list out, I figured I would do some searching for Miss Gold Digger. I thought about how the two women were different: Miss Manhunt needed wealthy men who wouldn't be freaked out by her urgency and intensity, whereas Miss Gold Digger needed wealthy men who were particularly generous.

For Miss Gold Digger, what about Paul, 39, hedge fund manager? No, as I recall, he is a small tipper. What about George, 44, magazine editor? Hmm, maybe he does come from big family money, could be interesting. Hmm, I know, the Troll. The Troll could be perfect!

For Miss Gold Digger's first official Table date, I went with the Troll. He has been around the New York social scene forever but has yet to get married. He comes from a *very* wealthy midwestern family and he has made a boatload of money on his own. Many a gold digger has tried to rope him in, but, alas, he remains unattached. His nickname is the Troll because he's short, maybe five feet six, and quite unattractive. However, as far as the gold diggers out there are concerned, mine included, he can stand on his money and get his teeth capped. The interesting thing about the Troll is that he actually likes gold diggers. He is perfectly willing to trade his money for women who trade their looks. So I put in a little call. . . .

Hello, Troll, how are you? I have the perfect Desperado—I mean gold digger, I mean woman—for you. This is how I work: you don't have to pay me anything right now, but if you marry my client you have to pay me a $25,000 fee. He said, "No worries. I have a lot of money and I've been dating forever. If only you could find me the One, I would love to pay you."

TABLE CHANGE

No more freebies for men. If I call a man from my database to introduce him to one of the female Desperados and he's interested, he gets charged a backend fee, as the Troll did. Backend fees can be any amount a guy is comfortable with but start at $25,000.

Monday, December 5

I went to an opening tonight at the new Louis Vuitton store on 57th Street. There were a lot of fashionistas, socialites, and wannabes. I spent much of the evening people-watching—there's always good people-watching at these things. I didn't pay much attention to the men there because most of them were gay. Of course, as usual, because I wasn't really looking, I met a cute guy who was definitely straight. He was manly, with broad shoulders, big hands, scruff on his face, and a loud, boisterous laugh. We got into a conversation, and I found out he was there because one of his best female friends from college worked for the public relations firm that had planned the party. We flirted for a while and were getting along really well. He even asked me if I would go with him to a work event that he had to attend next week.

And then the subject of what I did came up. Tonight I decided to go with the truth because I knew quite a few people at the party and I remembered the disaster with Soho House Guy and the scampering girl. So I told him and he exclaimed, "No shit. Wow. So you have a department store of women. Wow. So who do you have for me?" *I thought I had me for you, but I guess I thought wrong.* I immediately went into work gear. "I don't know you at all. I really wouldn't be able to say." He insisted, "Well, just try it. We have been talking for a while. Who would you set me up with?" The light went out of my eyes. "Listen, I need to use the rest room. Here is my card. I'd be happy to sit down for a consultation with you if you're interested." *I guess you are no longer taking me to that work event of yours!* I walked away and left the party.

On my walk home, I felt my eyes tearing up. *Why is it that men are such pigs? Why is it that I was interesting enough for that guy initially, but then when he heard that I had access to lots of hot women, I alone was no longer interesting enough? Aren't I a pretty woman anymore? Why would a man rather hear about a lot of amorphous women with whom he might or might not hit it off than continue to get to know me, who he already has chemistry with?* I wiped away a tear as I walked into my building.

BACK TO

The Girl I Always Thought Hated Me

She called and said sadly that she definitely wanted to go forward with the dating coaching—she needed it. Not only did she feel uncomfortable on her Samantha's Table dates, but she thought she was bombing the dates she found for herself. She needed help. She asked me, "Well, how would it work?" *I have no idea. You are my first coachee.* I said, "The first session would be over lunch. We would discuss conversation topics that would and should work for you on dates. And the second session would be the two of us really delving into to some of your dating issues." I was making this up as I went along. She said she wanted to buy a makeover day. How much was that? Five hundred dollars, I decided, and she said fine.

TABLE CHANGE

Effective immediately, I do dating coaching. I charge $250 a session, with a two-session minimum, or two sessions can equal one introduction if you are a registered Desperado. In addition, I charge $500 for a half-day makeover session during which I will take the Desperado to my hair and makeup person.

Note to self: Find my *hair and makeup person.*

And then I take them to one of the five "Bs": Barneys, Bloomingdale's, Bendel's, Bergdorf's, or Banana Republic and help them pick out clothes.

Note to self: Find my *personal shopper at each store.*

NOT FOR ME GUY

Not Even for the Database Guy

I hadn't been on such a bad date in a while. One of my new friends (a woman who wants me to set her up) gave my number to this guy. I have no idea why I trusted her, but I did. Big mistake! He showed up wearing dark jeans, a belt that had a huge gold horseshoe on it, and white ostrich cowboy boots. He was a throwback to the John Travolta days in *Urban Cowboy*! He kept trying to make jokes that just weren't funny, but he'd crack himself up and slap his hand on the table for effect. I stared at him, wondering, Am I pickier than I used to be? Or is he hopelessly unappealing? *Who knows?* All I knew was that I didn't like him, not even a little bit. I'm not even sure that I would enter him into the database and keep him in mind for one of my little chicks; he was that bad.

And to add insult to injury, once he heard what I did for a living, he wouldn't stop grilling me. He even asked me the question that I detest and hear more often than I would like: "How is it possible that you're a Matchmaker and you meet so many eligible men and yet you're still single?" *Jesus Christ, just because I am a Matchmaker doesn't mean I get an express ticket to the Marriage Promised Land. Unfortunately, I need to go through the pains of dating like everybody else, which means going out with losers like you.*

Note to self: Revisit the how-can-you-be-single *question and come up with a better response, something that I can live with and that moves the conversation along.*

Thursday, December 8

Got back from my date with Mr. Not Even for the Database feeling quite depressed. And to make matters worse, there were three e-mails and three messages from Miss 39, telling me it was an emergency. I needed to check out a guy she had been e-mailing on JDate and tell her whether or not I thought he was crazy. She also asked me to check out her profile and tell her what I thought because she wasn't sure it was attracting the kind of men she wanted to meet. I went over to my desk and turned on my computer. *Does my job as a Matchmaker never end?* I went online. I punched up her guy: NYhotguy137. He was good-looking, his profile seemed literate, he definitely didn't seem crazy to me. Then I went to her profile: Queen Bee. *What kind of name is that?* The profile seemed very much like Miss 39, direct, to the point, and a little humble. It was the photos that concerned me. She had a photo of herself holding a little baby *(a sure way to scare off the men),* a photo of herself in corporate business attire with no smile on her face *(not so welcoming),* and a full-length photo in a ski parka that completely covered her cute figure *(she should be showing off that body of hers!). What was she thinking? I need to have her change her pictures, pronto.* While I was checking out her profile, I got an instant message from Cruiseman64, then another one from EFGeorge, and then another one from Checkmeoutguy, and then still another one from Iamgreat. My God, this is overwhelming, but kind of fun. *Who are these guys? Are they normal? Do I know them? Do they know me?* Last month I said I would try this and of course I didn't, and now this month I am still single, still having horrible dates, and I still have not tried it. Maybe it's time . . . *maybe.*

DESPERADO #17

Miss Boobs

A new client walked into the Regency today, and when she took off her coat, all I could think was, What a rack! *Have I become a man, analyzing women first by their boobs?* This woman was tall and had a flat stomach but she also had huge breasts. I mean *bizungas galore.* It was hard not to notice them first. I could think of a ton of guys who would go crazy for *that.* I mean *her.* The funny thing about her, though, was that she was oddly self-conscious about her looks. She explained that she was meeting with me because she was having trouble meeting quality men. She felt as if she only met men who were obsessed with boobs, and she was more than boobs alone. *I, too, had already forgotten about the rest of her. Maybe it's not fair to call her Miss Boobs?*

BACK TO

Mr. Gazillionaire and Miss Manhunt

I spoke to Mr. Gazillionaire a little bit ago. He is crazy for Miss Manhunt. He doesn't want me to introduce him to anyone else right now—he is smitten. He has even been to her fixer-upper house, and he loves that she bought it. *Yippee*. Then I heard from Miss Manhunt with an update. She loved Mr. Gazillionaire, and Dot-Com Guy was just okay. Okay, that's not so bad on our first shot. Great, I said, so keep me posted on how it goes with Mr. Gazillionaire. I was about to hang up when she shouted into the phone, almost as an afterthought, "Wait, don't hang up. I want to keep seeing him but"—she paused— "I want to meet another two men as well."

I decided it was time to give Miss Manhunt a little lecture. I dove in. "Miss Manhunt, if you loved Mr. Gazillionaire, why not focus a little bit on him and see if it can go somewhere? I think your problem is that you are too focused on going on as many dates as possible, as quickly as possible. You're missing the person standing right in front of you."

She got upset. "That is not a problem. I can stay focused on him and I still can go on other dates. We are not married, we are not exclusive, so why should I wait?" "Miss Manhunt, I don't want to upset you. I am simply saying that you have been out with Mr. Gazillionaire six times, which is a lot, and maybe you will have more success with him if you focus on him and on the two of you. He told me that he doesn't want to get set up with anyone else right now because he likes you and wants to see where it's going." Then, in a timid voice, she said, "He said that? Really?" She paused. "Well, if he actually said that, then maybe, well, maybe I will say that, too." I smiled to myself and said, "It's our little secret that he said that. Don't tell him that I told you. But, yes, he's into you and I think you should focus on being into him, too, so you don't blow it."

It dawned on me that Miss Manhunt's frenetic dating pace was all a defense mechanism. She didn't want people (especially her guy) to know she was truly interested. Once she heard that he was into her, she was more than willing to slow down. *I can respect that.*

Tuesday, December 13

Tonight I ran into a guy I went on a date with about a year ago, during a time when Jerkoff was being a particular jerkoff and I decided to date. I ran into him at Zitomer pharmacy while I was buying tampons, of all things. He was a struggling novelist whom I had met at a friend's thirty-fourth birthday party. We got into a conversation, and the subject of my business came up. Now that I am the dating expert, he asked me to give him a little critique and tell him what he did wrong on our dates, since I was now the dating expert. I started looking toward the door for my escape route. "I don't think that would be a very good idea," I said. He laughed and playfully nudged my arm. "No, no, no, I can handle it. Lay it on me." *Oh boy, he so won't be able to handle it. Guys can't take criticism, especially if it has to do with a physical attribute.*

But he was insistent. I took a deep breath and very quickly said, "You had bad breath every time I saw you, and the thought of kissing you was very unappealing." I don't know what sort of critique he was expecting, but from the expression on his face, he wasn't expecting me to say that. He turned bright red, his eyes got that embarrassed, hurt look, and he started hurling insults back at me. "Well, you know, I only went out with you because I had nothing else going on. I wasn't even attracted to you. I wasn't even going to attempt to kiss you. Maybe I knew my breath was bad and maybe I didn't care because I had no interest whatsoever." *Right, yup, you are a struggling writer. You were on deadline for some spec script and you just figured you would waste time and money that you didn't have to take me to three expensive restaurants just for the hell of it. Sure!*

Whatever. I am a fool, and I am a stupid dating expert. I should have known better. I know that I can critique my clients because my criticism is objective and I am only relaying it. But never, never again will I pass along personal criticism to my own dates. No one wants to hear it. Telling him about his bad breath accomplished absolutely nothing because he didn't even hear me say it. He rationalized it away and now I have this guy walking around thinking that I am rude. *What was the point?*

BACK TO

The Girl I Always Thought Hated Me

Today was our first coaching session. We met at the Regency. I sat at my usual table and ordered the chicken noodle soup with mini grilled cheese sandwiches. She showed up in what I suspected was her date outfit—black pants and a low-cut sexy top that hugged her waist nicely. It seemed like she thought of this as a practice date. *Good idea. I should tell the peeps to come to the coaching sessions in their date garb so I can evaluate what they wear.* We spent an hour going over different dating scenarios. Since this was my first official dating coaching hour, I experimented a little, but The Girl didn't seem to spot it. I figured I would role-play date questions with her to start.

First I complimented her on what she was wearing. This made her smile and put her a little more at ease. Then I started in, "So how do you know Samantha?" (I figured a lot of the dates must start with that question because I probably provide some common ground.) She answered, "Well, I knew her in college. She thought I hated her, though. In college everyone thought I hated them." I rolled my eyes and said to her, "Think about the impression you are giving of yourself if you answer like that. If you say that everyone thought you hated them, he's going to think you're some kind of she-devil. Maybe it would be better if you say something cute or positive instead." She looked panicked. "What should my answer be?" "Well," I said patiently, "how about: 'I knew her in college and now, after all these years, we ran into each other again. When I heard what she did, I immediately felt comfortable hiring her since we had known each other for so long.'" She retorted, "But that's not really the truth. We didn't know each other at all, and you thought I hated you." I took a sip of my Diet Coke to give myself a minute to find my patient voice again. "Yes, but we do have history, and this is a good thing. The guy sitting across from you doesn't need to know the specifics, and we are friends now, and you don't hate me and I don't hate you." She nodded in agreement. I explained to her that on dates you have to monitor what comes out of your mouth, and you should only say the things you want them to believe.

I moved on, role-playing again. "So, tell me about your family." She livened up a bit. "Well, I have two brothers, and my parents are divorced. My dad is a jerk and I don't really see him." She wrinkled her nose in disapproval. "My mom is pretty self-absorbed, but she's my mom, so I deal with her, but we aren't close." She laughed a bit. "I have a great relationship with my brothers, though." She smiled and pushed her hair behind her ears. "How was that?" she asked. I wanted to say awful, but that wouldn't accomplish anything. Instead I said, "Well, what do you think the guy is thinking when he hears what you just said?" She didn't know. I explained, "What he is thinking is that you don't have a real relationship with either of your parents, so either you are not family-oriented or you have a lot of mom-and-dad issues, which can make a person very dysfunctional." She was distressed. "But that's the truth. That's what my relationship is like with my parents. We are not a Beaver Cleaver family." I countered, "That's fine, and eventually he will know that and have to deal with it. But he *doesn't need to know that on the first date*," I said with emphasis. "On the first date, you can be vague, and you can keep some of the scary stuff for later. Maybe it's better to answer by saying, 'My family is all in the New York area—a typical, dysfunctional modern-day family. My parents divorced when I was young, but I have two brothers and we're superclose." I took a beat and asked what she thought. Again, she said she guessed that she could say that but she didn't think it would change things. She looked so depressed and sad.

Okay, this role-playing thing does not seem to be working. Maybe that's for the second session. I changed directions and asked about questions that were stumping her, or other things that she thought might be inhibiting her on the dates. Her tone became serious and a little melancholy. "I just don't think I'm coming across in an interesting way. I always feel like the guys are bored. How can I fix that?" *Hmm, maybe body language and physical disposition was the real session one.* I said, "First, you need to smile more. When you smile, you light up and become much more approachable." She smiled a little. Then I told her, "You need to sit up straight so you seem alert and interested in what is going on, instead of seeming bored." I leaned across the table and pushed on her lower back to get her to sit up straighter. "And you should try not cross your arms across your chest. This also makes you seem unapproachable." She shuffled in her chair a bit again—much better. I then told her, "I am going to e-mail you a list of conversation topics and ask you to do a little homework. I want you to come up with light answers and cute comments, and we'll go over them and practice at our next session." She laughed and said okay. "Is this really going to work or am I hopeless?" I said of course it was going to work *but . . .*

Note to self: The first hour of dating coaching is a lesson on body language and asking the client what topics they get stumped on. Session ends with my handing them a date question list to review and asking them to come up with answers that we will review at the next session. Remember to create list of date questions.

Saturday, December 24

Went to a wedding tonight and ran into an ex—not Jerkoff, another one, Mr. Indecision. He used to drive me crazy. The SAT word *vacillate* was invented for him. He couldn't make a decision about anything, from things as small as what to order off a menu to bigger things like what he wanted to do with the rest of his life, careerwise. He was maddening. Of course he was still up in the air about his career. And of course he was still single, which wasn't surprising, because most men can only settle down with a woman when they feel content about their work situation.

I knew he was going to be at the wedding, and I was sort of curious how I would feel when I saw him. It's been a long time since we broke up, over four years, but he was definitely the hottest man I ever dated. He had the cutest smile and amazing dimples that gave me goose bumps when I saw them. I wondered if I would still think he was hot. I also wondered if we would wind up going home together.

He was still hot, and he still smelled exactly as I remembered, yummy. So we flirted a lot, and I would have gone home with him, just to see if it was still there sexually, but he was too chicken to put his money where he mouth is, so to speak. He flirted all night, but when it came time to the do-or-dare, he was on the fence about it. *A shocker.* I could have, I would have, but we didn't. He's still Mr. Indecision and I still know I made the right decision, even though I still think he is hot.

BACK TO

Looks Good from Afar Guy

I have sent this Desperado out on several dates. It is not going well. After his initial freak-out about his first date's voice, he's been very happy with the women I've been setting him up with. The setups aren't going anywhere, however, because the women aren't interested. They all think he's cute initially, but then they find him boring or rude and don't want to go out again. He had his fifth date last night, and he called today to find out what the woman said. I decided that today had to be tough-love-from-me day. How I hate those conversations! He asked me how last night went, and I started, as I usually do, by saying, "She said all great things about you, but unfortunately she didn't feel that romantic chemistry, so she doesn't want to waste your time going out again." As I said it, I was wondering if he remembered that this was the exact same sentence I had said to him about the last three women.

He paused. I paused. "That is the exact same thing you said to me after the last three women. I can either play stupid or ask you point-blank: am I doing something wrong?" I smiled in relief that he had been the one to open the door to this conversation. "Are you open to some constructive criticism and some advice?" (I've learned that I need to ask clients before I give the advice or they get pissed.) I heard him shuffling in his seat and then he said fine. I took a breath. "Well, a lot of the girls have found you to be very handsome and are very excited to get to know you when they first arrive, but then as the date progresses, they say that they get a little bored or think you don't behave well on the date." I paused and started playing with my hair—I was a little nervous. *What will I do if this guy starts to cry?* Women's tears, I'm starting to get used to, but, guys' tears are a whole new frontier. He seemed okay, though. So I continued. "I think you need to go to the dates with a repertoire of interesting things to talk about, fall-back conversation topics so that there won't be a lull in the conversation."

"Like what?"

"Ask her if she has any trips planned and then talk about where you would like to travel next. Ask her about her favorite travel destination and make sure you have an interesting place to describe that you have traveled to as well. Talk about favorite restaurants and come up with one or two to mention that she might not have been to so she thinks you like to do interesting things. Come up with a funny story from childhood that you can share."

"Hmm," he said thoughtfully, "I usually don't bring those things up. I usually just talk about my work or things that are bothering me and current events. Is that bad?" *Yes!* "Well, apparently it's not working. Why don't you try to come up with some of these lighter things to discuss and try them out on the next date, and let's see how it goes." Agreed. *Dating 101 accomplished.*

DESPERADO #18

Miss Kid Waffler

This Desperado came through a referral from one of my previous Desperados who is now in a relationship. It's good to know that the peeps give me good press. This woman was very peculiar. Quite pretty, thin, about five feet seven, with straight dark hair, very bright. Works in pharmaceutical sales, is sweet but says that she can't seem to get into a relationship. I was surprised because, at first glance, she seemed better than the average girl. It wasn't until we got to the children discussion that I was able to figure out what wasn't working for her. Most of the female Desperados who come to me are dying to have kids; usually the problem is their baby fever is too obvious and scares off men. I always need to spend a lot of time coaching these women on how to seem nonchalant about their biological clocks when in fact they are in a state of panic. This is no easy feat; in fact, it's my greatest challenge.

Now my current Desperado turned out to be exactly the opposite of most of my chickadees. She wasn't sure if she wanted to have kids at all. "How do you handle it if, on a date, a guy asks you if you want to have kids?" I asked with genuine curiosity. "I say that I am not sure if I want to have them. That's the truth so I just tell them that." *Ah-hah! We have discovered the Achilles' heel.* I tried to be empathetic. "Let me ask you something, Miss Kid Waffler. Is it that you definitely don't want to have children, or is it that you are *not certain* whether you want to have kids?" She looked at me curiously, gave my question some thought, and answered, "I don't know. I guess it's more that I'm uncertain. Why?" I nodded my head. "Well, I think that by answering the kid question that way, you're effectively stating that you don't want them at all, because most women would never say that they aren't sure if they want them. So what I think is happening is that the guys you are going out with are getting turned off because they think that you are a woman who *won't* have children." She started getting annoyed. "Really. Well, why would they think that if I am saying maybe. Maybe should mean *maybe.*" I nodded my head in agreement as I explained patiently, "You're right, but it's a funny, crazy balancing act in the dating world. Men don't want the women who are desperate to have kids tomorrow, but they also don't want the women who don't want kids at all, because most men want kids. So to get a man, you need to make it clear that you *can* be the mother of their children but you don't *need or want to be* the mother of their children *tomorrow,* even if that's not true." "So what are you saying?" she asked curtly. "I am not saying to lie, but I am saying to be more careful about how you represent yourself."

Furthermore, I told her, men immediately jump to assume that a woman who doesn't want kids isn't family-oriented or has a bad relationship with her family. Miss Kid Waffler was indignant. "I have an amazing relationship with my family. I talk to my parents every day. I am such a family person. That's crazy." "Exactly," I said, "you are giving off the wrong vibe." I told her, "Men are looking for the mother of their children *and* they are looking for family-oriented women. They take your reply to mean that you're not a good wife candidate and that you have family issues. I know it's not fair and it might not be true, but this is the way men think. Trust me, they tell me."

Finally she relented. "Okay, fine. What do you want me to say?" "Say, 'I love kids, and when I find the right person who I am going to spend my life with, we will figure it out.' This is the truth, but a little more palatable for a guy." "I can do that," she said with a smile, so I took her on as a client.

BACK TO

Miss Boobs

I wanted to find some good men for Miss Boobs. (I'm still calling her that but keeping in mind that she is not boobs alone.) I pulled out the NG (Nice Guy) list.

What about Jerry, 38, an orthodontist, very intellectual? No, might be too boring for her. There's Ben, 35, would probably die for her figure,

but he would never see beyond her boobs. Maybe Pete? Yes, Pete could be
good. Oh wait, Nick. Nick is perfect.

Nick would be an easy sell because I knew that he was a total boobs guy, but I thought—*thought* being the operative word—he would be more than that, too. When I called him, he gave me a bit of hard time at first, saying that if she was as hot as I was describing, why would she need to use a dating service? He thought that only ugly, fat chicks would come to me. I got pretty defensive on behalf of my female clients.

Note to self: Don't get defensive, get used to it!

I bawled him out and told him that now he didn't get to meet Miss Boobs. He was being punished, and he would always wonder just how hot she was. Then I hung up. *Oops, now the database is down again.* If I'm not careful, I won't have anyone left to set people up with.

I stuck with Miss Boobs for a while and made another call on her behalf. This time, jackpot. Peter, choice number two, was ecstatic to meet her. Great.

NOT FOR ME GUY

Mr. Retired at 36

I went to the newest hip lounge this weekend. When I got there, I ran into a woman I used to be friendly with. She is very sweet, but we just lost touch. She and her friends had a table, and a table is a key thing to have at a crowded place like this one, so I was especially glad to see her. She invited me to sit down.

Seated at her table was a guy I had gone on a date with a gazillion years ago and had not liked. I was in my I-am-so-cool phase then, and he just wasn't cool enough. These days, however, I'm stuck in my I-can't-get-past-date-one phase, and he would be more than cool enough. Funny how things change. Actually, I am not giving him enough credit: he had really come into his own. He was six feet two, with jet-black hair that has started to recede and a really welcoming smile, and he'd grown into a confident, funny, well-dressed, athletic guy. He had also done very well for himself financially. He built an Internet company during the Internet boom and sold it for millions, and now he's retired at 36. I looked across the table and found myself wondering if I could rebound and strike up something with him now.

I started flirting a bit and—surprise, surprise—I found him flirting back. But I also sensed a bit of territorialness coming from my former friend. *Hmm, the plot thickens. Were they together? Was he inappropriately flirting with moi? Was I imagining that he was flirting with moi?* No, didn't think so. We wound up in a heated debate/discussion about my business and how he thought that only losers would spend the money to hire someone like me. I explained that my clients were not losers—so much so that he wouldn't even make the cut. He was relentless in his criticism to the point that my former friend told him to tone it down, that everyone knew that my clients were actually really cool, that I had built a substantial business and that he was being rude. It was nice of her to defend me. Then Mr. Retired at 36 felt bad. He looked sheepishly at me and apologized, saying that he was just teasing, that he really respected me, that he knew my business was great, that he got carried away. I brushed off the whole thing. I wasn't offended at all. People have all sorts of ridiculous misconceptions about my biz. I milked it a little though, and I told him that he could feel free to send me flowers and that I prefer purple tulips. He laughed.

When I got up to leave, he jumped to his feet and gave me a kiss on the cheek. I tousled his hair a bit and said teasingly that I'd look forward to the flowers on Monday. He asked if dinner would be an okay substitute, and I tousled again, winked at him, and left. I thought about him when I got home. I couldn't figure out if it was innocent flirting or the real McCoy. I thought it was the real McCoy. I also didn't know if he was dating the woman I used to be friends with. If he was, I didn't want to be a home wrecker. The next day, I did some digging, and most of our mutual friends said they weren't involved.

On Monday I decided to go out on a flirtatious limb. I sent him an e-mail saying simply, "I thought you might need my address for the flowers." And I typed my address and signed my name. And I waited.

He e-mailed me back almost instantly saying he was very impressed with the fact that I had his e-mail. He asked where I got it, and I assured him I was quite resourceful when it came to getting purple tulips. He e-mailed back that he thought he could opt for dinner in lieu of flowers and I typed back, one word: "When?"

We wound up having dinner twice this week. We started making out at the table within thirty minutes of sitting down on our first date. There was a lot of chemistry between us. We went for drinks afterward, and we were all over each other on the couch at the bar. We had fun.

But . . . I've decided not to see him again. He's 36 and retired. I know that should be a good thing, but My Guy works for a living and My Guy doesn't retire at 36. I just think it's odd. I love working and I want to be with someone who works. *Is that crazy?* He thought it was. He insisted that most women would love the fact that he didn't need to work. I explained but he just didn't understand that it felt unusual for me to work and for him to do nothing all day. What I didn't say was that he had nothing to add to our conversations because he wasn't coming in contact with people or doing anything new. He was wealthy, he had three homes, he was presumably smart, and I was physically attracted to him, but I found him to be empty, uninteresting. *Maybe I am making a mistake, but I don't think so. . . .*

BACK TO

Miss Boobs

Got a nervous call from Miss Boobs. What should she wear on her date? "What do you usually wear?" I asked her. She said jeans and a sexy top. I told her that sounded great—she was going to look beautiful. So funny, now I am a fashion stylist, too.

January

After September, January is probably the hottest Matchmaking month. It's freezing in New York, nobody wants to go out, there are very few social events taking place, people have broken up over Christmas and New Year's, and many people are very depressed that they are starting a new year alone *again*. My phone rings off the hook this month.

BACK TO
Mr. Metrosexual

I set up Mr. Metrosexual a number of times last month. Turns out he is very picky, no big surprise. Ironically, the women find him to be too difficult and he's finding them to be not difficult enough. *What is wrong with this guy?* Didn't he tell me that he didn't want such high-maintenance girls, and didn't I tell him that I thought high maintenance would be better for him? And now he is complaining? I don't think this guy knows what he wants.

I asked him again to describe his ideal woman. This time he admitted, "I guess you were right. High maintenance is better for me. We complement each other better. Neither of us is really high maintenance actually—we are just 'challenging.'" I laughed to myself as I listened to his description. I decided it was time to have a little heart-to-heart with him. I launched in, "Mr. Metrosexual, in my opinion, the only way you are going to get the kind of girl you want is if *you* tone down the metrosexual act a notch. Just because the term *metrosexual* is part of the vernacular around New York City, it does not mean that you have to be the president of the club." He chuckled. "That's funny, Samantha." I got stern. "I'm not trying to be funny. I agree with what you said before, that most relationships work better if there is just one high-maintenance, very demanding person in the pair, but that person is usually the woman." His voice rose a notch. "Samantha, I want what I want, and I want there to be two metrosexuals in my couple, she and I! She's out there, I just know it." *Okay, great. But can you give me a hint where she might be because I am running out of ideas!*

Mr. Cuticles

I accepted a blinder with a guy that my old boss offered up. Interesting-sounding guy, he was mid-thirties, very entrepreneurial, sort of an old soul. He wasn't into the bar scene. He preferred dinner parties to "ragers," and he wasn't living with Ikea furniture from college (a recurring problem among otherwise eligible men in and around New York City). We had a nice conversation on the phone, and I was actually looking forward to meeting him.

We went to dinner at Mr. Chow, his choice, and a very good one considering it's my favorite restaurant in the city. We ran into a friend of his who was out with a woman I knew. The friend lived in a downtown loft with a huge outdoor deck and a hot tub. He invited us back to take a dip. Was I game, my blinder asked? Hmm, was I game? Not sure. *I was game as long as he and his friends didn't have something kinky in mind.*

After dinner, we all headed downtown. The other guy broke open a bottle of vino, put on some sultry music, stripped down to his boxers, and jumped right in. Obviously he was used to this sort of thing; it was his hot tub, after all. My guy went next. I could tell he wasn't as comfortable, but he did his best to seem nonchalant, and he hopped in as well. Unfortunately for me, Mr. Hot Tub had a much better physique than my guy, but I didn't really care. I am in search of a husband, not a bodybuilder.

Next, the other woman and I took off our clothes at the same time, down to our bras and panties, and slid in. I was thankful that my mom taught me when I very young to always wear matching bra-and-panty sets.

The hot tub was large, so my guy and I were on one side and Mr. Hot Tub and his babe were on the other. Clearly they had been dating for a little while, or maybe they were just more daring, but they started making out right away. I guess I should have expected that. So we started making small talk and trying not to notice the other couple, but they were hard not to notice. Finally, I guess my guy got up some courage and he put his hand on my leg under the water and starting kissing me. I figured a little innocent kissing wouldn't hurt.

His hands felt kind of rough, but he was good kisser and I liked the fact that he didn't start pawing me all over. After about thirty minutes, he got cold and suggested we go inside and towel off.

We went inside and sat down on the bed. With the lights on, I just happened to glance down at his hands. His cuticles, actually his entire fingers, were raw and peeling, which must have been why his fingers felt so rough. I had never seen anything like it. Before I could stop myself, I blurted out, "What happened to your fingers?" He looked down, embarrassed. "Um, I pick at them and chew them sometimes." For some reason, I was repelled. The thought of him touching me *you know where* with his raw and bleeding fingers was really more than I could bear. I told him that I was tired and wanted to go home. It was freezing outside, and as we left, I was grateful for my gloves, so I didn't have to feel his fingers when he held my hand.

When I got home I decided that it would be very shallow to never see this very nice guy again just because of his cuticles. He called me the next day and asked me out. I decided that I could probably buy him that thumb medication—the disgusting-tasting liquid that they use on children to stop them from sucking their thumbs. How hard could that be? He did say he doesn't always chew them, just sometimes.

We went out again last night. I hate to say it, but the cuticles became the deal breaker. They were worse than the first night. Whenever he was lost in thought about something, he would randomly pick at them without even noticing what he was doing. I realized that it was not a chewing-on-them thing. It was a picking-at-them thing, which meant that the thumb medicine wouldn't work, and I wasn't sure what would help them. And then I found myself thinking about him putting his hands on me again, and, uh-oh! No, so not happening. That was the end of Mr. Cuticles.

Miss Gold Digger

She called this morning. She went out with the Troll four times. She really tried to give him a chance, but at the end of the day, she didn't think she could date a guy that everyone refers to as the Troll. "Did you know that the Troll is his real nickname?" she asked accusingly. I felt a little guilty. I wasn't sure how to answer. I went with the truth and said, "Yes, I knew, but what does it matter? Let's be real. He can stand on his money!" She groaned. "Yes, that's what I kept thinking every time I went out with him, but in the end, it didn't help. Will you break up with him for me?" she pleaded. "No, Miss Gold Digger, I won't! One of the rules at the Table is that if you have gone out with a person more than the initial date, it is your responsibility, not mine, to end it appropriately."

She agreed, but I continued to scold her and told her to make sure she did the right thing. "I promise, but now can we move on to an-other guy? Can you pick a guy who doesn't have a nickname this time?" she asked me hopefully. Unfortunately, in my world, they all have nicknames, but she didn't know that, so I said of course. I threw her Dot-Com Guy, but I called him Michael, his God-given name, the guy that Miss Manhunt didn't want. I told Miss Gold Digger about him, and she said great.

Miss Boobs

I got a phone call today from Miss Boobs. She is ready for her next date. She went out with Peter, the guy from my database, a few times and she's decided that she doesn't want to see him again. "Why?" She started listing the reasons. "Number one, he always expects me to pick the place we go and to know of all the good places. Why can't he do that? He's the guy. Number two, his parents are divorced and I really don't want to be with a guy whose parents have split up. And number three, he likes football too much and it's annoying." *She is even pickier than I am!*

I began massaging my temples. "Okay, Miss Boobs, I don't think that any of those reasons should be deal breakers if you like the guy. Let's talk about it." I took the phone with me as I went to get a bottle of water. I opened it and took a few gulps, then said, "I myself used to judge men on where they took me on the date. I used to judge them on whether they spent time picking a place, whether the place was in the proximity of my apartment, whether the place was new and trendy, and whether it was expensive or not. However, now I know that it's more important that a guy would be *willing* to go to a trendy restaurant or an expensive restaurant or a restaurant that requires us to take a taxi. At the end of the day, when people get married, most of the time the woman winds up picking the restaurants, making the reservations, and planning the nights out, so to me, he just has to be willing to go." "Hmm." She paused to consider what I said. "I never thought of it that way. Maybe you're right," she said thoughtfully.

I took a few more sips from the bottle and launched into her second complaint. "As for his parents being divorced, one of my friends used to consider that a deal breaker, but I personally don't because there are just as many screwed-up, commitmentphobic people who grew up with *loving* married parents as there are people from divorced families. Also, I have found that many men who grew up in perfectly happy families have problems actually getting married because *no relationship* they get into ever lives up to their parents' relationship." She was pensive again. "Hmm, I could see that."

"And on the football subject, I've been there before. I once had a boyfriend who actually made me cut short our trip to Eastern Europe so he could get home in time to see an exhibition game, which is a practice game and doesn't even count!" I laughed at the memory. She insisted, "I just don't want to be with a guy who is so into something like that." So I continued on my tirade. "I feel your pain, but is he into football at the expense of being into you, or can he give you what you need and still love football?" She paused for a moment, and after a beat said she didn't know. I told her maybe she should give him a second chance and find out. Finally she agreed.

In the end, her session helped me a bit, too. I think I'm becoming much more accepting of men's quirks and issues. I used to be like Miss Boobs, someone who found fault with everything. Now I just don't do that anymore, or at least I try not to. *So why am I still single?*

TABLE CHANGE

This whole thing of my assistant answering the phone and talking to all the would-be Desperados is not working. Now she wastes all of her time when she could be helping me with the current peeps. Effective immediately, my assistant does not answer the biz line. Instead, there is a recording that asks the peeps, nicely, to send an e-mail to me explaining who they are and what they are looking for. We will respond to all requests within a week.

DESPERADO #19

Miss Excuse

Miss Excuse is the daughter of a friend of the family. Her mother called me directly and offered me $10,000 to work with her. She told me that the extra money would be our little secret: she didn't want her daughter to know, but she was offering the extra amount to ensure that I was properly motivated to help her daughter get a man. She even offered me a $50,000 bonus if I actually got her daughter married. *Wow! What a good mom.* I knew who her daughter was, and I had heard that she was difficult, but for $10,000 and a bonus I was willing to try.

From the second I sat down with her, all I kept thinking was that this girl was in serious need of a full-on dating makeover. She looked like the women in *Extreme Makeover* before the makeover. She was overweight; wore baggy clothes that made her look like a potato; had long, straggly hair; and wore a lot of inappropriate, almost clownlike makeup. Under all of it, however, she had what looked like good bone structure, clear skin, and really intense crystal blue eyes. She also had a great wit and an upbeat personality. As the lunch wore on and as I listened to her make one excuse after the next about her appearance and how she didn't care if she met a man, I decided that I wanted to do a little experiment to see if I could in fact perform the ultimate dating makeover and get this woman married. She was screaming for help even though she wasn't asking for it.

Finally I asked her, "If you don't really want a guy, then why are you sitting here with me?" She looked at her hands and said, "The only reason that I'm here is because my mother made me come. She helps pay my rent and threatened to stop giving me money if I didn't come to meet you and let you help me." *Wow, you go girl, Miss Excuse's mother.* I loved the idea of helping this one. She was the ultimate challenge.

I decided that with this woman I was going to learn how to be brutally honest and still be kind. I wasn't going to let up until she was the best that she could be. I told her sternly, "I like you a lot, but"—I looked directly at her—"the only way I can work with you is if we do a complete dating makeover." "What does that entail exactly?" she asked cautiously. "I need you to trust me implicitly. I am going to change your whole look so that you can attract more guys. I do this all the time with lots of my clients. You should think of it as an adventure." To my surprise, she said, "Why not?" I don't know if it was *why not* because she had no choice, or if it was *why not* because she liked me and wanted my help. I guess it didn't really matter as long as she was on board.

DESPERADO #20

Conflict of Interest Guy

I knew it would happen eventually. Sooner or later, a Desperado would contact me and I would want to date him myself. It was inevitable: I am single, I want to be in a relationship, and I run a Matchmaking service. It was only a matter of time, and it happened today.

This guy was someone I was supposed to get set up with on a blind date a few years ago, during a tumultuous Jerkoff time. *There have been way too many tumultuous Jerkoff times.* He's in his early forties, from New England, same hometown as my college boyfriend. He's an Aries (I seem to gravitate toward them—they're powerful men). He runs two companies, has a graduate degree, and is really funny. I had heard that he wasn't the best-looking guy, but that there was something sexy about him. I guess I never forgot his name because he sounded so good at the time.

Anyway, a few days ago, in came an I'm-interested-in-your-service e-mail from the unrequited blind date from years past. I recognized his name right away. I read his stats, and he seemed perfect for yours truly. I was stumped. *What do I do? How do I handle it? How do I get him to want me instead of wanting all the great women in my database? How do I handle it so I don't seem sleazy or cheap or unprofessional?* I had no idea. Friends think that I'll probably meet my husband through my business—it's inevitable, he will walk through the door wanting to be a client and then he will meet me and want me and want to marry me, and I will want him and we will live happily ever after. I admit this fantasy has crossed my mind, but when most of the Desperados sit down, I usually learn too much information too quickly to be romantically interested. Most of them immediately pour out all their heartbreak and dating issues and all the intrigue is gone. In some ways, it's like being on a first date and hearing every single dysfunctional issue in this person's dating life. *Big turnoff!*

I guess it might be possible that someday one of the Desperados might be a little more "baggage-free" than all the others, and then who knows? *Let's say today's the day and that this is the guy. I am not pre-*

pared. I don't know what to do. I decided to call my dad. I said to him, "Daddy, I have a problem. This guy contacted me and wants to hire me. I think I am going to like him for me, not for another woman. What should I do?"

When I was younger, my mother was always the person I went to for relationship advice. She would sit for hours and hours listening, consoling, and advising. And unbeknownst to me, my dad always felt a little left out that I never talked to him about my boy problems. When I moved to New York, broke up with the first real love of my life, and started calling home again crying, my dad answered the phone and asked me straight out why I always immediately asked for my mother. Maybe he could help and give me some good advice. Well, that was all he needed to say and I started bawling to him for fifteen minutes without coming up for air once. When I did finally take a breath, he interrupted me and stammered, "Um, um, let me go get your mother." He obviously didn't know what he was in for when he told his devastated daughter that she could cry on his shoulder! Now, as an adult, I don't get heartbroken as much and I also know what my dad can handle. Hysterical crying? Absolutely not. But a rational, business-related question—there he's a pro.

Anyway, my dad warmed up to the task this time. He said, "Look, go to the meeting, do what you usually do, and if you think that there is really something between the two of you, at the end of the meeting, instead of telling him about becoming a client, tell him that you think there seems to be something between the two of you and suggest that the two of you go out." *No way.* "Daddy, I can't say that!" I complained. "So what's my second choice?" He got serious. "Well, your second choice would be that if he offers you the money, you take it and take him as a client and as you get to know him, if you really think that you are the right girl for him, then on his second or third date, you tell him to look for a brunette and you show up." *Right, that sounds like a romantic comedy.* I laughed. "I don't know about that, either." He started getting impatient with me. "Look, Samantha, just go and meet him. Maybe you won't even like him at all and then all your worrying will be for nothing." He had a point.

Today was the consultation and, for better or for worse, I liked him. He was interesting, worldly, very attractive to me, and, for the moment, even baggage-free. He liked me, too. I could tell. He was flirting with me through the whole meeting. I wish I could tell you that I was confident enough to try my dad's first suggestion and tell him that I thought we should go out, but I wasn't. So we sat and we flirted and the consultation ended. I took his consultation fee and he said he wanted to sign up. *Oh boy.* I said great, welcome aboard, but I wondered if I would be able to set him up objectively. I guess we will see.

BACK TO

Looks Good from Afar Guy

Looks Good from Afar Guy asked me to sit down with him to go over what I thought was going wrong on his dates. I reviewed each of his dates and told him very candidly what the women said went wrong. "Date number one said that you got to the date late and took five or six phone calls during the hour that you were together, and every time you got off the phone all you did was obsess about business." He looked perplexed. "But, but I *was* having a work crisis and the phone calls couldn't be helped." I waved my hand to dismiss this idea. "Whatever. Looks Good from Afar Guy, we all have work crises, but either you need to cancel the date or go and not seem distracted. Also, no answering the phone, especially not six times! If it really is an emergency, you need to tell the woman upfront that you will need to answer your phone and apologize that you have to do it, so she thinks you are being polite. You only get one chance to make a good first impression." He sheepishly said okay.

"Your second date said that you were in a bad mood and snapped at the waiter and that it made her nervous about your temper." Again he started defending himself, but I cut him off and said, "I am not judging you. I just want you to hear how women are perceiving you. You can't be rude to people, period. I don't care what happened to you during the day. If you are in a bad mood and really can't pull it together to be pleasant, I would prefer that you cancel at the last minute. I will make up some excuse for you rather than have you go to the date all pissed off and angry. Furthermore, you cannot snap at the waiters or the busboys or the taxi drivers. Women notice this and they think that if you are snapping at the hired help today, it is just a matter of time before you will be snapping at them directly." "Fair point," he said.

I looked at my notes. "Your third date said that all you talked about throughout the date was the tumultuous relationship you have with your family, specifically your mother." Again he interrupted, "But on that day, there *was* a big family issue." I stopped him again. "But it's not of interest to your date what spat you had with your sister or how your mom showed up at your apartment and rearranged your furniture without asking. Deal with these issues with your family members directly or discuss them with a friend. Leave your date out of it. No woman is interested in marrying a guy who doesn't seem to have a good relationship with his family, so if you don't have a good relationship with them, you need to think about faking it!" He laughed. "Also she told me that you gave her a hard time about ordering dessert." He looked down at his hands. "Do not ever, I mean ever, tell a woman what she should and shouldn't order. That is death on a date, because she will think that you think she is overweight and doesn't need the calories." He looked at me wide-eyed. "I know that sounds crazy, but it's true."

"Moving on. Date four said that you seemed distracted and not interested in sharing anything about yourself. She said you kept peppering her with questions, and when she would turn the questions around to you, all you gave her were yes-or-no answers. Looks Good from Afar Guy, you can't do that. It's boring, and you need to share a little bit." He nodded in agreement and said I was right, he would try.

I glanced at my notebook again. "Dates five and six said pretty much the same thing, that they thought you were just a little dull. They both complained that the conversation didn't flow, that the topics you brought up were boring, and that they just didn't have enough fun to warrant going out again." I looked up. "Do you want me to review the conversation topics that I think are good for dates again?" He got a little embarrassed and shuffled in his chair. "No, I remember them and I am already working on my pop culture factoids, a few funny stories from my childhood, and I have been thinking back on some trips that I have taken." I smiled. "That sounds great, and if all else fails and there is a lull in the conversation, you can always go with a compliment. Women love compliments and compliments make them forget lulls in the conversation."

I concluded by saying, "Listen, Looks Good from Afar Guy, you are not a dating disaster. You just need a little work. When you go on dates, you need to think just like you would when you're in a business meeting. In a business meeting, you wouldn't take six phone calls, bitch about your mother, or yell at the secretary. So keep that in mind on your dates, too. And try to be yourself, fun and engaging and interesting, and then you'll be great." There was a silence, a lull. Then he said, "Thank you, I'll give it a try. And Samantha, I really like your shoes." He winked at me.

MAYBE FOR ME GUY

Soul Mate Guy

I just had another crappy dating situation come to an end. I met him through a friend. He came on very strong right away. I know that I should have thrown up a red flag, but he seemed so genuine and so into me that I got hooked. I'm a fool, I know. I always admonish my female clients about getting carried away with a guy who comes on like a bulldozer, yet I got carried away. *Why do I always think that I am immune to my rules? Why do I think I am different from the rest of the female population? Shouldn't I have learned by now?* But in my defense—*and here comes the self-rationalization*—I don't think it was completely my fault. He did tell me how great I was, how he could see us being a couple, how I shouldn't go house shopping because we would be living together in three months. He said I was his soul mate.

The bottom line? I, like all women, sit around waiting for a guy to come along who will recognize just how great I really am, a guy who hangs on my every word and who is supposed to be my Prince

Charming and my happily ever after. So even though I know better, even I can get carried away by Cinderella fantasies. Look, a girl should have her fantasies.

This guy was very attractive to me physically. He was about five feet nine and had almost crystal blue eyes, a calming voice, and a sweet smile. He dressed like he didn't care about dressing, yet he looked good in his simple duds. The first week, he was so enthusiastic that he told every single one of his friends about me. He threw a party at his apartment, and I soon realized that everyone there knew who I was. I wondered how this guy found the time to tell them all about me. *Did he send out a mass e-mail alerting them?* The second week he wanted me to meet his family. The third week he suggested we go apartment shopping together and see each other exclusively. His intense interest was flattering, but I found myself a little wary because I do know men, and most normal, emotionally available men do not come on so strong. However, he seemed like a legitimate, stable guy and, as much as I hate to admit it, I got lured in. *Big mistake!*

By week four I figured I should let my guard down a little or this guy was going to get fed up and move on. So I started seeming a little—*I mean a little*—more responsive. I mentioned to him that I told *one*—not ten, but one—of my friends about him. I said in passing that I *might* want to bring him to a wedding, and I hinted at *some* of the dysfunctions in my life—just some mild stuff so he could feel like I was sharing with him. And call me crazy, but as I started seeming, and the operative word is *seeming,* more interested, he started seeming a little more distant.

Then we went on our next date and had a good time. He still appeared to be very into me: he brought me flowers, he told me his parents were going to be in town next week and he wanted me to meet them, he suggested that we plan a trip together over the summer, and he kept telling me how beautiful I am. Again, some doubt was creeping in. *I may be great and everything but why is this guy soooo into me?* His devotion unnerved me and actually kept me from appreciating him. We went back to my apartment after the date and were fooling around a little and then at about 3 A.M., he left. When he left, I thought to myself that I wasn't really sure that I was feeling *it* with this guy even though I really wanted to feel *it*. So as I washed off my makeup and looked in the mirror, I made a promise to myself that I would spend the entire weekend with him and really focus. At the end of the weekend, I would decide to become exclusive with him, since he kept asking, or I would move on to another guy. I know the whole thing seems very methodical and strategic, but somehow love doesn't naturally flow that well anymore in today's world, especially for women in their thirties. With the plan in place, I went to sleep.

Next morning, he called sounding all upset. "Can you come over to my apartment?" he asked urgently. Sure. I went to his apartment, a loft on the other side of town. He opened the door immediately. He was freaking out, sweating, and pacing around. His behavior was very strange. He asked me if I could be his friend for a minute. I looked at him funny and hesitated. *What the hell does that mean?* But I said yes, because what was I supposed to say? "Last night after I left your apartment and I was walking home, I walked past the apartment of my ex-girlfriend, the one I dated for two and a half years and broke up with eight months ago." *Uh-oh this sounds bad.* "And before I could stop myself, I walked into her building, breezed by the doorman, went up in the elevator, and started knocking on her door and calling out her name." *Okay, psycho, what were you thinking?* His voice was shaking. "She never came to the door and eventually the doorman came up and told me I had to leave or he would call the police. So I went home and woke up this morning to a message from my ex telling me that if I ever did that again she would get a restraining order against me!" *Yup, so would I!* I sat pulling on my upper lip and shaking my head in confusion. My guy is devastated because he can't believe that he was in love with a girl for two and a half years who would threaten him with a restraining order. *She probably can't believe that she was in love with a guy for two and a half years who would show up at her door at 3 A.M. after eight months of not speaking.* And he is starting to realize that he never mourned their breakup from eight months ago and is beside himself.

I continued to sit on the edge of his couch with a blank look on my face. I crossed my arms across my chest as if to shield myself from him. My mind started racing. *Okay, what am I doing here? When he felt the urge to "phone a friend," why did he phone the girl he's been dating and professing his very strong emotions for? The fool. Why didn't he phone a real friend, a guy friend, and have his freak-out moment with him!* Instead of compassion, I started to feel anger. "What am I really doing here? Is this your way of trying to end things with me?" He was on the verge of tears. He looked at me pleadingly and claimed that this had nothing to do with me. "Oh, really," I said. "It seems suspect that as soon as I start focusing on a relationship with you, you conveniently freak over your ex, out of the blue." I stood up and told him I was leaving. He begged, "Don't be mad at me. I don't know why I am feeling this way, but I feel so emotionally unavailable. I can't even think about dating anyone. It feels like I just broke up with my ex yesterday." I flung open the door and spat at him, "Well then, you must be having a banner week because you broke up with your ex yesterday and me today." And I walked out. *How do I find these guys? Am I being punished for something?*

BACK TO

Conflict of Interest Guy

I have been putting off setting him up. I have gone through my database again and again and again, and I can't find anyone to set him up with. Either they aren't good enough for him or they are too good, which means he might like them and then he won't be marrying me. I realized I had two choices: come clean and let him know that I was personally interested in him, or set him up and hope for the best. I wasn't ready to profess my interest—I was still smarting a little bit over Soul Mate Guy—so I scheduled a date for him. I picked a woman named Sydney. She is 31 years old, pretty without trying to be, one of those girls who can just get up on a Saturday morning throw on jeans and a T-shirt, no makeup, and run out the door for breakfast and look terrific. *I hate girls like that!* My professionalism made me pick the kind of girl he would like, but my territorialism made me pick a girl who might not like him back. I figured if we were fated to be together, he and Sydney would not work out. Their date was scheduled for 7 P.M. tonight. At 5:45, Sydney called and said she had a work emergency and needed to cancel. I called Conflict of Interest Guy to let him know. He surprised me and said, "Well, since you ruined my evening and now I have no plans, you need to come out and have dinner with me." I found myself saying yes and rushing to cancel my plans. *Why not? Soul Mate Guy just treated me awfully. Isn't a girl entitled to a little spontaneous fun?*

We went to dinner. We laughed, we flirted, and Sydney's name didn't come up once. He walked me home and on the way he asked me how much it would cost to date the president of the Matchmaking company, and I joked and said, "A lot more than you've paid me." He joked and said he thought he could afford it. He dropped me at my door and gave me a kiss on the cheek, but very close to my mouth.

BACK TO

Brad Pitt Guy

He e-mailed me this morning. I hadn't heard from him in a while. I learned very quickly that if the Desperados don't come a-calling, I should not bother them because when they are single and want to get set up, they get in touch pronto. Case in point, this morning, Brad Pitt Guy. He sent me an e-mail and asked who I had for him. I said, "Well, I haven't heard from you in two months so I don't have anyone lined up right now, but I will certainly give it some thought. How's it going? Where have you been?" He had been dating a girl he met on JDate. Her favorite movie star? You got it, Brad Pitt. Her hairstyle? A Jen Aniston cut. So what happened? I asked. "She thought I was too pre-occupied with Brad." *Imagine that!*

BACK TO

Miss 39

She called me crying this morning. It is her 39½ birthday and she is still alone. *I know, Miss 39, we are trying.* "Why is it that you've set me up with eight guys and I'm still alone? Why isn't this working? You are supposed to be the best Matchmaker out there. Why haven't I gotten married yet?" I felt attacked. I responded, "Well, Miss 39, I do need to remind you that you have liked every guy I set you up with, and you have gone on more than one date with each one; to me, this is successful." She did an intake of breath. "Now maybe we need to work on getting you past the first few dates and getting you to give the guys a real chance. What do you think?" She paused for a moment and seemed to be considering what I said. "What does that mean?" she asked. "Maybe we should sit down for a regrouping session to go over the dates, and I will give you some constructive criticism on things you could have done better or differently," I suggested hopefully. Her voice was still trembling, but she agreed to sit with me.

BACK TO

Conflict of Interest Guy

I called him today to thank him for dinner. This was the polite thing to do. He flirted with me on the phone. As I was hanging up, I couldn't resist. I asked him if I should reschedule the date with Sydney. He said sweetly that he was okay for the moment. We both paused. He didn't elaborate, I didn't argue. Then in a bit of a shy voice, he told me about these tickets he had to the symphony and asked me if I would be his date. I didn't know where this was going. I felt a little funny being his date again and having his money, but I found myself saying yes. The money thing was strange. I couldn't offer it back to him without seeming like I was trying to define what we were doing, but I would only be able to last so long, going on "dates" with him and keeping his money. . . .

Mr. Large Adonis

I met with this Desperado earlier today. It never ceases to amaze me just how much information the peeps choose to share with me. This guy was very handsome, nearly gorgeous. I found myself a little distracted and giggly, that's how hot he was. He was tall, well over six feet, with a great physique, and well dressed. I could only imagine that there was no shortage of ladies for him.

He filled out the questionnaire and then I asked my typical first question: "So tell me what has been going on in your social life that prompted you to get in touch with me." He shifted in his seat and said, "It's very embarrassing for me to tell you this," and then he paused, as if uncertain of whether to continue. I prompted him by saying not to worry, he could trust me. I guess that did the trick because he went on, "As I was saying, it is awkward for me to tell you this, but I feel like the only way you are going to be able to help me is if you know the whole situation. Obviously, as you can see"—he brushed his hair off his face—"I am a very attractive guy." *Yup, I'll say so!* "Well, girls like me a lot, and because I am so tall and well built they also expect me to be, um, well . . . well endowed, you know, *down there.*" He pointed to his crotch. Then without making eye contact with me, he continued, "Well, I am not well endowed *down there.* As a matter of fact, it's sad to say but I am actually not very well endowed at all, sort of much smaller than the average bear." He stopped talking and flushed. "There I said it." He flagged down a waiter and ordered a Ketel One on the rocks.

I thought my jaw was going to fall open with surprise. I took a sip of my Diet Coke to give me time to compose myself. Then I said, "Okay, so what? So you aren't the largest guy in that area. I don't get it. Do women actually stop seeing you because of it?" "Yup," he said, looking sad. "It seems that women develop high expectations, and when they learn that I'm not this perfect Adonis of a man, they actually get upset and leave. It's happened several times. It's humiliating, and it definitely doesn't help with performance anxiety, either." I asked, just to clarify, "But you can perform, right? I mean, it's not a sexual issue—it's an appearance issue, right?" "Yes, I can perform, but at the end of the day I still am only attracted to hot women, and I can't find one who will like me *for me,* not for the huge dick, pardon my language, that she is expecting to find when I take off my clothes." He took a long swallow of his drink. "Can you help?"

Oh boy, who'd a thunk it? Mr. Large Adonis, not so large. I found myself still wondering if it was really this guy's penis or something else. I inquired again, "And you are certain that it's your penis and nothing else that's making the women run for the hills? I'm concerned that the penis issue might be causing a confidence issue, which might be the real culprit. If we work together, we would need to work on that." He didn't actually confirm that this was part of the problem, but he nodded in agreement.

Now that I had him on board, how would I handle this situation? I mean, I couldn't call up a woman and come right out and tell her that I have this great guy but be prepared, his you-know-what is small. I would have to pick women who wouldn't care so much about the size, who wouldn't be turned off and leave him. But how could I know for sure which women would stick around? And what would happen if my women reacted just as his past girlfriends had? Hmm, sounds like a difficult Desperado. Maybe I should turn him down. No, how can that be? He is so handsome and so sweet. There must be some women who wouldn't care. Would I care? I would want to think I wouldn't, but who knows?

I stalled for time by writing down some notes. Then I looked up and studied him more closely. *Yes, he is amazingly handsome. There must be some women I can find who wouldn't give him a hard time.* I told him that I would be willing to try to work with him, but I couldn't guarantee that my women would behave any differently. I told him that, absent my telling them the situation up front, which obviously was not an option, I would really have no idea how to prevent history from repeating itself. I told him I would try to pick women who were nice and sweet, real, unaffected, and hopefully they would stick around. He said okay.

TABLE CHANGE

I am raising my prices. Effective immediately, I charge $5,000. Much better. My Desperados are all very wealthy and more than a few are a little nutty. I should get paid more to cover the extra services I offer the peeps and to keep me outfitted in cool vintage handbags.

BACK TO
Soul Mate Guy

I am feeling unsettled about what happened with Soul Mate Guy. Conflict of Interest Guy has been a bit of a diversion, and it's been a little over a week, but I can't stop thinking about our confrontation. At 3 A.M. on Thursday night I went to sleep wondering if this guy was for me and deciding that I would take the weekend to find out, and then ten hours later, I was unceremoniously dumped by the same guy, who turned out to be a freak. It was bugging me. I don't usually get dumped. I wasn't actually dumped by him, but because he suddenly became emotionally unavailable, the decision of whether to be or not to be with him was taken out of my hands. I was left feeling very incomplete. As I got dressed this morning, I became very girly, questioning whether I looked pretty the last time I saw him, whether I had bad breath, or whether any other thing was the real reason this happened. I needed one more date to end things on my terms. I don't like things ending on someone else's terms—it doesn't work for the control-freak side of me.

I decided to e-mail him about something trivial, just to open the lines of communication. As I did it I thought, *Oh God, I am still so high school.* My e-mail was innocuous and ended with, "How are you?" He e-mailed me back almost immediately, saying that he missed me. He missed hanging out with me and laughing with me and talking to me. He knew that I probably was as disgusted and disappointed with him as he was with himself, but he wanted to see me again. I sent back a very uncharacteristic e-mail and said that I missed him, too, and that he shouldn't be so hard on himself. And I reminded him that he had invited me to be his date at his friend's engagement party. I asked if I was still invited and joked that I wouldn't mind having a little fun. Two hours later, he called and asked me to go.

February

February is up there as one of my most popular Matchmaking months. In the first part of the month, I get a slew of calls from freaking-out females who feel suicidal because Valentine's Day is a few days away and they don't have a Valentine or even a date. In the second half of the month, I get a slew of phone calls from depressed women and a few men who broke up on Valentine's Day proper and are now alone. Valentine's Day is a funny holiday: a lot of people insist it's a romantic holiday, but it might be better described as the breakup holiday. Thousands of relationships end on that day, all because of unmet expectations.

BACK TO
Miss Excuse

Today was our makeover day. Her mother gave us her car and driver to cart us around from place to place. I had scheduled four stops. We started at my hairstylist. He's the perfect hairstylist because he does whatever I ask and never goes all *"I'm a creative genius"* on me. We decided that he should cut about eight inches off her hair and color it.

She had long, straggly dark hair and random highlights. He cut her hair shoulder-length, gave it some modern angles, and rinsed it with a medium brown color. The result was glossy and chic. On the way out of the salon, Miss Excuse kept stopping to look at herself in each mirror that we passed to make sure it was really her.

Next stop, Francesca, my makeup artist and eyebrow lady. It took her over an hour to tweeze Miss Excuse's brows—they were a mess. Then Francesca gave us a makeup lesson—no more glittery eye shadow, no more self-tanner that turns the skin orange. Instead, she suggested subtle, tinted moisturizer, daytime eye makeup, shiny, kiss-me lip gloss. Miss Excuse looked terrific.

Then we made an unscheduled stop at Starbucks for a latte for her and an iced tea for me. I noticed a few guys checking out Miss Excuse, and she must have noticed as well, because she started blushing and looked a little flustered, probably because she wasn't used to the attention.

Next stop, the contact lenses store. Out with the glasses and in with the contacts. I complimented her on her brilliant blue eyes. She smiled. On the way out she went up to the glass of the window and again admired herself shyly in the reflection.

Last stop of the day, my nutritionist. After a lot of cajoling and many reminders that she wouldn't enjoy sleeping on the street when her mom pulled her allowance, Miss Excuse agreed to go on a four-week healthy-eating plan. The nutritionist put her on a modified South Beach diet. In the car on the way home, I reminded her, "No more late-night snacks, no more bingeing after smoking pot. You want to smoke, fine. I will deal with that in phase two, but when you have the munchies, you munch carrots, not Chubby Hubby ice cream!" We agreed that when she lost her weight, we would begin phase two, shopping for more flattering clothing.

It was remarkable what a haircut, a little makeup, some plucking, and contact lenses could do for a woman's appearance. I noticed a little change in her disposition, too: Miss Excuse seemed much more confident and content. This made me smile.

BACK TO

Soul Mate Guy

Last night was the engagement party with Soul Mate Guy. I showed up looking hot. I wore a low-cut top, no bra, and a very sexy short skirt. He gave me a full head-to-toe glance when I walked in, and his eyes lit up in appreciation. He escorted me to our table and acted like his freak-out had never happened. We both drank too much. He was all over me within fifteen minutes, telling me that I was the hottest girl he had ever dated and that he wanted to take me home to make love to me. *So much for being worried that he wasn't attracted to me.* We continued to flirt all night. People at the dinner asked us how long we had been living together—that's how cozy and normal we seemed. I asked him if he was working through his issues. He said that he was trying not to think about them. *Great.* Nevertheless, we ended up going home together and fooling around all night. I didn't want him to sleep over, but he insisted. Again I asked him about his freak-out and he told me he was still emotionally unavailable but he was feeling better. At this point, I didn't really care. *Was he a man or a mouse? These were girly issues, not men's issues. Grow up!* I listened with half an ear. Now that I knew he was attracted to me and my self-esteem had recovered,

I wondered if I had ever been into him in the first place. Had I been trying to force it because he was so enthusiastic and I had been so lonely after Jerkoff? *Probably.* I'm out of here.

DESPERADO #22

Mr. How About You

I ran into this one at a few social events recently. He's 47, divorced, and has a young child. He's fit and he's a young and contemporary dresser. He looks good for his age but seems like a lost soul, a loner. And he's always at the events alone. A few days ago, he called me and left a message saying that he wanted to talk to me about my biz. I was surprised to get his call. He didn't strike me as a guy who would spend money to meet someone. Actually, he struck me as a cheap-skate, but you never know, so I called him back.

When he picked up the phone, instead of asking me about my biz, he said straight out, "I find you to be interesting, intriguing, and impressive. Are you yourself available for a date?" Even though we all know just how available I am, I was taken aback and quickly answered that I wasn't available. I said this because every time I saw him out, he struck me as one of those creepy older guys who was looking for hot younger women. And he seemed like one of those guys who already had one child, saw that as an inconvenience, and would not have any-more. Also, I was insulted. I felt he was undermining the profession-alism of my business by pretending to be interested in hiring me in order to get a callback. It's funny, I didn't mind it when Conflict of In-terest Guy was flirting without admitting that he was interested in me, maybe because I was interested in him as well. Yet this guy's admission bugged me. *Go figure.*

Still, we spent some time on the phone after I said I was unavailable. I started thumbing through my database haphazardly as he described the type of women he was interested in. He told me that he was only interested in very accomplished and financially secure women. He mentioned a literary agent who interested him—a woman who had an Ivy League degree and came from a nice family. I happened to know the agent he was talking about, and I told him that if he wound up becoming a client, I could probably introduce him to this woman and many others like her. I guess that cinched it because he agreed to a consultation.

Today was the consultation, about an hour ago. Funny thing, as soon as he started talking about himself, I began thinking that maybe I shouldn't have been so quick to judge. I liked him more and more as he told me about his interest in travel, his ability to speak three foreign languages, and the fact that he's a world-renowned public speaker on the subject of finance. And the fact that he had a child started making him seem more stable once he told me that he definitely wanted to have more children and that parenting was his favorite part of his life. This was a different kind of attraction than what I had felt for Conflict of Interest Guy. I didn't anticipate it, it just happened. He wasn't sounding so dysfunctional anymore, and I rationalized that he had been interested in me first, the service second, so maybe I should consider him. *Maybe it doesn't matter that he is 47 and goes to a few social events alone. Maybe he's a possibility for me and I tossed him into the water without even a lifeboat.* It was probably pretty difficult to ask me out, the Matchmaker herself. I found myself fixating on how to rectify my mistake. I decided the best thing to do was to start complaining about a recent blind date I had been on, which would probably prompt him to ask about me again.

Sure enough, he looked at me inquisitively and said, "I thought you weren't available." And for once I decided to be up-front, which made me feel very awkward and shy. I smiled at him a little to soften the criticism and said, "I only said that because I'm put off when men call under the guise of hiring me only to ask me out on a date." He looked a little embarrassed but nodded in comprehension. And then more tentatively I said, "I would be interested in getting to know you better on a date if you still want to." I cast my eyes down to my notebook. I was proud of myself. I had never put it out there so honestly before. The good feeling was short-lived, though, because he cleared his throat and said, "I find you intriguing and would certainly like to explore things with you, but before we end our session, do you think you could just tell me a little more about the Ivy League literary agent?" *Very nice!* Can you imagine, I allow myself to be vulnerable, I tell him that I would like to go out with him, and he says, yes, he's interested, but at the same time as he explores his interest in me, he wants me to help him pursue the other girl! *Whatever. He is still almost 50 and he still goes to events alone.* I don't know what I was thinking. I must be feeling particularly lonely these days. I should trust my first impression. My gut instincts are always right!

TABLE CHANGE

I stepped up to the plate this week and added a New Client Registration Form to my website. Yippee. Effective immediately, when you call my biz line, the recording says go to the website *www.SamanthasTable.com,* fill out the form, and send a photo. Then the form automatically comes to me. I read it at my leisure. The form provides me with all the preliminary information I want on the peeps. I study their photos and then I get back in touch by e-mail. There is also an automated message that is sent if they don't include the photo. *Ain't life simple?*

BACK TO

Conflict of Interest Guy

We have been out four times. Tonight's our fifth date, and he invited me over to see his apartment and to cook me dinner. I think this was the night he was planning to make *the move.* I brought with me a check written out to him. I figured if and when we fooled around, that was probably an appropriate time to give back the money. Otherwise one could say that I was turning into a very high-priced hooker!

He had a beautiful apartment on Park Avenue, a classic seven, as they call them in New York (meaning two bedrooms, a study, a kitchen, two baths, and a dining room). The décor was magazine perfect: clean minimalist lines, brown mahogany floors, mostly white furnishings. He cooked or someone cooked a homemade meal: a tricolore salad with a champagne vinaigrette dressing, filet mignon with asparagus tips and rosemary mashed potatoes, and a chocolate soufflé for dessert. Afterward we sat in the living room, talking. I felt like this was the first time we really talked without flirting and being silly. He started telling me things that he had never told me before. He said, "I want to have five kids, and eventually I want to move back to the Midwest." My heart dropped. Then somehow we got into a sex conversation—I don't recall how—but the next thing I knew he confided that he liked anal sex and threesomes—a lot! I thought my eyes were going to bulge out of my head. I got up and started clearing the dishes. *Oh boy, maybe there is no more conflict of interest.* Things became clear for me very quickly. I started talking very fast, and I admitted that I did not want to have five kids, and the only places I would ever even consider living were New York and Los Angeles. I also told him, as casually as possible, that anal sex was not my favorite and the whole threesome thing *made the bed a tad too crowded for me.* He laughed at my attempt at a joke, and I laughed with him but felt dejected. Then, always the professional, I smiled as sweetly as I could and said that maybe I should get back in touch with Sydney. He seemed disappointed, but he said maybe. I left his apartment with his check still in my purse and a lump in my throat.

BACK TO

Miss 39

Today was my "sit-down" with Miss 39. I brought tissues. She was dressed in one of her serious corporate outfits again, this one navy blue with beige piping. And she was still clutching her handbag, though this time the bag was a Prada with a zipper, which she kept playing with haphazardly. We made some small talk, she ordered a chardonnay, and I launched in. "Okay, Miss 39, let's review your dates. Date number one, Mr. 50, we already covered him, right?" She chuckled and nodded. I looked down at my notepad. "Okay, date two was 45, a nice guy. He didn't try to have sex with you like Mr. 50 did, and he liked you a lot but you said he was too short for you. Date three was 44, much taller, worked in finance but you didn't like that he grew up in Queens. Date four grew up in Manhattan. He was a very funny doctor, but you said you don't want to be a doctor's wife. You were concerned that he might bring home a disease. Date five was a lawyer, no diseases, nice-looking and very sweet to you. The two of you went out twice, but then you refused a third date because you said he wasn't active enough for you. That brings—" She interrupted me with a yell. "Stop, Samantha, stop. I've heard enough. Don't even tell me about the rest of the dates. It's all too depressing. I can't listen." She put her head in her hands. I felt bad, but she needed to hear this. "Okay, Miss 39, we'll just focus on the guys I have already brought up. Okay?" She slowly raised her head. I looked at her seriously. "Basically, Miss 39, you are just too picky. All the guys I have introduced you to are really good guys. They liked you, they were smart, they want to get married, and you had a lot in common with each one, but every single time you found a fault and couldn't see beyond it. This is why you are 39 years old and you have never been in a long-term relationship. You need to be less picky and you need to try to see the bigger picture or you are going to be alone forever." *There, I said it.*

Tears started to well in her eyes, but I was resolved. "Look, Miss 39, the tears are not going to help. It is ridiculous that you didn't give date two a second chance just because you prefer five feet ten and he was five feet eight. You are only five feet six. I know you would like to marry a jolly green giant, but you can't wait around for him forever. And date three, who cares where he grew up? He is not living there now, he is not asking you to live there, so why does it matter? This is a stupid reason to dismiss him." She was sobbing now. "So why didn't you say something then? Why didn't you make me go out with him again? Maybe you're right, and I did kind of like him except for that one thing." "Miss 39, I *did* say something. We battled about it, but you refused. What am I supposed to do, kidnap you and lock you in a room with the guy? You are an adult. I can't force you to do anything."

I turned back to my notes. "Date four, I know you don't prefer doctors, but this doctor was atypical. You got along with this doctor. And date five, so he isn't as active as you are. Maybe he could become more active, or maybe he's active enough, but you didn't even give him enough opportunity to express that to you. You can hold out for a more active guy, but by then you might not be as active yourself because you'll be old and gray. Date six—" She held up her hand to silence me as the tears flowed down her cheeks. "Sorry, I forgot." I put my hand on her arm and said quietly, "Miss 39, it's foolish to not go out with someone again just because they don't fit the fantasy you have in your head about your Prince Charming. That is only a fantasy. The reality is that you cry yourself to sleep because you hate being alone, so you need to be realistic. Enough with the tears, Miss 39! Promise me you will give the next round of guys more of a chance. Seriously, promise me!"

She sobbed harder but she promised. I felt bad that I was so tough on her, but somebody needed to be tough on her or she was going to be alone and miserable forever.

Thursday, February 9

After my powwow with Miss 39, I started thinking about myself. *Am I too picky? Is that why I am alone?* Should I have dealt with Mr. Cuticles's cuticles? What about Mr. Retired at 36? Most women would think that his retirement is a good thing. Should I have just dealt with it? What about Dr. Touchy? Being affectionate is a good thing. Should I just have been happy that someone, anyone, wanted to touch me? How do you know when you're being too picky? When should you just accept certain things about a guy even though you don't really want to? And if you accept unacceptable things, are you settling? *If I am so hard on my female Desperados, shouldn't I be just as hard on myself?* I went to sleep pondering all those questions.

Saturday, February 11

I was contacted by YPO, the Young Presidents' Organization, to speak at their singles retreat. I feel honored. The people who belong to this organization are mostly men from all over the world, mostly owners of companies that are worth more than ten million dollars. These people are real heavy hitters. *A slam dunk,* a perfect target audience for me, and the organization is actually paying me to speak! Yippee. It's funny, some of them are already my clients (which ones, I will never tell), and some of the members I've dated (again, I will never tell who they are). I am planning to read them the riot act because, as successful as some of these people are in business, some are equally as bad at dating. Should be fun!

Jerkoff Again

He called. When I saw his name on my caller ID, my heart went aflutter, as it always does, and I self-consciously brushed my hair out of my face. He purred into the phone, "Paris for Valentine's Day?" "No f—ing way," I retorted. "I just went with you to Paris and I know that you know that I love it there, but I can resist you this time because we were just there." He misses me terribly. No other woman compares to me. *I know that, you schmuck, but unfortunately you don't really get that because if you did you would treat me like gold and marry me.* He needs to see me. *No, no,* I can't, I won't, I told you, lose my number, nothing has changed!

Silence. Then, "I'm . . . I'm in AA, and I am seeing a shrink." Silence at my end. *I needed to sit down. What did Jerkoff just say? I feel a little light-headed. Is Jerkoff lying to me just so I will see him?* Oh my God, Jerkoff is getting some help. "That's great. I am proud of you, but I am still not going to go with you to Paris." I paused and said softly, "Happy Valentine's Day." I hung up the phone thinking *maybe. . . .*

BACK TO
Conflict of Interest Guy

I called him and told him that I was going to give him back his money. I told him that I felt funny setting him up right after we had dated. The truth was, I felt like I knew too much about him and I wasn't certain if any of the women I knew would like his kinkiness, but I didn't tell him that. He said he respected my decision. Funny how things happen. *I thought I would be giving him his money back for a very different reason. . . .*

Valentine's Day

I didn't schedule any consultations for today. I learned my lesson last year when I witnessed too many emotional breakdowns. I sent out a very cute e-card wishing all my peeps a happy Valentine's Day and love in their life for years to come. In the morning, a lot of them e-mailed back with updates—Miss Manhunt and Mr. Gazillionaire still going strong. *Yay.* Mr. Priority is still hot and heavy with Miss TV Reporter. She isn't so annoying anymore and he loves that everywhere they go people know who she is.

Miss Boobs, but not boobs alone, gave my guy Peter another chance, and they really like each other. She decided that I was right: a football-watching guy from a divorced family who is clueless about trendy restaurants is not so bad, especially when he's teaching her about football, he's affectionate, and he figured out how to make a reservation at Le Cirque for Valentine's Day. Heard from Brad Pitt Guy. He made a nervy request: he asked if I could get him a reservation at Jean Georges or Daniel for tonight. "No, Brad Pitt Guy, I cannot. I don't *do reservations.* Plus, people make those reservations three months in advance at a minimum. It is impossible to get in there tonight." He complained, "You are supposed to be cupid and it's Valentine's Day. You should have some pull. Brad Pitt would be able to get in." I shook my head and laughed at him. "Yes, you're right, Brad Pitt probably could get in, but you or I probably cannot." It's funny, Mr. Gazillionaire asked me to help him get into a restaurant as well. I started thinking that I should hire someone to book reservations at the top romantic places in town for Valentine's Day, then sell the reservations to the highest, most desperate bidders. Not a bad idea, right? I have been thinking of doing this for a long time, but how much would someone really pay? *I guess it would depend how desperate they were for a reservation.*

Mr. Metrosexual checked in. Didn't I have a set up for him

tonight? I laughed. *My clients are funny.* "What, are you crazy, a blind date on Valentine's Day? That's romantic suicide." Why? he asked. He could handle it, he didn't have any plans, he'd even bring her flowers. No, Mr. Metrosexual, nothing doing, no woman wants to go out with a stranger on the most romantic day of the year! Miss Excuse wrote back. The diet is going strong, only seven more pounds to go. She is feeling great! Looks Good from Afar Guy tried some of my suggestions on his last few dates and things are definitely looking up for him. He thanked me. Miss Gold Digger got an Hermès scarf and perfume for Valentine's Day, plus three dozen yellow roses from Dot-Com Guy (she calls him Michael). She's pleased. The Girl I Always Thought Hated Me is still alone and ready for another date, but she is feeling more confident after our coaching session. The only unhappy chickadee is Miss 39—she cried on my shoulder again. She has no plans, it's Valentine's Day and she doesn't want to be alone. *I know, Miss 39, me neither.*

I stayed in by myself and wrote a profile to put up on JDate. I figured, what the hell. I'm all alone with no good prospects, I may as well try something different. I decided that I would put it up over the weekend. *It seems pathetic to put your profile up on Valentine's Day.* At the beginning of the evening, I decided that I didn't care that I didn't have a date for Valentine's Day. After all, I had been fortunate: this was my first and only Valentine's Day without a date. Nonetheless, when the phone rang during the course of the evening, I didn't answer it. I decided no one needed to know that the Matchmaker was without a match, especially on her signature holiday. Jerkoff sent me purple tulips and a purple tulip pendant with amethysts on it. A note was attached: "Are you sure you don't want to come to Paris with me?" I threw the note in the trash, but later in the evening I fished it out, read it again, smiled a little, and put it in my keepsake box. *I can't help it; I am always a romantic at heart.*

BACK TO

Soul Mate Guy

Okay, I'm laughing. I ran into Soul Mate Guy on the street today. He asked me why I hadn't returned his calls. I gave him a perplexed look and said that I didn't see the point. He told me that he had called me because he thought that it was only fair for him to tell me that HE MET SOMEBODY! *Excuse me, Mr. Freak-Out Freak, you met somebody? You slept over at my house ten days ago and told me that you were emotionally unavailable and now you've met somebody? And why are you telling me anyway, just to annoy me?* I asked him this and he said with conviction that things just happen, and besides, our whole situation was such a long time ago. I was irate. "A long time ago? You freaked out about your ex two and a half weeks ago and you slept in my bed ten days ago. How is that a long time?" I shook my head in disgust. He said that he just felt like it was and he was feeling better and now he has a new girlfriend. He shrugged. "A new girlfriend. How long have you been seeing her, a day?" I scoffed. "A week," he said, trying to look casual.

He is such a freak, I am speechless. And I am disgusted that I listened to his story about how much he liked me because obviously he likes any girl he meets. I offered him a few more rude comments. He said that he knows I would like him to tell me what it was about me that made him lose interest, but there's nothing. He still thinks I'm terrific, but he just met this girl and that's what happens. He suddenly looked shy and said, "Well, the truth of the matter is this. I am embarrassed to say it, but I think that this girl is my soul mate." "Your soul mate." I looked at him incredulously and started laughing uncontrollably. "You told me that you thought I was your soul mate, too. What is wrong with you?" He went from thinking I was his soul mate and wanting me to meet his parents to freaking out about his ex and thinking he was still in love with her to finding another girl who was his soul mate, all in three and a half weeks, and he didn't think this was crazy, erratic, insane behavior. I needed to leave. I looked at him again as if I were seeing him for the first time and said, "Good luck with everything. You are going to need it." *I can't believe I thought I liked this guy!*

NOT FOR ME GUY

Mr. Serial Monogamist

Had a blind date tonight. I hadn't been on a blind date in a while, or any kind of date for that matter. Soul Mate Guy spooked me a bit, and after seeing him yesterday, I almost canceled. However, I knew I needed to get back on the horse. At least that's the advice I would give one of my female clients, so I dragged myself to meet him. This guy was a doctor, a well-known brain surgeon. I had run into an old friend from college on the street, and when she heard I wasn't seeing anyone, she shrieked and said that I had to meet her husband's best friend; he was terrific and was looking for a relationship. *Great, we will have that one thing in common at least.* I didn't want to go, not really, and I told my friend that, but she insisted that I had to go, this guy was different. Okay, I'll go. *She was the only person who offered this week so I guess I have to.*

I met him for the drink at the Regency. Maybe I shouldn't meet my own dates at the same place where I meet with all my Desperados, but it's convenient, I know I can get a table, and I like it there so I don't care. The doctor was there when I arrived. He was seated at my regular table in the corner. I guess one of the waiters put him there thinking he was one of my peeps. *I hope the waiter didn't make some sort of Desperado comment.* At first glance, he was handsome. He was well dressed in a conservative suit and a blue silk tie, with a big smile on his face. I admired his straight white teeth. I introduced myself and sat down. Right away, he seemed to have the need to explain that he wasn't a big dater and that he rarely went on blind dates. He went on to tell me how he's a serial monogamist and that he'd had five serious relationships, one right after the other. I asked him if he thought that was a good thing. He said haughtily, "Of course it's a good thing. I am not a player, I don't go out on tons of dates with girl after girl after girl. I meet a great girl and I get into a meaningful relationship with her." "Right," I said, almost to myself, "and then you can't commit to her so you break up and do it again with someone else." He said, "Excuse me, what did you just say?" *Oops, I think I just said that out loud.* I closed my eyes hard, then opened them and said, "Oh gosh, I didn't mean to verbalize that. It's just that I dated a serial monogamist once and I've heard it all before." He looked at me funny. "What is *it,* what have you heard all before?"

I hesitated before I answered. After all, we were on a date. To me, first-date conversation is supposed to be fun and light and vapid, nothing serious, nothing too probing, and definitely no relationship talk. This guy clearly didn't subscribe to my brand of dating conversation. "Look, I don't think it's right to get into it on a date. Maybe we should just have some vapid date talk for a while." I smiled hopefully. He wanted none of that. "No, you're the dating expert and you opened the door. I want to know what you meant." *Okay, I'm not feeling like the dating expert at this moment. Why did I even start?* I shifted in my seat. I figured that since I had already determined that I wasn't interested in this guy at all—I don't "do" serial monogamists—at least I could give him some advice. I plunged in, "In my opinion, being a serial monogamist is not a good thing. As a woman, I run to the hills from serial monogamists. To me, they are far worse than players because they take their dating much further than players do. They lead the women on for longer, actually make them believe that they are about to walk down the aisle, but then because serial monogamists are typically unable to commit, the relationship ends. The monogamist is devastated, but almost immediately gets right back into another relationship with another unsuspecting female." I looked straight at him to see his reaction. He was listening closely.

I continued, "I have an ex-boyfriend whom I dated for two and a half years. We started dating right after he had just broken up with another girl he had been living with and was supposedly devastated about. Then when we broke up, my guy was supposedly heartbroken, hysterically crying that he couldn't live without me. But less than two weeks later he got into another two-and-a-half-year relationship. Then he broke up with that girl, same devastation. Less than two weeks later there was a new girl, and now he's living with her and she has no idea that it's only a matter of time before they break up and he is onto someone else." I stopped to gasp for breath. He was speechless. He said a little too forcefully, as if trying to convince himself as well as me, "That's not me at all. I just haven't met the right person. I am not scared of commitment. I like relationships and have every intention of getting married. Maybe your ex-guy is the same way—maybe he just hasn't met the right girl."

I shook my head. "I am not saying that every serial monogamist is exactly like my ex, but why do you think that, at age 42, you have been in so many long-term relationships and not one culminated in marriage?" He shrugged. I continued, "My ex finally admitted that he does have a commitment issue and that he thinks he could have been happy with any of his serious girlfriends. He said it wasn't the girl but the commitment that was wrong for him. He's in therapy now." My date look alarmed. I felt bad then. "Maybe we should drop the subject, but it might just be that you are a little scared of taking the next step and making a commitment." I took a sip of my Diet Coke and looked away. Then he put his drink down on the table and sheepishly asked, "Do you know the name of the therapist that your ex is seeing?" *Men!*

Tuesday, February 21

I got home after yet another bad date and decided it was time to put that stupid profile up on JDate. I had already decided that putting up a photo was beyond the realm of possibility, but at least I could post the description of myself and see what happened. It's anonymous, so who would know? Then, if and when guys wrote to me, I could decide whether or not I wanted to proceed. *Sounds like a plan.*

BACK TO
Mr. Large Adonis

I needed to come up with my first date for the not-so-large man. I pulled out the 25- to 35-years-old *NG* (Nice Girls) file. . . .

Hmm, what about Dara? Could be interesting, seems very sweet. No, she probably isn't pretty enough for him. What about Marjorie, the invest-ment banker? She is really friendly, has midwestern values, and is cute—she's a good one. Wait, oh, Beth. Beth is interesting, 31, a graphic designer from Texas, really wants to get married. Yes, Beth. No, I know, Suzanne. Yes, Suzanne is perfect.

Suzanne is a really pretty girl who for some reason doesn't realize just how pretty she is. She is five feet eight, with a boyish figure. Clothes fit her perfectly. She's a brunette with a pixie-girl haircut and twinkly green eyes. I think she's a little insecure, which should be good for my guy. I figure he will like her looks and she'll be okay with his you-know-what. A perfect match.

DESPERADO #23
Mr. Teeth

Finally Mr. Teeth, my ex-date, decided to bite the bullet and hire me. And guess what? He got his teeth done. I'm sure he knew that he could never come sit down to hire me unless he got his teeth whitened, so he did it, and now here he was. As soon as he sat down, he flashed them at me and said, "Look what I did," like a little boy looking for his mother's approval. I clapped my hands in appreciation and told him that they looked great. Then he filled me in on the past few months. He had been dating a girl who grew up in Brooklyn and didn't graduate from high school and worked a part-time job in a laundromat but had no other career aspirations. I frowned. *What? Mr. Teeth, you are a double Ivy League graduate, an ambitious guy from Manhattan. What is up with that?*

He told me that, because he was insecure when it came to his inexperience with women, it was easier to date uneducated girls who didn't put so much pressure on him. I patted his hand. "Okay, Mr. Teeth, that was yesterday, but as of today, you are going to date educated, appropriate women who are sweet and kind and who will not make you feel insecure. I am going to find them for you and coach you on how to make the relationship work. Got it?" He looked at me with gratitude, smiled, and said okay.

Thursday, February 23

I got home and found that I had gotten fifteen responses to my profile on JDate. I spent some time looking at them. JDate is fun, at least it seems fun initially. E-mails pop up on my screen to say I have mail and then I get to go to the JDate site and see the e-mails that these guys have sent me. They all say that they think I sound great, which makes me feel really good. But . . . then I read about them, and they themselves are not so great and then it's not really so much fun anymore. *Oh well.* Some are too young, some too old, some uneducated, some have written the most uninteresting profiles, and some can't spell, which really bothers me. *What happened to spell check?* I realized that I need to be proactive and pick the guys, instead of letting them pick me. *That might work better.* So tonight I spent all night watching television and going through profile after profile and putting the good ones into a folder they call Your Favorites. I came up with fifty-three favorites after four hours. *This is very time-consuming.* Then I went into my favorites and read the profiles I had chosen. Upon closer inspection, a lot of them didn't seem so favorable, so I began discarding. They should have a Maybe box, too, for the ones I might contact in the future.

I finally settled on four guys to contact, but then I got nervous. *Maybe it is too weird for me to be doing this.* I was on the fence about it. One side of my brain was saying, What do you have to lose? So what that you own a Matchmaking service? And the other side of my brain was saying, Don't do it. You're a Matchmaker. You should be able to match yourself. People will think you are some kind of loser. A dilemma. Then the phone rang. It was my best friend. I confessed to her what I was doing and I asked her opinion. "Samantha, you should go for it. You are a great Matchmaker, and anyone who knows you knows that you couldn't be further from a loser. And if you recommend to everyone you work with to exhaust all avenues when trying to meet someone, then you need to practice what you preach. Don't you always tell me that just because you are a Matchmaker does not mean you have an express ticket to marriage?" I laughed as she quoted my famous line. "You should just take ownership of the fact that you think it is fine and cool and normal for you to try out online dating, and everyone will just think that, too." *My best friend is very smart!*

I decided to go for it. Screw it. It would probably be good for me to have the experience. Maybe it will work for me, maybe it won't, but I should just give it a try and stop spending so much time obsessing over it. With that I pushed the SEND button.

Saturday, February 25

I spoke at the YPO singles retreat today. It was exhilarating. For two hours, I really harangued them about how, in order to be successful in dating, they needed to take it seriously. I told the story about Miss Manhunt with the upstate New York fixer-upper house, and I told the story about a YPO guy I knew who couldn't get into a relationship because he overextended himself with charity commitments. I explained that taking lengthy trips *outside* their hometowns might be fun but didn't demonstrate a commitment to meeting their significant other *in* their hometown because they weren't there long enough to meet someone. I talked about how meeting someone once and then expecting that person to fly to see them, even if they pay for the ticket, doesn't cut it: most people won't fly to a destination until they know that they won't be stranded and miserable in a foreign place. When I looked out at my audience, I was happy to see that they were enraptured. I really felt like they got something out of my lecture. I ended with dating do's and don'ts, and a question-and-answer period. A few people raised their hands and asked whether I could continue going with more do's and don'ts. The moderator said no, but I promised to e-mail them a full list, which seemed to please them. And after I finished, a guy came up to me, introduced himself, and asked me to guess where he lived. I told him I had no idea, and he said upstate New York, right near Miss Manhunt, and he would love to meet her. *Go figure!*

March

March is a busy Matchmaking month because I get the Valentine's Day aftermath. I get the people who broke up on Valentine's Day—there are a lot of those. And I get the people who were depressed because they were alone on Valentine's Day and took a few weeks to get up the nerve to give a call. Also, March is a cold month, at least in New York, so people are still looking for someone to cuddle with, which always works to my advantage.

DESPERADO #24

Osmosis Man

This guy contacted me a few months ago. He's someone I have known socially for a while. First he didn't want to fill out the online form, then he insisted on talking to me and not my assistant, Vanessa, on the phone, and now he wants to meet with me directly but he doesn't want to pay the consultation fee. *Tough! You must pay to play at the Table!* Couldn't he just take me to dinner and discuss the service? Why did he have to pay just to meet me? He's a doctor and he doesn't charge a consultation fee. I told him that was his choice, but how I work my business is that I charge a consultation fee. *You want to pay, I am happy to sit down with you and listen to all of your requests and all your neuroses; you don't, well then, Adios.* He said he would think about it.

He called me back the next day and obsessed some more. "Tell me more about the service. The prices are steep. How do I know that you'll deliver?" I said, "Quite frankly, you don't. You just have to trust me. But if you don't hire me, how else are you going to meet your wife?" He said defensively, "I have no trouble meeting women; I have dates all the time." I tried to smooth things over. "I am sure that you do, but obviously whatever you're doing to meet women isn't working, because you're contacting me." I paused to see if he would interrupt me. He didn't, so I continued. "So if you don't hire me, how do you plan on doing things differently so you have different luck?" There was a long silence and then he said he didn't know. I pressed on. "Are you interested in doing online dating?" He answered quickly, "No interest in that, it's not for me." "Okay, well, are you planning any trips to places where you could meet women, maybe to a ski resort?" Again, a quick answer. "No, I don't have time to get away right now." "Well, do you have any blind dates on the horizon or people you can tap into to provide you with blind dates?" He chuckled. "No, not right now. I think my friends have introduced me to every woman they know and then some." I thought about my own string of bad blind dates and laughed aloud. "Right, and what about the bar and party scene?" I already knew the answer. He responded with contempt, "I'm definitely not into that, I'm more low-key."

"Let's review," I said, trying not to patronize him. "No online dating, no time for trips, no blind dates on the horizon, and you hate bars. How, pray tell, do you expect to meet a woman, through osmosis?" "Hmm," he said, obviously mulling over the question. "When you put it that way, I don't have an answer. I guess I just think it will happen." I nodded, then closed with the zinger. "Well, it might, but chances are you will be calling me back in three to six months, standing in exactly the same social void you are in now, and signing up for the service." I gave him the hard sell because I knew he could afford it and because I figured that, like most of the Desperados, he contacted me because he really wanted to work with me but just needed some reassurance. I went in for the kill. "Why not do it now and save some time?" There was silence, and I thought I had succeeded, but he said he would think about it. *Think away, Osmosis Man. You'll be back, of that I have no doubt!*

Wednesday, March 1

I got a return e-mail from one of the guys I wrote to on JDate. He said I sounded interesting and he would love to see a photo. Hmm, now comes the do-or-die. Do I send it? *What happens if he knows me?* I got my best friend on the phone again for moral support. She told me to send it, just think of it as an experiment. So I sent a sexy but somewhat blurred photo. He e-mailed me back an hour later. No mention of knowing who I was—he told me I was hot. *Thank you!* Did I want to talk on the phone? *Not really!* I told him maybe a few more e-mails would be better. So we e-mailed back and forth all day, playful and witty notes. He called me "Sam I am" from Dr. Seuss and I called him "the Road Runner" because his profile name was RunnerNY182. I kept my profession out of the e-mails. I figured it was better to tell him that in person, if we ever met in person, so I played coy on the job topic. I told him I was employed, self-sufficient, and that I used to be a lawyer. He seemed satisfied with that answer. I realize that women care a lot more about the guy's occupation than guys do about the women's.

He was getting a little impatient about the talking on the phone thing. I wasn't sure what I was waiting for. I guess I figured that once we spoke on the phone there would be no turning back. Finally I bit the bullet and told him I would take his number and call him. He didn't understand why I wouldn't give him my number. I explained to him that I was a good Jewish girl and needed to be careful—he was a stranger. He seemed annoyed. I wasn't sure why he would be annoyed. Wouldn't every woman dating online ask the guy for his phone number instead of giving out hers? I advise all my ladies to do that. *Don't be annoyed, Mr. JDate. If you want to talk to me you need to play by my rules.* Eventually he relented, and I said I would call him later.

I soon realized that initiating a phone call to someone of the opposite sex was not so easy. I began to pity men, and the fact they have to make that first call. I procrastinated most of the day and never called. *Maybe tomorrow.*

Miss Kid Waffler

I started the ball rolling with Miss Kid Waffler last night. I sent her out with Rick, an old friend of mine. I heard from her by e-mail this morning. She really liked Rick. She was nervous about going initially and couldn't imagine who I was going to come up with for her, but she was really impressed—he was a really good guy. *Of course he was. That's what you pay me for. Have some faith!* Then I e-mailed Rick. He asked me to call him. Uh-oh. I have learned that whenever they ask me to call them, it's not good. I dialed his number slowly. Rick is a sweetheart of a guy. I met him when I first moved to New York at an "in spot" on the Upper East Side. He hit on me, he hit on my best friend, and he hit on pretty much every other girl we knew. Eventually we realized he was just a character and we all became fast friends. He was very pleasant on the phone, and we made small talk for a while. Then I asked about Miss Kid Waffler, and he said, "She seemed really terrific, just my type in the looks and personality categories. But I thought that you knew that I really want children, and a girl who doesn't want to have kids is just not for me." *Oh, Miss Kid Waffler, we reviewed this already. Weren't you listening?* I thought that if I offered predate coaching, it would prevent the Desperado from screwing up the date itself. No such luck with this one.

I asked him, "Did she say that exactly? Did she actually say that she doesn't want to have kids, or did you just assume that from the conversation?" "Um." He hesitated. "No, she definitely said that. The topic of children came up and I asked her how many kids she wanted to have and she made a joke and said none. Then I gave her a look, as if to imply that I didn't find her funny, and she changed her answer and said she didn't know, she hadn't given it much thought." "Hmm." My mind was racing. "Well, maybe she was just kidding around." I wanted to try to salvage this date. "Samantha," he said, "I've never met a woman who would joke around that way if she wanted to have kids. I could definitely see her joking around and saying she wanted fifteen or twenty, but to say none? You and I both know that there's an element of truth in everything anyone says. Plus, I just sensed it. She was serious." *Fair point.* He asked me to be straight with him. So I admitted that she was a kid waffler, plain and simple. "She just isn't sure yet, so she is not saying no, but she is also not saying yes." I told him that I thought that once she was in love, it would become a yes. He said maybe, but taking that chance wasn't for him. I understood.

My next call was to the Waffler herself. I launched right in. "Miss Kid Waffler, we have a problem. Rick liked you a lot until you made a joke about not wanting kids. Didn't we talk about how this scares men off?" Her voice tensed up. "Yes, Samantha, but I was only kidding around. It was an innocent little joke." I shook my head and took a long breath. "Miss Waffler, you cannot, cannot, cannot make jokes of that nature, not once, not ever. Do I make myself clear? This guy doesn't want to go out with you again because of your innocent little joke. If you really want to meet someone, you need to listen to my advice." *Then the lightbulb went on for me. Did Miss Kid Waffler really want to meet someone? Or was she using this whammy as a convenient way to sabotage potential relationships? Too soon to tell, but we shall see. . . .*

BACK TO

Mr. Teeth

Mr. Teeth has been a little difficult to set up. He is very inexperienced with women. He doesn't know what to say and what not to say or how to move from a friendly encounter into a relationship. He needs some major coaching. I also think he has a crush on me, which is not good, because now that I know the real him, I am never going to date him. I've set him up with some unassuming women who will appreciate how smart he is and won't mind his awkwardness. But now all of a sudden, because he paid his money, he's getting really picky. It's funny, before he signed up with me, he was dating women who didn't even graduate from high school, and now he's started demanding pretty sophisticated women who would never ordinarily give him the time of day. I am not sure what to do. I need a good-quality woman who will also give him a chance, or a woman I can force to give him a chance. Then it hit me. *Miss 39!* Mr. Teeth was the guy for Miss 39. He was as inexperienced as she was. They could learn together! And he is not short, not from an unacceptable place, not a doctor. He's active, a big tennis player and biker, too, and he is very close to her age! Oh my God, how happy would I be if I could actually get Miss 39 married. I started to daydream. I don't want her to screw this one up.

NOT FOR ME GUY

The Boy Toy

I found my first real boy toy—a guy who has no long-term potential but offers a lot of temporary fringe benefits. I figured if Demi and Cameron can do it, so can I. I met him at a party. He's hot, he's 25, great body, smells really good, and is very sexy. He's just out of school, in and out of work, trying to act and write, and he doesn't want anything from me except to have fun. *I deserve a little fun for a while, right?*

BACK TO

JDate

I bit the bullet and went on several JDates. I figured it would be good research, if nothing else. My overall experience? I didn't really like it. Don't get me wrong, I think the service is amazing. I wish I had invented it, but it's too time-consuming and too anonymous. Obviously, I'm all about the personal introductions through an intermediary. JDate does not have that component. Also, it freaked me out a bit that I didn't know who any of these guys were. There was RunnerNY, the first guy, an international entrepreneur; Hiyasexy, the 38-year-old sales trader; NYeastguy, the 42-year-old partner at a law firm; Yaleguy32, the 40-year-old who owns his own company; and a few others. They were all unique, but it bothered me that I didn't know anyone who knew them personally. It also bothered me that they were all able to hide behind e-mail, and I couldn't assess their real personalities. I learned quickly that a lot of men who were confident and eloquent and funny writers weren't so confident or eloquent or funny in person. I told some of them I was a Matchmaker. I told others that I was a lawyer. Some of them asked me what I was doing on JDate, some asked whether JDate was the competition, a few thought it was cool that I was a Matchmaker, and a few I flipped into my database once I figured out that they weren't for me. I might try JDate again when I have more time. You never know. . . .

BACK TO

Mr. Large Adonis

He went out on a few dates with my girl, Suzanne. She called me this morning. "I have been out with Mr. Large Adonis a few times and I really like him, but [*there it is again, the* but], well, we fooled around a little last night and, well, his . . . *his thing* is really small, like supersmall. I was . . . uh . . . sort of turned off," she said, her voice low. I played stupid. "Hmm," I said. "Well, is it a deal breaker? I mean, he's a great guy and if you like him, is it really all that bad?" She snorted. "Samantha, I don't want to seem shallow, but once I fooled around with this guy and he was so small that when he was inside me, I didn't even know it. Suffice it to say, that was a very embarrassing situation. Who wants to have sex if you can't even feel it?" I tried to seem understanding. *She had a point.* "So what are you going to do?" "I think I want to stop seeing him. You tell him, okay?" she begged. "You can say whatever you want."

This girl was not one of my Desperados, so I couldn't tell her that she had to break up with him on her own. I said I'd take care of it.

Saturday, March 11

I went to a wedding tonight. It was a couple that I had introduced before I *went professional.* I found myself observing the socializing process again. Women definitely go to weddings hoping to meet a man there. They figure that the marrying feeling is in the air, and if they meet a man who is good friends with the groom, the domino effect might happen. I tend to agree that weddings are good places to meet someone because the wedding of a best bud is a "triggering event," as I call them, an event that inspires an urgent desire in a man to get married.

Other triggering events? you ask. Well, when a younger sibling gets married, engaged, or has a baby. Or when several work superiors make one too many jokes about the fact that a guy is the only single guy at the executive table. Or when there's a sickness or death in the family. Or when the guy injures himself and doesn't heal as quickly as he thought he would and realizes that he's getting older. Unfortunately, falling in love is not a definite triggering event for men, the way it is for women.

Think about it. How many times have you seen a guy you know in a relationship with a woman who seems perfect for him, and they seem so happy together, yet they eventually break up because he isn't ready to commit? And then he dates another woman who seems so terrible for him, who doesn't even hold a candle to the first woman, and the guy goes and marries her and leaves all of his friends stumped. Why did he marry the second one and not the first? I don't think it's because he was more in love with the second one; I think it's because he experienced a triggering event and all of a sudden he was absolutely ready to get married, and that bride was the one in front of him. Some people think this theory is crazy, but I've seen it proven time and time again. We all want to believe that when a guy catches marriage fever, the perfect girl, the One, is standing in front of him. I'm sure sometimes that's the case, but other times it's just dumb luck. So my advice to women is to fall in love with a man who has already had his triggering event and is ready. How do you know? You don't, sorry. Men and women are very different creatures. Sometimes I wonder, if it weren't for procreation purposes, would we even be together?

BACK TO

The Boy Toy

I came to a realization today. Sex complicates things and sex makes you like someone you don't really like. I had sex with my boy toy. *I fig-*

ured *I should. After all, isn't that what a boy toy is for?* He is for sex and my personal pleasure, right? I figured I could have sex with him without having *feelings* for him because I knew that he wasn't for me, and I knew I didn't want him to be my boyfriend. I tell a lot of women not to have sex unless and until they're certain that they want to be with that guy because—here comes another theory—as soon as women have sex, they become attached and look at the man and the relationship or situation differently. A lot of women, myself included, claim that they can have unattached sex just for the fun of it, but from what I have seen time and time again, I don't really think we—*I* can.

I have always thought of myself as more like a guy in that I can handle casual sex without feeling and attachment. *I now realize that's a big fat lie.* I had sex with the Boy Toy and actually started contemplating whether I could be in a real relationship with him. *Am I insane?* The guy is 25 and out of work. We have nothing in common except for good sex. Intellectually I know I could never be in a real relationship with him, but nevertheless I started having all these *closeness* feelings about him. So I either need to stop having sex with him or find a way to have sex with him and not get attached. Wow, I guess I am just like all the other single women out there. Sex really does cloud my brain. *I need to practice what I preach.*

BACK TO

Jerkoff

I called him tonight. I never call him, but I wanted to know how he was doing. It took a lot for him to tell me that he was seeing a shrink and that he was in AA. I realized that I would advise a Desperado to be supportive of his decision, and I wanted him to know that I was supportive of him as well. Four times, I dialed his number three-quarters of the way before I finally let the call go through. I guess I was a little nervous. "Hi, Jerkoff." "Samantha? Hi, I'm surprised to hear from you. I mean, it's good to hear from you. I am just surprised." He sounded a little flustered. I asked him if I had gotten him at a bad time. "No, not at all, um, just hold on for a minute." I heard some movement and it sounded like he was getting out of bed, and I heard a voice. *Oh shit, I called when he was in bed with someone. I want to throw up.* "Are you in bed with someone? Am I interrupting sex?" "No, Samantha, no. I am happy to hear from you. She's no one." "Look, if she is someone or if she is no one, it's not my business. I was just calling to see how you were doing, to see how AA and therapy are going. I shouldn't have called. It was a mistake. I gotta go." I hung up quickly. *Now I feel like shit again. Why am I still not over him?*

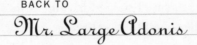

Mr. Large Adonis

I called him today to break up with him for Suzanne. Right away, he asked me if it was because of his you-know-what. I figured this time I didn't need to upset him, and Suzanne did say that I could give any reason I wanted, so I said that I didn't know, that I had heard that she recently ran into her ex-boyfriend. *Good excuse.* I figured if the same thing happened with the next girl, then we'd have to regroup, but until then I could spare his feelings. He seemed okay with that answer. *Maybe he didn't want to hear the truth.* I told him I would be in touch soon with a new date.

BACK TO
The Girl I Always Thought Hated Me

She called today, very excited. Her voice was all singsongy. She met a guy on her own. She has been using my dating technique suggestions and they have been out about fifteen times. She doesn't know if she will need our second coaching session, or at least she doesn't right now. She thinks things are going well. "That's terrific," I said, genuinely happy for her. Then her enthusiasm seemed to wane a bit and she said, "Before we hang up, I need your help for a minute. I really like this guy but I'm just not sure if he is as into me as I am into him, and I'm not sure how to find out. Can you help?" "Sure," I answered. "Have you had the relationship talk yet?" "What would that mean exactly?" she asked, confused. "Well . . . you would talk about your relationship and decide where it's going and whether you're seeing only each other or if you're still seeing other people." "Oh no," she insisted, "we are *not* seeing other people." "How do you know that?" I asked. She replied with conviction, "I am not seeing other people, so of course he isn't, either." "Look, I don't want to burst your bubble, but there is no guarantee that just because you have stopped seeing other guys that he's done the same. He might still be seeing other girls, you don't know, and until you know for sure, you should still be seeing other guys so you can keep this situation in perspective." There was silence as she processed what I said.

Then she asked me what signs there would be if he were still seeing other women. "Do you see each other every weekend and both weekend nights?" I asked. "No, not every weekend," she said. "Have you met any of his friends?" "One only, but that was by accident when we ran into him at a restaurant." Her voice started to drop. I asked, "How did he introduce you to that friend?" She said that he called her "his friend." "Has he met your family or you his?" As if she was beginning to see what I was getting at, she said more slowly, "I asked him to come to dinner with my parents twice, but he said he had to work both times, and when I asked to meet his family, he said his family was difficult and he didn't want to subject me to them."

Her voice started trembling. "What does this mean? Now that you ask all that, it doesn't sound so good." "Don't panic," I reassured her. "These things are just clues about where he is in the relationship, and I agree they don't sound wonderful, but it's still early and it usually takes men longer to get exclusive. Why not just ask him?" She said she was nervous and she didn't want to screw things up. I became stern. "Look, you either need to ask him or you need to keep dating. You're accepting a double standard if you sit around waiting for him and he does as he pleases. And it's better for you to stay busy than to sit around obsessing. Guys can sense that *obsessing vibe,* and you don't want to give it off." I could hear her tapping her pen on the table while she weighed her options. Then she agreed reluctantly. I pressed on, "Maybe if you seemed a little busier and a little less available, it might prompt *him* to have the relationship talk." I told her I was sending her out on another date, just to keep her busy. She paused again, trying to make her decision. Then she said she was nervous but willing.

When I got off the phone with The Girl, I thought about her situation. It's a pretty common one for women. A woman will fall for a guy, get all excited and fantasize about her wedding, and along the way forget that actions speak louder than words. She'll forget to pay attention to the signals the guy is giving. Those signals might be that he doesn't see the relationship in as serious a mode as she does. However, a woman won't even notice this because she will get so carried away with her fantasy of happily ever after with a particular guy. And most of the time, even if someone like me points out the indicators she is missing, she will rationalize them away. Or she will continue to call friend after friend, describing the same situation until she finds that one friend who will interpret things the way she wants so that she can still believe in the fantasy that her guy is perfect. *And there is always a friend out there who will give exactly the right interpretation.* The interpretation that she chooses to believe is the one in which concrete proof is not what it seems, and there is some other logical explanation for the fact that he hasn't called in five days, didn't come to her party, didn't invite her out with his friends, or didn't introduce her to his parents.

Unfortunately for us girls, men usually know exactly what they are doing, and it's no accident that they behave the way that they behave. If they are doing all the wrong things and not behaving as interested guys would, most of the time it's because they don't want to behave that way and aren't ready to be the kind of boyfriends that women want them to be. This is usually because they are just not interested enough in the particular woman to step up to the plate. *We've all been there.* This is the harsh reality that most women don't like to accept, so they start the rationalization process to give the jerky guy the benefit of the doubt and say he isn't ready when the real question is, Will he ever be ready with them? *Reality sucks!*

BACK TO
Jerkoff

He sent me a dozen purple tulips. I am starting to hate purple tulips. *No I'm not.* He wrote two words: "I'm sorry." He's always sorry and I am always upset. *Why?*

BACK TO
Soul Mate Guy

I ran into him on the street again. I wish the streets were wider or I knew a different route or lived in a different place. I hate running into him. We were making small talk when his phone rang. He got a smile on his face and said into the phone, "Hi, yes, I called you. No, not on your cell, on *our* phone. Yes, I will be *home* in thirty minutes. I miss you, too." And then he turned back to me and said, "It's tricky for two people who work for themselves to be living in the same space." I was taken aback. *You are living with her now? A month ago you wanted to live with me. What is wrong with you?* I didn't give him the satisfaction of saying that out loud. I think he somehow wanted to torture me. I told him I needed to go, bye. Clearly he just wanted to be living with a woman as quickly as possible, and I guess he found someone to fill the slot. I am glad it's not me because he is an unstable, needy guy. But I have to admit, I am a tad jealous. *Why can someone like him fall so easily for so many people and I can't even find one?*

Monday, March 13

I got an e-mail today from Mr. Bonus with the Pinkie Ring. Remember him? When I saw his e-mail pop up, I got so excited. *Maybe he broke up with his girlfriend, which of course would be very sad, but then he would need me to set him up again, and that would be a very happy ending, at least for me!* No such luck. He started the e-mail by telling me that he is still very happy with his girlfriend. However, he was thinking of me because he wanted to refer a friend, a guy who lives in New York and London. "And, Samantha, I told him how I incentivized you to find me great women. I hope you don't mind." *Mind? I love you, Mr. Bonus. You are my hero!*

DESPERADO #25

The Hundred Thousand Dollar Man

Today I met with Mr. Bonus's friend. I was very excited, I was about to have a new Mr. Bonus Desperado. *I was singing in the shower as I pictured my new apartment!* I met him at the Regency. Unfortunately, he wasn't as nice-looking as the original Mr. Bonus. He was kind of tall and broad-shouldered and looked like an absentminded professor, with messy hair, a bow tie and pocket square, and old-fashioned oxford-type lace-up shoes. No pinkie ring, *thankfully*. He was also a bit of an intellectual, had a Ph.D. in Russian literature from Stanford. He was a money guy now, a very wealthy money guy who had started and sold several businesses. His financial stability would appeal to the ladies, but at the end of the day, he was still a quirky intellectual, and being "bi-city" complicated the picture even more. I had no problem taking him as a client because I was anticipating that large bonus, but I knew he was going to be a tough one.

I told him that I was fine with taking a bi-city client as long as he gave me his word that he would take my service and my efforts seriously. *It's ironic, it used to be that the clients gave me a hard time about taking my own job seriously, but now I give them a hard time about their job, which is to be available for the dates and make meeting someone a priority. There's nothing worse than when I spend all this time picking a great person for a Desperado, and I learn that they had a great date, and then I hear they blew it because they had no time to follow up and go out again.* This guy said he understood and gave me his word that he would be in New York for close to a week or more at least once a month, and that getting married again (he was divorced) was a real priority.

Then he got a little hung up on seeing the women's photos before he met them. I explained to him that this was not the way the service worked. I didn't have photos of all the women in the database, and my setups were based on a wide range of criteria, rather than looks alone. He was relentless, though, insisting that he wanted me to keep in mind all of his criteria but he also wanted to be able to see what the women looked like before he met them. I started to sense that he might not sign up as a client if I didn't come up with some sort of compromise. Then it dawned on me. *I could run a search ad for him. All the Maries do it, and I have always wanted to give it a shot.* "We can compromise," I said. "I will introduce you to some of the women already in my database, and those women you will meet without seeing their photos." I looked at him intently. "Then I will also run a search ad in one of the local magazines asking women to respond and send in letters and photos. Once I get those responses, you can look at them with me, and we can decide who you are going to meet. How does that sound?" The more I thought about it, the more I liked this idea because he was a bit of a quirky guy, so an ad in which I asked for a particular type of woman who would be well suited to him might be helpful.

He wasn't so keen on that at first. He said, "But I thought you are a Matchmaker. You are supposed to have all these women. Why would you need to run an ad?" I gave him a not-to-worry look and explained to him that I do have tons of women, but I wanted to find special women for him, women who were exactly right, and besides which, this would allow him to see what the women looked like. He shrugged and said, "Well, if that's the case, let's start with the ad first and get to your database afterward." *Fine with me.*

Then he asked me how well I knew Mr. Bonus #1, and I said that I worked with him for a while and got to know him pretty well, why? "Well, what did you think of him?" He sat forward in his chair and paid close attention. "Nice guy." I smiled. "Sweet and kind and very generous." "Did you think he was good-looking?" he inquired. *I didn't know where he was going with this.* I chose my words carefully. "I thought he was a great guy and, yes, a nice-looking guy." "Do you think I am better looking than he is?" he coaxed. "Um, I don't know. I haven't really thought about it. You are very nice looking, too." *What was going on here?* He pressed on. "Think about it. Am I better looking than he is?" "Um, well, you have a better physique than he does and such pretty blue eyes. Yes, I guess I would have to say that you are better looking than he is." He seemed satisfied with that answer. Then he asked me which income box the other guy had checked on my questionnaire, and he asked if he himself had checked a higher box. *Okay, this is getting ridiculous. Why does it matter? Why was this guy so competitive?* I told him I didn't recall and, besides, that's not something I tell people. He seemed to accept that.

He then rendered me speechless by saying, "I know my friend offered you a $60,000 bonus, but I want to offer you a higher one." *Okey dokey, guy!* He smiled, took a sip of his drink, and said, "How does a $100,000 bonus offer strike you?" *It strikes me fine, A-OK!* "But do you promise that you will introduce me to much hotter women than you ever introduced him to?" My eyes lit up. "Absolutely!" *Anything you want!* I saw *Pretty Woman,* and he seemed to want some major sucking up, so I basically told him that he was the hero, and the man, and so much cooler, brighter, and hotter than his friend could ever be! *You are The Hundred Thousand Dollar Man. Forget about Mr. Bonus and his $60,000— he was so yesterday!*

MAYBE FOR ME GUY

LA Guy

I went to Aspen for some spring skiing and met a guy. He was little boyish in his looks, kind of like Matthew Broderick except that his hair was more curly than wavy, and he was a lanky six feet three. We had a lot of fun together, but the whole time I couldn't help wondering, Is this vacation chemistry or real chemistry? Could we have a relationship in the real world, or do we just like each other in vacation world? He seemed to think that we could be a real thing, but there was one minor technicality: he lives in Los Angeles, I live in New York. He didn't think that would be a problem. I wasn't so sure.

When I got home, he immediately called and said, "Where are

you?" I thought, *What do you mean, where am I? I am in my apartment in New York, freezing my ass off.* "Why aren't you here?" *Because I live here and you haven't invited me there.* "You should come to L.A. this weekend." I stopped to think about it. Five minutes later, I had thought about it, and I told him I'd come. *Very smooth, Miss Matchmaker / Dating Expert, way to go. You didn't try to get him to miss you even a little bit. You didn't even make him wonder for fifteen minutes whether you would come or not.* "When will you come?" he asked. "When do you want me to come?" *Smooth again—why am I making it so easy for him? Maybe I should have insisted that he make the first cross-country trip. The guy should do that. Maybe he shouldn't think I will fly across the country on his whim.* Oh God, I am such an idiot, but I am "in like," and being "in like" makes you do impulsive things. No matter, I will be sure to be at the top of my dating game once I go there. We made plans for me to visit next weekend. Let's hope I can find some playing-it-cool pills to take before I leave.

DESPERADO #26

Mr. Emaciated

This guy plain offended me. He was a big braggart who loved talking about all of his money and all of his fancy toys. He did it in an obnoxious way, as if he had something to prove. And all he cared about was meeting a hot-bodied woman. He didn't care what her face looked like, what her personality was like, what she did for a living, where she was from, only that she had a great body. And that great body needed to be waiflike. Not curvaceous, not just sexy, but truly waify. He only wanted to date women who are under a size four, meaning only size two and size zero. He thought that a size six was fat. I totally understand a guy wanting a girl with a hot body, and I can and will deliver that every time if requested. However, thinking that a size six is fat is just plain irritating. The kicker was he could probably afford to lose twenty-five pounds himself. I asked him flatly, "Mr. Emaciated, I am not really sure I understand this. Why are you so hypercritical of the female body when you don't seem to hold yourself to the same standards? His answer was equally obnoxious, just three words: "Because I can." *Well, Mr. Emaciated, maybe you can with some people, but business is really good these days. I can afford to be picky, and I am not picking you.*

Friday, March 24

I threw a party last night. I called it the lock and key party. I invited three hundred people and when they walked in the door, all the women were handed locks and the men were handed keys. They had to walk up to one another and see whose key opened whose lock. I made it so that more than one key would open each lock so there would be more matches. I came up with this idea as an ice-breaker, and it seemed to work. Everyone complimented me on what a great party it was and what a great hostess I am. The bartenders told me they heard a number of people talking about me, asking who I was specifically, and commenting on how attractive I am. I should be riding high. But at the end of the day, throwing a party like this when I don't have a boyfriend makes me feel really sad. It's no fun to have this great success, make so many matches, and go home alone. It makes me feel sad and lonely. I don't get that lonely feeling often, but last night I had it.

BACK TO

Mr. Large Adonis

I sent him on several dates since Suzanne. He thinks that all the women are beautiful but that they don't have enough edge. I have listened to his complaints and told him that I understood and would try to come up with someone edgier, but the truth is, I think an edgy girl is going to freak about his little you-know-what. He called me this morning and complained again. As I was in an "advising" mood, I told him, "I think the reason that the girls of your past have given you such a hard time about your *little* problem is because they have been bitches. Yes, they might be edgy but they were also not understanding. In my opinion, and you are paying me for my opinion and expertise, you need to give the nicer girls a chance because the nicer girls are going to fall in love with you and stick around when they see that your Johnson is not as large as they expected." He was taken aback. "Do you really think so?" I nodded to myself. "I obviously can't be certain, but I do think so, so it's time to get over your bitch fantasy and move into reality, where you and I both know that you have an extenuating circumstance." He said he respected my candor and would give Katie, last night's nice girl, another shot. *Great!*

BACK TO

Miss Fantasy

Heard from Miss Fantasy today out of the blue. It didn't work out with her best guy friend. She sounded sad. "I thought things were going to work out at first. He was completely interested in trying it.

We spent every day together and became like an old married couple almost immediately." "That sounds great, so what happened?" I asked. She paused, as if not certain that she wanted to continue. I urged her on. "Don't worry, you can tell me anything, everyone does." She paused again and then said, "Well, we started having sexual issues. He claimed that he was suffering from something called the Madonna/Whore syndrome. Have you heard of it?" *I hear about it all too often, unfortunately.* "I think so," I said cautiously. "It's a syndrome where a guy puts a woman up on a pedestal and thinks so highly of her that he can't have sex with her because he thinks its almost sacrilegious, right?" "Yup, you got it, and it's worse than that, apparently these men are only able to have sex with girls that they don't respect, whores, but they can't get it up for girls they love and respect." Her voice dropped.

"Samantha, it was so terrible, he couldn't get an erection with me. We kept trying and trying and he just couldn't. And then the more times we tried the worse it got because I guess he and I both were focusing on it so much that of course he was going to have performance anxiety." I wasn't sure what to say to her, so I just continued to listen. "For a while I wondered if he was gay. I still think he might be. I just don't know. All I do know is that my self-esteem is pretty low right now, it was just shocking that he couldn't get it up for me. Guys always think I am sexy, I have never had that problem before." Her voice was shaking now. I quickly tried to change the subject so that she wouldn't lose it on the phone. "Listen, Miss Fantasy, that sucks, but you need to move on. How about I set you up with a guy who will definitely think you are hot and sexy? I have this guy, Brad Pitt Guy. . . ."

DESPERADO #27

Mr. Bigger Better Deal

I have known this Desperado for a while. He goes to every party, has three sets of plans every night, and is never satisfied with the woman he's with or the party he goes to because he's always wondering if there's something or someone better out there. He never really has fun where he is because he's too concerned about what he's missing. I see this type a lot, and I was surprised when he called and said he wanted to have a consultation. I scheduled him today and decided to be very up-front with him. "Mr. Bigger Better Deal," I said, "I am going to be honest with you. We have known each other for a while, and I see you run around from party to party and from woman to woman to woman. You are a classic example of the *Bigger Better Deal Guy*. I think you know what that means. I need to know what has changed or what's going to change to make you behave differently with *my* women." He ran his fingers through his hair and responded, "It might seem like I'm that way, but that's not really me. I just like to have fun and to know a lot of people. But I also would like to have a relationship. There has to a woman out there who likes having a good time and knowing a lot of people, too."

I looked at him more closely. *Will I really be able to work with Mr. BBD? Hmm, he is a nice-looking guy, tall, about six feet two, lanky build, dirty blond curly hair, and a lopsided smile. He's cute and he's sweet. I'll try.* I said to him openly, "I see your situation differently. Let me tell you about a little theory I have. I call it the 85 percent theory. When someone is dating a person they actually like, that person usually has 85 percent of the things they are looking for, but there is about 15 percent remaining that they wish was different. In most towns and cities across the country, normal people are satisfied with the 85 percent and take the plunge and get married because, if you think about it, 85 percent is pretty good. But in New York, people are obsessed with perfection. They are complete overachievers and they won't settle. So time and time again, they throw back 85 percent in an attempt to get 100 percent, but when they "go fish" again, they just get *another* 85 percent, a *different* 85 percent of the things they want in a person." I paused to see if he was listening. "They keeping trying and trying, and throwing back and *fishing* again, and as a result a lot of people stay single. Mr. Bigger Better Deal, I don't want you to be that guy." I smiled at him sweetly and waited to see what he would say. He looked impressed and said, "Interesting theory." And he committed on the spot, surprising me. *I guess he no longer wants to be that guy, either. . . .*

April

April is probably one of my most uneventful Matchmaking months. It's the start of spring, so people are feeling particularly optimistic about meeting someone on their own. They begin looking forward to summer, when they expect to meet a new crop of singles out and about, so they aren't thinking about hiring a Matchmaker to help them. But don't cry me a river yet, because there are always those triggering events that keep my phone a-ringin'. . . .

BACK TO
LA Guy

Just got back from L.A. I like LA Guy, a lot, probably too much, because I'm not even 100 percent certain that he's so into me. I think that I need to play harder to get and see if he responds, if he starts to feel like he can't live without me. You know the drill.

I arrived in L.A. on Friday. He picked me at the airport. I was really nervous. Doubts kept racing through my mind. *Let's say I hate him, let's say he's not as cute as I remembered, let's say his apartment is disgusting, then what?* I got off the plane and made a pit stop to fix my hair and makeup. I wanted to seem casual and a little mussed since I just got off a cross-country flight, but also irresistible. He called while I was primping. "Sexy, where are you? I am waiting outside." My stomach was in knots as I walked through the airport. What do I do when I see him? *Do I kiss him hello? On the lips or on the cheek? Give him a hug? Do I run to him? Do I smile?* The walk through the airport was torturous. I got outside and he wasn't there, so I presumed that the cops chased him away. As I waited, I found myself wondering what kind of car he drove. I decided it would be an SUV. I was right—up drove a Porsche Cayenne. And then all of a sudden he was there. He got out of the car and lifted me in the air for a hug; it was very romantic, very romantic-comedy. I was glad he took control because all my overthinking and planning had fried my nerves.

He was still cute (curly brown hair, little dimples, about six feet three, lanky tennis player build). *Thank god.* He took me to his apartment. It was a typical I-haven't-moved-since-college bachelor pad with old furniture and a lived-in look, but it was very clean and he, I soon discovered, was compulsive about keeping everything organized. He told me he was waiting to buy a permanent home until he met the woman he was going to spend his life with. *Okay, here I am!* (I hear this from men a lot: they say they don't mind living in a crappy apartment because they are rarely home and they believe that once a woman is in the picture she will make them move anyway, so why spend the time and money buying now? Somehow it doesn't dawn on them that they could live well while they wait and then once they meet a woman, they could jointly decide whether to stay put or move.) I, for one, own my apartment. I am not going to sit around waiting. *At this rate, who knows when my significant other will come along?*

Anyway, getting back to LA Guy, we hung out for a bit and then went to a party. He seemed to know everyone while I knew no one, which was a refreshing change from my New York life. I was happy to be anonymous. He was very affectionate, and it turned out to be the perfect initiation to Los Angeles.

After the party we went back to his apartment and immediately started fooling around. There was intense animal chemistry between us. I loved the way he kissed and I loved the way he smelled. I cuddled up next to him and asked, "Are you surprised that we actually click now that we are away from Aspen?" He turned over, looked at me oddly, and planted a kiss on my lips. "Not at all." *Maybe that was just a girl question*. We stayed awake most of the night and fell asleep spooning.

The next day he took me all around Los Angeles, showing me things, being affectionate and very *boyfriendy*. I know I shouldn't have, but I started envisioning myself living in Los Angeles with this guy. I even started putting out feelers about the Matchmaking business, trying to get the lay of the land. Call me sappy, call me girly, and call me an idiot, but the first twenty-four hours were so perfect that I got swept away.

On the second night, we went to dinner and had good conversation. Everything was great until we went back to his place and got into bed. I was very much looking forward to another hot night. However, I soon found out that he was not. I started snuggling up against him and he pushed me away. *Uh-oh, what is happening?* I waited a few minutes and tried again. Again, I was rebuffed. I wanted to say something, ask him if everything was all right, but I couldn't find the words. I was too nervous to begin a don't-you-want-me conversation—it seemed a little premature. I would probably advise a female Desperado to stay away from it, so for once I took my own advice and just rolled over and went to sleep.

The next day he went to work—he owns his own advertising agency—and I hung out around Los Angeles. That night he came home in good spirits and was sweet and affectionate, so I figured last night he was just tired and nothing was wrong. We got into bed and, wouldn't you know it, the same scenario played out. He didn't want to fool around. *I don't understand this. You're a guy. You're supposed to be permanently horny. I am naked, and you are supposedly crazy about me. What's going on here?* These were the thoughts racing through my head. They were so loud I was sure he heard them. I lay there trying to decide what to do. I was leaving tomorrow. I really liked this guy but if he wasn't into me anymore, I would rather know that than go back to New York unsure. However, I didn't want to have a serious relationship conversation when everything between us was so new. I didn't know what to do. Finally I decided that I had to say something. I was driving myself crazy. I rolled over, tousled his hair a bit, and said, "Is everything all right?" "What do you mean?" he said, stroking my arm softly. I said, "I just wanted to make sure that everything was all right between us because you didn't want to fool around last night, which wasn't a big deal, but now you don't want to again and I just wanted to make sure everything was all right." He stopped stroking and sat up, annoyed. "Why do we have to fool around every single night? Why is it such a big deal if we don't fool around? Why does that mean that something is wrong?" *Well, I'm here for only three nights. I'm leaving to-morrow, and most guys would want to fool around as much as possible, espe-cially on my last night. I'm starting to think that either you're weird or you aren't attracted to me.* Instead, I said, "It's not a big deal. It just caught me off guard, and since I am leaving tomorrow, I just wanted to make sure we were okay." He then rolled over and started to touch me again, but all the while, I wondered if it was because he wanted to smooth things over or because he was into me. I wondered that on the whole plane ride home.

BACK TO

Mr. Large Adonis

I checked in with him today. He has been out on a number of dates with Katie, the last woman I introduced him to. He gave her a chance and has come to believe that she's not only attractive but even a little edgy. *Goody.* He launched in, "She has even seen my penis and she's fine with it. She likes the fact that when she puts it in her mouth——" I interrupted him, wide-eyed in disbelief. "Hey, hey, Mr. Large Adonis, this might be a little too much information for me so early in the morning. I'm glad that the sex is working for the two of you, but I'll pass on the play-by-play!" He laughed. "Okay, I'm sorry. I guess I see you as my priest. I can confess anything to you." *Thanks, I think.*

BACK TO

LA Guy

He called me almost as soon as I got back from L.A. When I saw his number come up on my caller ID, I got butterflies in my stomach. *Was he calling to break up with me?* But he acted like everything was fine and again asked me why I wasn't in Los Angeles. He wanted to know when

I was coming back. "When do you want me to come back?" I asked a little too anxiously, looking for reassurance. He said, "Why not this weekend?" I really wanted to go back immediately—I couldn't get him out of my head. He was acting like everything was fine, but still I was feeling a little insecure. He wanted to fool around only one of three nights, and that's odd for a guy—*no, for anyone*. He repeated that he really wanted me to come back this weekend. He told me he missed me. I said I would think about it, that I had just gotten back to New York and needed some time. In truth, I was ready to pack my bag and get right back on the plane. He called me every night this week. I got butterflies every time. I decided to wait a week before going back, to play it cool and be a little hard to get, at least for the moment.

BACK TO

Miss Excuse

I had my follow-up makeover session with Miss Excuse. She looks amazing. I am so proud of her. She lost almost all the weight that she needed to lose, and now that her face is thinner, you can see her high cheekbones. Her skin is glowing and her body is toned. We went shopping at Barneys and her mom gave her carte blanche on the American Express card. We spent several hours at the store, and I picked out outfits that I thought would complement her newly svelte body. I would say that she went from a three to an eight in the looks category. Not bad! I picked out low-cut but respectable tops that would accentuate her great breasts but also cover the tummy she still had. I chose some A-line short skirts that would show off her legs but wouldn't hug her rear end, which still needed some toning. She looked awesome. She hugged me when we left and started to sniffle a bit. This time I didn't mind the tears.

Thursday, April 13

I just got home from one of the New York big charity parties, this one at the Metropolitan Museum of Art. I marveled once again at how people socialize. They go to these big parties, sometimes private events and sometimes charity benefits, like tonight. Their habits are usually the same. People go with their friends and talk only to their friends the whole evening. They might look around and check out other people, but rarely do the groups of friends interact unless one person in the group knows someone in the other group.

Most single people think that as long as they place themselves in one of these *singly* socializing environments, even if they go home meeting no one time after time, they have still made the appropriate effort and there is nothing more that they can do. They kid themselves into thinking that they have done what they are *supposed* to do to try to meet someone. I guess they don't know that there are no "supposed to's" in dating. What a colossal waste of time! And all the single people do it. Stop and look around any crowded party. *They could probably using some coaching!*

BACK TO

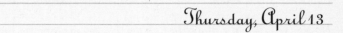
Miss Excuse

It might be time to rename her Miss Proactive. I think she's ready for her first date. I spent some time thinking about who should be bachelor number one. I wanted a guy who would be very sweet to her, since she probably wouldn't feel as confident as her looks would suggest. I pulled out the 30- to 40-year-olds NG (Nice Guy) list.

Hmmm, what about Harold, the nice lawyer with the lisp? No, she deserves a cooler guy than that. What about Lawrence, the guy who speaks really fast? No, I think he's too annoying for her. Hmm, what about Bill, the tall guy with the big nose? He is really funny and nice, maybe him. Hey, what about Larry? Wait, Larry is Looks Good from Afar Guy. What is he doing on this list? He should be on the client list, but that's okay, he actually might be good for Miss Excuse. Yes, let's start with him.

Looks Good from Afar Guy has been so humble recently and is trying so hard to be a better dater, I bet these two will get along. Miss Excuse has always had the most upbeat personality—she can talk to anyone—and now with her new look, she's a great catch. She should be interesting for Looks Good from Afar Guy. Let's give them a shot.

DESPERADO #28

The Troll

The Troll signed up today. He bit the bullet and scheduled an appointment with me. He asked me to come to his apartment instead of meeting me at the Regency. I usually don't travel to the peeps. I like them to come to *my* office, the table in the corner. But I've always wanted to see The Troll's apartment, so I made an exception. The trek downtown was well worth it. His apartment was outstanding, a duplex with an elevator, complete with an unbelievable contemporary art collection and an amazing view of the whole city. Immediately after we finished the grand tour, he started obsessing about his privacy. He didn't want anyone to know he had hired me. He was very hung up on this subject. "Well, Troll," I said, "if they don't know that you hired me, how will I set you up?" He looked at me imploringly. "Why can't you just say to the women that you are setting me up as a favor?" He was willing to pay me extra—double actually, $10,000— but in return, he didn't want me to tell people he was my client. Did I agree? *Hmm, I wasn't sure if I agreed. He was asking me to lie, and I wasn't sure if I wanted to do that, even for double my fee. Besides, let's call a spade a spade. Pretty much everyone around town knows what I do for a living, so won't people just assume that he is my client? After all, I am the Matchmaker and he's The Troll. He might as well wear a sign on his forehead. Maybe deep down, he realized this too, which was why he was so hesitant.*

I felt bad for the guy. So I gave him a look of understanding and said, "This is what I'll do. I am not going to agree to lie for you. However, I will be vague about it. I won't announce that you are my client, and I won't start my pitch with, 'I have a client I want you to meet.' Instead, I will just say, 'I have a great guy I want you to meet.' And if women ask how I know you, I'll say that we'ven been friends for a while, and I'll try to avoid saying that you are my client." *After all, I do have friends who I set up just because, and they don't pay me any money at all.* He seemed to like that response. "However, if any of the women comes straight out and asks if you are my client, I will have to say yes." He frowned a little. "But"—I paused—"I promise I will try to avoid getting to that question. And of course if anyone else asks, we're friends, and that's all. I will say absolutely nothing else. Can you live with that, Troll?" He stared out the window, weighing his options.

Then, realizing that he didn't really have any, he said okay. I guess he, like most of the Desperados, had already made up his mind that he was going to work with me before he even came to the meeting.

TABLE CHANGE

Effective immediately, people pay $10,000 total for the service. This includes the twelve dates but also the dating tips, the grooming, the coaching, and the feedback, because they all need that. The Maries have been charging that amount or more for a while, and it seems like these days all the clients offer that amount anyway, so I might as well ask for it. After all, you can't put a price on love. . . .

BACK TO
LA Guy

I went back to Los Angeles this weekend. I needed to. I couldn't get LA Guy out of my mind. I thought about insisting that he come to New York, but I really love Los Angeles. *And if we are going to get married and have babies and live together in Los Angeles, I need to get used to Los Angeles.* I know I'm ridiculous to fantasize like that after only a few weeks, but he's been calling me every day, we stay on the phone for hours, he says all the right things. *He gives amazing phone.*

He picked me up at the airport again. Again, big swirl in the air, big hug and kiss, and he held my hand all the way home. He attacked me even before we got into the apartment, and my clothes were off within seconds. *So much for my worrying that he was no longer attracted to me.* We fooled around all night and fell asleep in each other's arms. It was paradise, and I found myself forgetting about the last time I was in town, figuring that was just a fluke.

On Saturday, he played golf with some friends and I did some more research about the L.A. singles market. I figured that soon I would be legitimately bicoastal, so it was high time to do what I had been contemplating doing for a while, open an L.A. office. I met with several party promoters and a few publicists to get the lay of the land. As far as I could see, there didn't seem to be too many Maries in La-la-land, at least not ones who subscribe to my brand of Matchmaking. There were several women who claimed to run a Matchmaking service but their businesses, in my opinion, was one step up from an escort service. These women, the "Jackies," collected hundreds of beautiful women, mostly struggling or out-of-work actresses and models (and God knows there is no shortage of those in Los Angeles) who wouldn't mind meeting a wealthy guy who could help make life a little easier. They put their photos in a bound book that reminded me of the Pig Book you received freshman year of college with everyone's photos and bios. The Jackies then traveled from one rich guy's office to the next, thrusting the book onto their desks and saying that any of the luscious ladies could be theirs for a price. The Jackies banked on the L.A. guys caring only about looks and nothing else when choosing a mate. I'm sure this works for some of the men in Los Angeles, but I found that most L.A. men could find their own "pigs" without the Jackies' books. What they couldn't find was quality women, the future mothers of their children. That was where I could come in. The market seemed wide open for a Matchmaker who would take the time to find women with beauty but also with brains and class. *Perfect, my business could be a huge hit in Los Angeles.*

My research done, I looked forward to my evening with LA Guy. Throughout the day, thinking of him brought a smile to my face and little butterflies aflutter in my heart. We went out to dinner at a trendy sushi restaurant and had a little too much sake. I found myself looking at him and at the surroundings and thinking, I could live here with him. When we got back to his apartment, I threw off my clothes and got into bed naked. He got in soon after and once again turned his back to me! I started cozying up next to him, and once again he pushed me away. Okay, now I am starting to think he is bipolar—*Friday night, a sex machine. Saturday night, cat got his penis? I don't get it. What is up with this guy?* I lay on the bed thinking about what to do or what to say and when I finally rolled over to talk to him, he was sound asleep.

The next day at brunch, I tried to bring up the subject, but he brushed it off, joking that I was some kind of nympho. He said that not everyone needed to have sex all the time, and he liked me for other reasons. I found myself getting defensive. *I am not a sex maniac, but two nights in a row, especially when we live in different towns, is not asking for all that much.* He got annoyed and didn't want to talk about it. During the ride to the airport, we were silent, and all I kept wondering was why the radio plays so many sappy love songs. He gave me a stiff hug good-bye, and it might have been my imagination but the light seemed gone from his eyes. When I boarded the plane, I felt very unsettled.

BACK TO
Mr. Teeth and Miss 39

I decided to micromanage this setup. I really want them to hit it off, so I decided to escort them on their date. I figured this way, I could direct the conversation, make sure neither one of them insulted the other, and eliminate the misinterpretations or awkward silences that were common occurrences on many first dates. I told them that I was going to do this date a little bit differently, a little more low-key, and we were going to go out, the three of us, and just hang out, no pressure. They thought it was a little odd that I was playing escort, and they both asked why. I fibbed and told them it was a new thing I was doing once in a while for all of my clients.

I took them to a fondue place where we could all be a little silly and loosen up a bit. The date started out pretty well. They were getting to know each other, asking each other a lot of questions, and whenever there was a lull, I would pick up the slack.

When Mr. Teeth went to the bathroom, I asked Miss 39 what she thought. She hesitated a moment and said that he was okay—this was a high compliment coming from Miss 39. I patted her hand and told her that was good, that I was glad she was trying to give him a chance. Then after he came back from the bathroom, things went downhill rapidly because I sensed Mr. Teeth trying to flirt with me. I wasn't sure if Miss 39 noticed. She was probably too much of a novice dater to notice, but I was growing alarmed. When Miss 39 got up to go to the bathroom, I turned on him. "Mr. Teeth, what the hell do you think you are doing? I am on this date trying to help you and Miss 39 get over that first-date dating hump, and don't think I didn't notice that you were trying to flirt with me. What are you thinking?" He got a little skittish and told me that he couldn't help it, he would love to date me. "Well, snap out of it, Mr. Teeth. You can't have me. I am not interested and Miss 39 is a great girl and she is interested, so don't blow it!"

He looked shocked and asked, "Do you really think she *is* interested in me?" And I quickly nodded and gave him the thumbs-up as she approached the table.

I can't say what it was, but something immediately changed. Suddenly Miss 39 and Mr. Teeth were expert daters and no longer noticed I was there. I wound up eating one too many freshly dipped chocolate-covered bananas out of boredom. Maybe Mr. Teeth just needed to know that someone was in fact interested in him, and Miss 39 just needed to feel that this someone was interested back. I realized that both of them fundamentally lacked confidence that a person of the opposite sex would be attracted to them. Once I let it be known that they were interested in each other, all the awkwardness went away. I have a funny feeling about this couple. . . .

Tuesday, April 18

I had dinner tonight with a guy friend of mine. I spent the whole dinner obsessing over LA Guy. *I am such a girl.* I went over every detail with him. I tried to rationalize and convince us both that LA Guy doesn't have a sex issue. My friend was a sweetheart—he listened for over an hour. He teased me about being the dating expert when it comes to all my clients and a novice when it comes to my own life. I told him that I epitomize that old adage: Those who can, do, and those who can't, teach. He said that was ridiculous. Of course I *could,* I just needed to practice what I preached. He said to me that I know the truth, I just needed to listen to it. *Yes, the truth is that LA Guy is screwed up, but the other truth is that so am I, a little, and I still like him. . . .*

BACK TO
The Hundred Thousand Dollar Man

I better get crackin' finding this Desperado a wife and pronto if I want that apartment on Park Avenue. I was glad we decided to run the search ad because, as I spent more time thinking about him, I realized that the ad might make it easier for me: his exceptionally high IQ, his Poindexter looks, and his travel schedule made him a little more challenging than some of the Desperados.

I decided I would write something like a personal ad. In it I would talk about my company. I figured that would provide some legitimacy. From there, I would describe The Hundred Thousand Dollar Man physically, add some interesting and alluring facts about him *(something other than the 100K bonus)*. Then I would describe the type of woman he was looking for and ask respondents to send in a photo and a letter. I'd highlight his pros and minimize his cons, as any *agent* would do. I'll call him a Renaissance man, point out his love of the opera, his propensity for luxurious exotic travel. I'd mention his home in Paris and his ability to speak three languages. I'd tell them that he's decadent and loves to spoil. And I'd ask for women who are *beautiful inside and out* and who love a little mental sparring with a quick-witted, spontaneous man. I convinced The Hundred Thousand Dollar Man to pay for the ad even though it cost $2,000. I promised that the ad would give us more women to choose from, and I told him he could look at the responses and the photos after I sifted through them. He agreed.

Miss Fantasy and Brad Pitt Guy

Guess what? Miracles of all miracles, they are dating. He prefers cold-weather vacations to warm-weather ones, and he's only five feet eight, but Miss Fantasy actually gave him a chance and now he's golfing with her dad, talking about skiing with her brother, and, from what I hear, having raging sex with her. *You go, Brad Pitt Guy!* And he says Miss Fantasy would actually cut it with Brad Pitt himself. *Wow!* I am so excited, superexcited!

The Hundred Thousand Dollar Man

Boy, have I gotten a lot of responses to the ad for The Hundred Thousand Dollar Man. I was convinced that I would get a better caliber of response than he, or any guy, would get on his own if he just ran a personal ad in a magazine, and I was right. I knew that the mere fact that my company was endorsing this guy would make a lot of quality women comfortable enough to respond, but I had no idea just how many would put it out there. I got hundreds of letters. I got responses from models and actresses and Harvard grads and triathletes, linguists, executives, artists—so many that I thought my head would explode. Some letters were funny, some were sincere, some were ridiculous, some were from women who were exactly what I asked for, and others were nothing like what I asked for but they clearly wanted me to keep them in mind for other men. Some letters had all the information I needed and some were incomplete. I found myself with two dilemmas: Number one, how do I decide who to introduce my guy to? There were so many great women. Number two, was it okay to poach from this group of women for my other clients? Many of the applicants wouldn't be good for The Hundred Thousand Dollar Man but would be great for some of the other Desperados. *Was that okay?* I figured that as long as I wasn't taking one of the women that The Hundred Thousand Dollar Man would want, then it was fine. After all, it was a shame to let all these terrific women to waste.

I started calling some of the most interesting ladies to see if they were appropriate for my client. My plan was to talk to a few of the good ones on the phone and do some screening. Then I was going to sit down with him and present the ladies I thought were best suited for him. Once we agreed on all *my* ladies, I was going to meet with them in person and verify that they were who I thought they were, and then I would arrange the dates.

I started making the calls. The third woman I called gave me a bit of a surprise. She told me that even though she had answered the ad, she no longer wanted to meet my guy. She said that she thought he was shady and unethical. I frowned. I asked her how she could say that, she didn't even know who he was. She said with conviction that all she knew was that he was two-timing me. She had seen an ad about him in one of the other local New York magazines from one of the other Matchmakers and, while she didn't know how I ran my business, she thought it was suspect. I agreed completely. I hadn't even seen the other ad and I was shocked. I felt my neck tensing up. *I couldn't believe that Hundred Thousand Dollar Man would hire me and one of the Maries at the same time, and let us both run ads in magazines at the same time.* I told her that something wasn't adding up. The guy was a really good guy and I really wanted her to meet him. I asked her if she had been in touch with the other Matchmaker. She said she had not, she had only contacted me. I liked that this girl was so ethical, and somehow I felt like she was going to be *his girl*. I told her I would get to the bottom of this and be back in touch.

I didn't know how to broach this subject with The Hundred Thousand Dollar Man. Obviously I had screwed up. I need to ask the Desperados if they are working with any other Matchmakers, and I need to have an exclusivity clause in my contract. I immediately found myself wondering what sort of deal the Marie had with him. *Did she get a bonus if she got him married? Was it higher than mine? Was it in a contract? Did she ask for it or did he offer?* I felt myself getting very competitive. I started tapping my purple pen against the desk haphazardly. I dialed his number slowly and when he answered the phone, instead of letting him know that I was upset, I told him I personally didn't care, but some of the ladies were getting turned off by the fact that he was working with two Matchmakers at the same time. He started apologizing profusely. He felt bad, I could hear it in his voice. He said, "I just really want to meet someone so I was doubling up." I told him not to sweat it, but then in a serious voice I said that when we sat down to review my ladies, he would have to initial something so there would be no confusion if he ended up with one of them. He seemed relieved and said no problem. We scheduled a meeting for the end of the week.

TABLE CHANGE

Effective immediately, there is a clause in my contract stating that the Desperados are not to work with any other Matchmaker while they are working with me. And it furthers says that, in the event that they do form a relationship with another Matchmaker, they must disclose such relationship and promise to keep all my information and my people proprietary to me, *i.e., no passing along my peeps.*

The Girl I Always Thought Hated Me

I got a panicked phone call from her today. "I had the *relationship talk* with my guy, and I don't think it went very well! Can you help me salvage things?" She was chomping on her gum at a frantic pace. I told her to calm down and tell me what had happened. She took a breath and began, "Well, last night when we were in bed having sex, I told him that I loved him and I asked him if he felt the same way. He immediately lost his erection and rolled away from me." *Uh-oh!* "What did he say?" I asked. "He yelled, 'Why would you possibly bring that up in the middle of sex? You just killed it for me. Now I am totally turned off.' I started to cry and then we got into the conversation. He was fuming and didn't say much." What did I think, did she really screw up?

Oh gosh, The Girl, still a dating disaster. Of all the stupid times to bring up the relationship talk, during intercourse was probably the worst. "Had you ever said *I love you* to each other before?" She said no, this was the first time. *Oh gosh again, The Girl saying I love you to the guy for the first time when the guy had yet to say it, and in the middle of intercourse. And crying in bed after the guy loses his erection—again the worst possible scenario.* "Did I really screw it up?" she repeated. I told her honestly, "Well, things aren't great at the moment." But I could tell that she needed to be reassured that she could still salvage things, so in my no-nonsense voice, I said, "Here's what you need to do. You need to call him back and make light of what happened last night—very light. You need to keep it really brief. Guys hate it when women give them long-winded speeches. Just tell him that you don't know what got into you last night—you are premenstrual and it must have been the hormones. Tell him you are sorry that you tried to have a relationship talk during sex. It was poor timing and you are an idiot. I actually want you to call yourself an idiot. And after you say this, I want you to immediately change the subject and start talking about a funny thing that happened at work today. Okay?" She thought about this for a moment, then said she would try. I told her emphatically that she had to promise me that she would only say what I told her to say and then change the topic.

She interrupted, "But I still don't even know where I stand with my guy. I still need to have the relationship talk." *This girl has a one-track mind!* "First we need to get you out of the doghouse, then you can have your talk! Can you call him now?" I asked. She said okay. I told her that I was going to call her in fifteen minutes so she would have an excuse to get off the phone. I said my next words with great emphasis: "And after you say what we practiced, you need to get off the phone, no matter what!" I wanted to make sure she didn't prolong an awkward conversation. I wanted her guy to believe that her behavior was just an anomaly, that she wasn't turning all girly and difficult. I asked her if she was ready. She took a deep breath said she was. I told her I would be talking to her in fifteen.

BACK TO

Mr. Metrosexual

I have sort of been avoiding him. I haven't had any good women for him for a while so I have been lying low. But today I started to feel guilty, so I shot him an e-mail to see what was going on with him. And to my surprise and excitement, he e-mailed back to say that he was dating the very first woman I set him up with. "We ran into each other at a party, and she was dressed to the nines. She had just been to the beauty salon, had her hair done, her makeup done, her nails done, and she was dripping in fancy jewelry and wearing Manolo Blahnik shoes. I was very turned on." It turned out that, on their first date, she had tried to downplay her love of labels because it was usually a turnoff to men, but Mr. Metrosexual thought it was terrific and she's unleashed it in full force ever since. He has been meaning to e-mail me to thank me—I did a great job picking this one for him, and he thinks she's "the One." *Mr. Metrosexual, I couldn't be happier for you!*

BACK TO

The Girl I Always Thought Hated Me

I called her back in fifteen minutes. She answered the phone, sobbing and hiccuping. *Oh God, oh God, she didn't listen to my advice. They never listen to my advice. Why do they ask for my advice if they don't want to listen?* I told her it was time to get off the phone, do it now. "But we are *in* the relationship talk," she said through tears. I reprimanded, "I told you not to go there. Why did you?" She wailed, "I didn't, he did. He said he thought we should see other people. I don't know what to say." She was hiccuping again. I ordered her to get back on the phone and say, "'Okay, fine. Let's try seeing other people and see what happens. I can be fine with that. I don't even know why I am crying. Let's speak in a few days and make some plans.' *And then hang up!*" I raised my voice a little for emphasis. "I promise this will throw him for a loop and he will be back. Do this exactly and then call me back." She swallowed hard and said she would try. And I hung up. I hoped she could do it, *but I knew better. . . .*

The Girl I Always Thought Hated Me didn't call back. I wasn't sure what to make of that. I tried her number, no answer. Suicide floated into my head for one second, but I pushed it away. *That would be crazy, ridiculous, right?* I started to get nervous and pace back and forth in my apartment. I didn't know her that well—anything was possible. I didn't know what to do. I left her several messages on her home machine, on her cell, and I sent two e-mails. I told her I was worried and that she needed to call me back. No response. I left two more messages. I told her that if she didn't call me back I was going to call the police or come to her apartment. No response. *I wish I knew her friggin' guy's name. I wish he had been one of my setups, then I would know how to reach him.* I started really worrying. I was so uptight. I had already picked all the chips out of the old container of mint chocolate chip ice cream that I had in my freezer. I called my brother Sean, the calm, rational one in my family, to ask what I should do. He said not to panic. By midnight I was panicking though. *Maybe I take my job too seriously?* I tried going to sleep but couldn't. Maybe it was all the sugar from the chips I ate. My mind was racing. *What if she really did freak out? What if she was lying on her floor from a drug overdose and I don't do anything? I will feel guilty for the rest of my life.* Oh God, *Oh God.* I called my brother again. "I am going over there. I have to, I can't sleep. What if something awful has happened?" My brother chuckled. "Call me after you find out that she's fine."

I went to her building in a panic. The doorman buzzed up, no answer. "Have you seen her?" I asked. No. Has anyone gone up to visit her? No, not on his shift. He kept calling up, no answer. Finally, I convinced him to walk me upstairs with her key. I was frantic, and even the doorman got nervous. We unlocked her door and tumbled in just as The Girl, in a towel with her hair all a mess, walked out of the bedroom. She was startled. "What are you doing here?" she demanded. "Oh my God, I have left you fifteen messages," I said, breathless. "I got panicked, and I thought you did something crazy. Where have you been?" Just then, her guy walked out of the bedroom. *I guess I now know who he is, what she has been up to, and how the conversation went.* She apologized. I felt like an idiot. I think I need to take another vacation—this job is getting to me. . . .

May

May is an unpredictable month for my business. I never know how busy I'm going to be. The weather is beautiful, there are lots of parties, and people are looking forward to the summer, hence many decide that they don't need my help. But May is also a very popular wedding, graduation, and homecoming month. People see friends from the past who have gotten married, and this inspires them to want to get married, so there are always those who decide they need a little extracurricular help. Overall, the month shakes out fine for me.

BACK TO
The Hundred Thousand Dollar Man

We sat down today to go over my choices of ladies for him. He showed up in his usual uniform: a blue blazer, a pastel-colored oxford shirt, a bow tie and matching pocket square. First order of business, I got him to initial the letters of all the girls I presented to him in case he had the same arrangement with any of the Maries. *I was dying to ask about his Marie arrangement, but I didn't.* We agreed on three women for him to start with: first, my *oh-so-moral* girl, the one who pointed out that he was a two-timer. He was iffy on her, but after some cajoling, he agreed. *I hope she agrees, too.* Second, a woman who used to model, has a law degree from an Ivy League school, has one child and big, big boobs. *Surprise, surprise, she was his favorite.* And third, a blond woman who was more of a granola type but who, like him, also has a Ph.D. He was very pleased. It seemed like this Desperado might prove to be one of the easier ones for me. After all, I do have a file full of fifty-two other very interesting women for him if one of these three didn't pan out.

Wednesday, May 3

Just got home from another party. Sometimes I get so upset about how little respect women have for themselves. I don't know if last night was a full moon or what, but I ran into two women who were both in awful relationships with wealthy men who treated them like crap, and for some reason last night they were all giving the guys yet another chance. I walked past the couples and in each case heard the guy asking for another chance, promising things were going to be different. The woman was saying that she didn't buy it, but her body language was saying that she did. These women are so naïve—they think things are going to change, that somehow this guy who has treated girl after girl poorly is going to act differently toward them. It's *just* not happening.

These women don't handle their men properly. They are well aware of the guy's reputation as a womanizer, and they have witnessed all the women before them who let this guy do whatever he wanted—lie, two-time, manipulate—and never said no to him. And even though they are fully aware that it was a big mistake for the other women to let him get away with murder, they do the same exact thing and don't put their foot down and don't command respect. One of these women is a really good friend of mine, and we talk about the situation again and again and again. She always says she's moving on, and then she just goes back to him, insisting that this time it will be different. But it's never different. And she keeps telling herself that he is so interested in her because he buys her decadent gifts and takes her on extravagant vacations. She won't let herself see that he is so wealthy that spending money on things like this means nothing. What would mean something was if he treated her with respect and like a real girlfriend instead of like a mistress of sorts. I feel sorry for her. She needs love, not money. She needs to take charge of the situation and tell him how she will and won't be treated, and if he can't adhere to that, then she needs to move on.

BACK TO

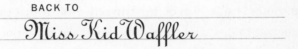

Miss Kid Waffler

I am at my wits' end with this Desperado. I have now introduced her to four men and, in some way or another, she has scared off each one. They all call me to complain, but she never says a word. It's as if she is rationalizing to herself that as long as she's going on dates with appropriate men, then she's making an effort, and it doesn't matter if the dates don't work out. This might be enough for her, but it is not enough for me. I want her to really meet someone and get into a good relationship. If I can't help her meet someone, then I want to give her her money back and part ways.

I have needed to have it out with her for a while, so I called her. She was excited to hear from me and immediately gushed on and on about how I was doing such a great job and how all the men I have introduced her to have been exactly what she was looking for—it was just a shame that they didn't like her. This caught me off guard. I knitted my brow in confusion and said, "But, Miss Kid Waffler, they *did* like you. They all liked you a lot at first, but then you sabotaged things every time by waffling about having kids. I don't get it. Why do you do this? Don't you want to meet someone and be in a relationship?" To my further surprise, she started to cry. "I don't know why I always do that. I want to be in a relationship so badly but then when I meet a guy who I could like, somehow I always screw up. I just get nervous about being in a relationship and thinking about whether it will work and whether I will ever be able to actually get married." She stopped to take a breath and blow her nose. "I just think too much, I guess, and it scares me. I always say the wrong things and do the wrong things. Sometimes I can't even control myself. I know that I shouldn't say and do certain things, and then somehow I am saying or doing them before I even realize." She sniffled again. "Do you understand what I am saying?" I felt bad for her. "Of course, it's the old mouth/brain disconnect. Your brain is thinking one thing and your mouth does a completely other thing. It happens to the best of us." She perked up a bit when she realized I could relate to what she was saying. "Exactly, and for me, I think I know subconsciously that the kid thing will scare the guy off and somehow if he is scared off then I won't have the opportunity to ruin things, and sometimes I think that's better. I am so bad at this!" Her voice started shaking again. I ran my fingers through my hair. "Maybe you just need to relax a little bit. Maybe you are just putting so much pressure on yourself to do everything right that you do everything wrong. Just try being yourself and see what you think of the guy in front of you." I said with more conviction, "It's just one date. Don't think so far into the future. Take it one date at a time. Can you try that?" She said she could and thanked me.

Monday, May 8

When I hung up the phone with Miss Kid Waffler, I considered whether I'd been guilty of the same missteps. Do I sabotage situations? Do I think too far into the future? Somehow I think I do. Even with LA Guy, we had one weekend together and already I was thinking about living in Los Angeles, being married, and having his babies. I shouldn't do that. *Why do I do that?* I also tend to go out with guys who would be good for me but somehow I fixate on the one bad thing about them and fixate and fixate and give them a hard time about it until I ruin things. And then after the fact, I look back and say to myself that maybe that one bad thing wasn't so bad. I need to work on not sabotaging, just like Miss Kid Waffler. *I hope both of us will be able to get over this hump.*

NOT FOR ME GUY
Tattoo Man

Even though I am a little obsessed with LA Guy, I am still dating in New York. I have to. Tonight's date was a setup through a friend of mine. The guy was hot. I haven't been on a date with a truly hot guy in a while. I don't care as much about looks anymore; I have become a typical woman in her thirties who cares more about chemistry and personality than looks. I dated my fair share of amazing-looking guys in my twenties, and the truth is, it didn't get me anywhere. So now I think I would rather be the better-looking one in the couple.

I remember when I broke up with my last great-looking guy. I asked my best friend to set me up on a blind date so I could *get back out there*. Her response was that she didn't know any guys who would be handsome enough for me. I asked her what that meant, and she said that it seemed like I only dated hot guys and she didn't think she knew anyone for me. I thought about that, and how insecure and off-kilter I always felt when dating the hot guys everyone wanted. Right then and there I decided that hotness was no longer a "must-have" for me. And I meant it; let the guy feel off-kilter for a change! The next guy I dated and every one thereafter was just okay-looking, but there was always chemistry.

Well, tonight's guy sent me back to my twenties. From the second I sat down, I wanted to kiss him. He had a mischievous smile, really white teeth, and cute dimples. *I am a sucker for dimples.* I was psyched; it seemed like it was going to be a good date. But then the date took a nosedive when I dropped my napkin, reached down to pick it up, and noticed a tattoo on his ankle. *Call me crazy, call me Miss Fantasy, but My Guy does not have a tattoo, not even a small one on his ankle. He wouldn't even be able to be buried in a Jewish cemetery!* I asked him about it. I thought that maybe he got it one drunken night in college and would be willing to get it removed, like Charlie Sheen did when he married Denise Richards. No such luck. He didn't get it one drunken night and it wasn't his only one. "I have two others as well, one on my hip and the other on my arm." "Oh cool," I responded with a fake smile. *Call me crazy, but My Guy doesn't have three tattoos, he just doesn't.* If I was just looking for a hookup evening, I would have been into this guy, but I could have that from my boy toy. I was on this date looking for My Guy. Oh well, game over.

BACK TO
LA Guy

I haven't seen him in about three weeks. I am not sure what to think. He calls me every day, e-mails me, flirts with me, sends me flowers, and acts like he's crazy about me. He keeps encouraging me to go through with it and open my L.A. office, insisting that I need an L.A. presence. *What is that all about?* Things are amazing when I am in New York and he is in Los Angeles, but when we are in the same town, things get weird. He invited me out to Los Angeles again, but this time I decided that I should play it differently. I told him that he needed to come to New York and see me. He is coming this weekend.

DESPERADO #29
Miss Interrupter

I knew this woman from around the city. A lot of people don't like her because she can be very annoying. If someone is telling a story, she inevitably interrupts and starts telling her own story or chimes in with her two cents right in the middle.

Now she was sitting at my Table wanting to hire me. I needed to be honest with her about this bad habit if I expected to work with her.

We started the consultation and, as if on cue, she interrupted and interrupted and interrupted. Finally, I said in a rush, "Miss Interrupter, we need to get something straight right now. You have a problem. You interrupt people. You don't let them finish what they are saying, you just interrupt and start talking. You have been doing it to me for the past hour." She gave me a perplexed look. "What did you just say? I have a problem? What does that mean, I have a problem? What are you talking about?" I couldn't believe it. She didn't even know that she did this, let alone that she was notorious for it. *How can someone get to their thirties and be completely oblivious to their most obvious faults?*

I guess it needed to be spelled out for her. I took a breath. "Look, maybe you don't realize this, but when people are talking, you interrupt them. Sometimes you talk over them. You—" She started to interrupt. I interrupted back, "There, see? You were just about to do it again. What I am saying is important. I don't want to be interrupted. I am trying to help you. Do you want me to help you?" Meekly, she said yes. "Okay then, you have to work really, really hard to not interrupt people. You have to focus on it and make sure you don't do it. You probably have been doing it for so long that you don't even realize that you do it." She started to speak again but I held up my hand to silence her. "I am not finished. When you interrupt people, you seem very self-absorbed. You imply that what you have to say is more important than what is being said by the other person, or that you don't find what they are saying to be interesting. I will work with you, but only if you give me your *uninterrupted* word that you will work on this problem of yours and take it seriously." She let me finish and she agreed.

Wednesday, May 10

I can't stop obsessing over LA Guy. *I am so dysfunctional.* I know he is wrong for me. I know it should be easier, I know it should just be right. I always find myself interested in the men I shouldn't be interested in, the ones who need major work. I always want to fix them, help them become the men I know they can be. I am a fool.

BACK TO

LA Guy

He came to New York this weekend. The same exact thing that happened in Los Angeles happened in New York. We had amazing sex the first night and then he didn't want to come anywhere near me on night two or night three. I didn't even bother saying anything this time. I realized that this was just the way it would be with him. And the fact that he wouldn't even talk about it just told me that he had a real intimacy problem and I either needed to accept the fact that he was like this or move on. I decided to move on. I like sex. I want to have the option of having it more than once a week. *Is that too much to ask for?* I was disappointed. He was the first real Maybe for Me Guy in a long time, and he made me forget about Jerkoff, at least temporarily. When I dated Soul Mate Guy, a part of me liked him, but a bigger part of me was only hung up on him because he ended it before I could. The Conflict of Interest Guy was part of my fantasy, a fantasy that my Prince Charming was going to walk through my Matchmaking doors and sweep me off my feet. *I should know better than to believe in fantasies.* But LA Guy—I liked him. I thought we could have something. I'm sad.

BACK TO
Mr. Teeth and Miss 39

They are actually dating. I give each of them weekly pep talks, especially Miss 39. Every time she tries to find fault with something about Mr. Teeth, I remind her of all his great qualities, and I remind her that she is 39 and cries herself to sleep. I am her conscience, her Jiminy Cricket. My cheerleading seems to be working: they have been out more than ten times. I really hope they stay together.

TABLE CHANGE

Effective immediately, I have hired an assistant to open an L.A. office for me. The assistant's name is Lindsay. She's a hip young publicist who just left her other job. She knows everyone who's anyone in L.A., and she said she would spend the next several months getting my name out there and paving the road. I realized that even if I'm not with LA Guy, I still should have a business presence in Los Angeles. The market is ripe, and people really seem to take to my concept. So I hired Lindsay, hooked up a business line, and decided that, at the end of the summer, I will become officially bicoastal and spend half my time in Los Angeles setting up the peeps. *Sounds like a plan.*

BACK TO

The Troll

Time to set him up with his first date. I pulled out the VHW (Very Hot Women) file again.

There's Melissa, 34, in PR. No, she probably knows him. What about Yvette, the advertising woman? She could be good for him, but she might know him, too. What about Beth, 37, divorce lawyer from New Haven? She would like a rich guy, but maybe they have a mutual friend. . . .

I started worrying that The Troll would already know all the women I know. *What do I do if they already know him? He is so paranoid about the people-knowing-him thing. How should I handle this?* I decided to cross that bridge when I came to it. I just needed to try to find a date for him. I went back to the list and decided to start with Beth. I e-mailed her and asked if she was dating anyone. She e-mailed back that she was engaged. *You go, Beth.* I crossed her off my list. Then I e-mailed Yvette. She was game. I told her about The Troll. No sign of recognition, good. I scheduled them for next Tuesday.

Jerkoff Again

It didn't surprise me when I heard from Jerkoff out of the blue the day after LA Guy left. Somehow Jerkoff and I have mutual radar. I knew that he would be able to sense that I had moved on from LA Guy and would call me. Sure enough, he did. He made small talk for a while, acted like we had spoken yesterday, not two months ago. He told me that he was still in therapy. Then he said a little nervously, "And my therapist wants to meet you. She told me to invite you to my session. So will you come with me?" Then his voice dropped almost to a whisper, "It would really mean something to me." I twirled my hair haphazardly. *Oh my god. Jerkoff is asking me to go to his therapist with him. That's big. Should I go? I don't know if I should. I am over him. I was just in a brief relationship with someone else. I am over him. No, I'm not. I am lying. But the question is, Should I go to his therapist with him? Yes. He asked, and it was probably hard for him to ask. I will go. I have already spent three years of my life on him. If he might be getting better, don't I owe it to myself and to him to see? Don't I?* I took a deep breath and said okay.

Mr. Bigger Better Deal

I set him up with Brooke, a 32-year-old teacher, fun and outgoing and very bubbly. She called me the next day, all excited. She had a great time with Mr. Bigger Better Deal. They went from drinks to dinner to more drinks to her apartment to walk her dog and watch *Letterman,* and they even kissed a little. All together, they were out for seven hours. *Sounds like a great date to me!* So I called Mr. Bigger Better Deal, expecting him to thank me profusely. He did not. "I wasn't into her *that* way," he said immediately. I was annoyed. "What *way* is that, Mr. Bigger Better Deal? You were out with her for seven hours. I don't get it. How can you say you aren't into her? You found seven hours' worth of things to be into her about last night." He was indignant. "She's a cool girl. She's fun, and I was having fun last night, so I stayed out with her. But I'm not into her. I don't want to date her. I was just having fun." I began to argue with him. "Look, I am not going to tell you that you can't have fun, but don't you think that maybe you led this girl on a *little bit* by staying out with her for so long and making out with her? It's not right." He stood his ground. "I didn't mean anything by it. I was just having fun. I didn't promise her anything." *Clearly he wasn't getting it.* Then I asked him why he wasn't into her. I pointed out that if he could have fun with someone for seven hours, maybe there was potential there that he was overlooking. He insisted, "Samantha, I have no trouble having seven hours' worth of fun with lots of people. Brooke was nice, but there is definitely someone better out there for me. I know it. So let's move on." *Surprise, surprise from Mr. Bigger Better Deal!* We moved on. *I wish I could find just one person that I could have seven hours' worth of fun with. I'm not greedy!*

BACK TO

Miss Kid Waffler

Got a call from her today. She had her third date with my latest guy. I picked a guy who wasn't sure whether he wanted to have kids. I figured this way Miss Kid Waffler wouldn't get freaked out. She was all excited. "Samantha, I like him a lot and I think I can try it with this guy because he is on the fence about the kid thing, too." I smiled. "We decided that if it works between us, we will figure it out together later on. I feel much calmer, Samantha. Thanks." *You're welcome.*

Mr. One Night Stand

I went to a wedding this weekend in Boston. One of my girlfriends from college was getting married. I went hoping to get my mind off Jerkoff and LA Guy. Even though I knew that I was better off moving on from LA Guy, I still wanted him and missed his daily phone calls, his charming e-mails, and the constancy of him. I went *sans* date since there wasn't anyone I really wanted to bring and, like any typical girl, I thought that I might find Him at the wedding. Or, at the very least, maybe I would catch the bouquet. . . .

I got to the wedding on Saturday night. I wore a very sexy pale purple halter dress that hugged me in all the right places and very tall rhinestoned Sergio Rossi heels. The bride whistled as I approached and said she knew the perfect guy for me. She introduced me to the one single guy, a childhood friend who happened to live locally. Luckily he was handsome and a very good dancer because he turned out to be my only real option for the evening. To me, nothing is more flirtatious or a better prelude to a sexy evening than some dirty dancing. We dirty-danced all evening. I drank a lot, I don't think I even realized how much, and he drank a lot, too. I wasn't really paying attention.

When the wedding ended, he suggested that we go to a local bar, and I was enthusiastic. He told me he had just gotten a brand-new sports car earlier that day, a midnight blue Aston Martin coupe, and he wanted to show me what it could do. We got into the car, he revved the engine, and we took off toward the highway. The next thing I knew he skidded on some oil on the exit ramp. The car did a 360, slid sideways, and crashed into a barricade. When the car stopped moving, I started to shake uncontrollably. *I couldn't believe how irresponsible I had been. It was so unlike me to let someone drive drunk and not even ask him if he was okay to drive, not even be concerned. I was so angry with myself. We were almost killed, and his poor car.* The crash happened so fast I didn't even realize what had occurred. I looked at him, he looked at me. Neither of us said a word. The car wasn't even eight hours old. Then, after about two minutes of complete silence, he started to cry. *How uncomfortable for him to be bawling in front of a near stranger.*

At that point, I wanted to say it's been fun and now I need to go back to the hotel. *But how could I just leave him?* Finally he composed himself. He took charge, got out of the car, pulled me out his side of the car since my door was bent shut. Then he called Triple A on his cell phone. They said they couldn't tow the car until morning, so he called a taxi to take us to his house. I was looking for the opportunity to escape, but I just didn't find it. I felt so sorry for him. When he told me that he was so glad someone was with him, I knew I was stuck going home with him. So I gathered my belongings and hopped in the cab. By the time we got to his house, I was completely sober. My makeup was streaked all over my face, my hair was hanging limp, and I had the beginning of a pounding headache. During the wedding I figured we would wind up fooling around at the end of the evening. After all, we were making out and dirty-dancing all night. But at 2 A.M., after nearly being killed, seeing a grown man cry, and winding up stone sober at a near stranger's home, the last thing I wanted to do was hook up with the guy. But again, I felt so bad for him. Let's just say I offered a sympathy fool-around, and *let's just say I wasn't satisfied at the end of the evening.*

Monday, May 22

I went to another charity party tonight, this one at the Central Park Zoo. I have finally figured out the perfect metaphor for socializing in a big city—it's like a moving sidewalk. Everybody is on one of those conveyor belts, the ones they have in large airports. People keep coming up to each other, taking about thirty seconds to talk, and then moving on by. This is why it's so difficult to meet people at these parties. Each person gets about thirty seconds of airtime to interest someone else enough to get them into a full-blown conversation. After thirty seconds, people get distracted, start looking around the room, and prepare to move on. You need to be pretty damn witty to grab someone's attention and keep it at a party. This is why I think the Matchmaking business is here to stay. When people use my service, the revolving sidewalk stops. They don't have to worry about being funny or witty or at the top of their game at any of the social events. I do all the work for them. All they have to do is tell me who and what they want, and I go to these parties for them and find them the dates. *Not to toot my own horn but, I'm telling you, if you can afford me, I'm a total deal.*

BACK TO

The Hundred Thousand Dollar Man

He called me first thing today. He has been out with each of the women that I picked for him, three times each. *He's been busy.* He likes them all so much that he isn't going to meet any of the women that the other Marie found for him—he has his hands full with my ladies. *Oh, Marie, I feel for you!*

The Troll

I set him up with Yvette. He e-mailed me first thing in the morning to say that he liked her a lot. She called me first thing and launched in, "Samantha, why didn't you tell me that his nickname is The Troll?" I was cautious. "Um, why?" She started laughing. "Well, when you asked me about him, I didn't know who you were referring to because I never knew his real name. Everyone in Manhattan knows him as The Troll. I can't date The Troll, how humiliating." I took a deep breath. "But, why?" I asked. "What is the big deal? Did you like him?" "Yes, he's a nice guy, but would you date him? He's like five feet two!" she exclaimed. I defended him. "He is not five two, he is about five six, maybe even five seven, and you aren't even that tall. If he is your Prince Charming, his height shouldn't matter." She was indignant. "My Prince Charming's name is Charming, not Troll. I'm sorry but I don't want to go out with him again."

Oh my. She said what Miss Gold Digger said. They don't want to date a man called The Troll. I guess you can't blame them, but he is so decent and such a good catch. *Didn't they see* Shrek? I shook my head in despair. *How am I going to get this guy coupled off?* There has got to be some girl in Manhattan who doesn't know his nickname. I pulled out the database again.

Hmm, Suzanne? No, she probably knows him. Maryanne? She loves money but she is very image-conscious. Wait, what about Victoria? She just moved to New York from Louisiana and probably doesn't know him, and I have an asterisk next to her name to indicate that she likes shorter guys. Bingo!

I called Victoria. She said yes immediately. This time I decided to mention that he had a funny nickname. She laughed and said she thought it was cute. *Go figure.*

Two-Timer Guy

The month ended strangely for me on a personal dating front. I met a new guy. I'll call him Two-Timer Guy. I met him when I went for drinks with my friend Celeste and some of her friends. He was nice-looking in a dark, brooding kind of way; he was about six feet tall, had thick eyebrows, deep brown eyes, and a goatee. He somehow seemed familiar to me. It turned out that we didn't know each other, but we had an instant rapport and became completely absorbed in conversation for about ten minutes. He seemed a little different from a lot of the guys I had been meeting lately, more mature and focused. But then he sat down next to Celeste and started playing with her hair, telling stories that ended with "and I hoped that by doing that, it would make Celeste like me more." That seemed odd, given our instant connection, but if they were dating, I certainly didn't want to get in the middle of it. The rest of the night I socialized with other people. Celeste didn't seem to be chatting with him either, but I didn't get a chance to ask her about him. Later in the evening, Two-Timer Guy offered to set me up with one of his friends, which I thought was a friendly gesture.

Next morning first thing, I got an e-mail from *guess who,* not telling me about his friend but asking me out himself. *Very strange.* I wrote back and asked about Celeste and mentioned his friend who was supposed to be so good for me. He said there was nothing with Celeste and he thought he was much better for me than his friend. A little cocky, but confident. I was interested. We had definite chemistry and as long as there was nothing between him and my friend, I figured, why not? We scheduled plans for Sunday night, five days away. I put in a phone call to Celeste so I could ask her what she thought of my going out with Two-Timer Guy, but I got her voice mail and she and I started playing phone tag.

As the week progressed, Two-Timer Guy came on really strongly. He had a kid, and right away he told me he wanted me to meet her. He asked if I wanted to go with them to the Museum of Modern Art. *Whoa, guy, move a little quickly, don't you?* I was surprised that he would want his daughter to meet every random girl he takes out. *Won't she develop major abandonment issues?* He called me every day that week, trying to move up our date, telling me he couldn't wait to see me, telling me I seemed so perfect for him. On one hand, he was a little freaky, very reminiscent of Soul Mate Guy. His enthusiasm seemed way too much, way too soon. But on the other hand, I felt a connection with him, so I was hopeful. I flirted with him throughout the week but wouldn't reschedule the date. I just told him that good things come to those who wait.

Saturday night rolled around, and Celeste and I got together and went to a party downtown. Afterward, we decided to go to the Regency and have tea. When we sat down and started talking, I said to her, "I have been wanting to ask you all week what you think of Two-

Timer Guy." "Why?" she asked, looking wary. I told her about our date scheduled for the next night. Next thing I knew she was shrieking, "Samantha, I'm dating him!" "What?" I shrieked back. "What do you mean? I asked him if there was anything going on between you guys and he said nothing." I slammed my hand on the table. "What a scumbag."

She went on to tell me that she had been out with him on Thursday night until three in the morning, making out with him. I admitted that he had asked me out for Thursday night and I had said no. She told me that he even asked her to meet his daughter and go with them to—I joined in as she said it—"the Museum of Modern Art." She looked at me, wide-eyed. "He asked you to do that, too?" "Uh-huh." Neither of us could believe the nerve of this guy. Then she groaned and said, "We need to do something to teach that guy a lesson." A smile spread across my face and I said I had an idea.

I pulled my BlackBerry (my wireless e-mail server) from my purse. We had been flirting via our BlackBerries all week, so I knew he would get the e-mail and answer right away. "What are you doing?" I typed in flirtatiously. He e-mailed me back immediately to say that he was supposed to have his daughter but she got sick so her mom had her for the evening. *Perfect,* I thought. "What are *you* doing?" he asked me. I laughed, raised an eyebrow, and quickly typed "thinking of you," and pushed SEND. He immediately e-mailed back asking if I wanted to have a nightcap. I let out a hearty laugh and e-mailed back, "Meet me at the Regency in 20 minutes." Then I looked over at Celeste, gave her the thumbs-up, and told her that we were about to teach our two-timing friend a little lesson.

Now mind you, it was 1 A.M., and Two-Timer Guy was coming

to the Regency for one reason and one reason only: a booty call, no doubt about that. What guy would come out of his apartment at 1 A.M. for any other reason? My friend and I sat in the corner of the bar area and waited. She sat in a big armchair, with her back to the door, so he wouldn't be able to see her when he walked in; I sat facing front on a couch so he would see me immediately. We were excited and nervous: excited to be teaching this scumbag a lesson, a lesson for all the two-timing, double-crossing jerks out there, but nervous because behaving like this was a little out of character for us both.

Finally he walked in the door. I got up to give him a kiss, and as he kissed me hello, he caught sight of my friend. *Surprise!* I invited him to sit down on a couch between us. He started blinking rapidly and running his fingers through his hair as he said, "What a surprise to see you both here." My friend said under her breath, "I bet." We made small talk for about fifteen minutes. He was getting visibly more uncomfortable as minutes ticked by. Finally my friend stood up and announced that she couldn't sit there anymore, that she needed to leave but she just wanted him to know that she thought he was a complete slimeball and she never wanted to hear from him again. He got indignant and said that he resented her calling him that.

Then she rolled her eyes, made a disgusted face, and said, "You are a slimeball for asking Samantha out when you were making out with me until two A.M. two nights ago!" He looked at her with a cocky grin on his face. "What's the matter with that? It's not like I was exclusive with you or anything." *Hello, what planet does this guy live on? He met me through her!* She asked him straight out why he did it. He looked over at me and then back to her and said, "Celeste, you are really fun to hang out with and a great kisser, but I started thinking"—he looked in my direction—"that I could have something real with Samantha, so I started pursuing her." I raised my eyebrows in surprise and cast my eyes downward because I was a little embarrassed for Celeste. She started tapping her foot on the ground. She seemed pretty offended, and I didn't blame her. And then I looked over at him with a plastic smile on my face and said, "You are a fool. I was actually interested in you. I actually thought that maybe we could have something, but you blew it big-time." I shook my head slowly. "Please don't ever call me again. I'm finished." And with that, she and I breezed out, leaving him holding his you-know-what. So much for his booty call.

When I got home I felt sad. *How could I have been so duped? How could I have liked such a bad guy?* I fished through my desk drawer and found a picture of Jerkoff and stared at it for a while. *Maybe he's not so bad.* By the time I went to sleep that night, I had received a two-page e-mail from Two-Timer Guy, begging my forgiveness. I responded with "I am not interested." The next day, he sent me gorgeous, I mean gorgeous, flowers from the most expensive florist in New York.

I almost relented. No I didn't. I said thank you, but no thank you. He left five messages on my voice mail, the fifth saying, "So I guess we are not still on for dinner tonight?" *What clued you in on that one, hotshot?* Maybe next time when you *need* to two-time, you'll be smart enough to pick two girls who don't know each other. *How am I supposed to become a married Matchmaker when all I meet are pigs and losers?*

June

June is another unpredictable Matchmaking month. The summer has officially started, so a lot of people opt to search for their special someone on their own. In New York, a lot of the singles have already started braving the traffic to the Hamptons and have spotted some cuties they want to keep their eye on as the summer progresses. Starting this month, however, I am omnipresent in the Hamptons, a constant reminder that I can be *your* Cupid for a price. So some people sign up nonetheless.

BACK TO
Miss Excuse and Looks Good from Afar Guy

They've been dating for about six weeks. As I do with Miss 39 and Mr. Teeth, I check in with them weekly to make sure things are full speed ahead. So far, so good—until this week, when they hit a love bump. Miss Excuse called me and said urgently, "We need to talk." *Uh-oh.* "I'm not sure what is going on with Looks Good from Afar Guy. We have been out seven or eight times, and I think he really likes me. But, well, he hasn't made a pass at me!" *Really?* I was surprised. "What does that mean? No kissing or no major fooling around?" She laughed at my question. "Well, we've kissed good-bye, but no tongue, and that's it. He never asks if he can come up to my apartment, and he never asks me to come to his apartment. Are you sure he's straight?" I realized I wasn't sure. "I think so. I don't have any reason to think otherwise. Maybe he really likes you and he's just trying to take it slow." I wasn't sure what to say. She said, "I guess, but it's been eight dates. How slow can a guy go?" I said hastily, "Well, let me see what I can find out next time I speak to him."

We hung up and I immediately called Looks Good from Afar Guy. "Hey, how's it going with Miss Excuse?" He sighed. "I don't know, Samantha. I'm conflicted. I think that she is an awesome girl. We have so much in common, but I just am not sure if I am feeling *it* in the romance category. I am trying, but I'm not sure if I am into her *that way*." "Hmm, have you fooled around with her yet?" I asked. "No, not really." I heard him rustling some papers on his desk. "Well, maybe you should. Sometimes it takes hooking up with someone to become sexually attracted. You've been out with her quite a few times, so you should just give it a shot. Maybe then you won't be able to keep your hands off her. You never know. Wouldn't that be nice?" He perked up. "You really think so?" I gave him more reassurance. "Yes, have a drink or two and go for it, you have nothing to lose."

Thursday, June 8

I was contacted today to do commentary on celebrity dating for the E! channel. They want me to be on camera and talk about celebrity makeups and breakups—why celebrity couples are good together or not so good together. *Sounds easy.* I said yes.

I think I spoke too soon about the easy part. They sent me a packet of close to seventy-five pages of background on all the couples they wanted me to be able to talk about. This was like homework. *Did you know that when Dave Navarro first met Carmen Electra, rumor has it that he was so taken with her beautiful eyes that he went out and bought over a hundred pairs of sunglasses for her to wear to cover her eyes whenever she left her house so no one would fall in love with her the way he did? Did you know that* Brad Pitt (the real one) *is a true romantic? It's rumored that on Valentine's Day one year, he filled Jennifer Aniston's trailer with hundreds of roses. And that when he was filming* Ocean's Eleven, *his costars asked him to go out for a drink on a Thursday night, but he said no, he had a date with his wife, and that date was to watch her on* Friends. *Did you know . . . ?* It took me the whole day to study. But now I am like a walking celebrity-couple factoid encyclopedia—you can ask me anything!

MAYBE FOR ME GUY

Credit Card Guy

I went to dinner with a friend of mine tonight. At the restaurant I couldn't help but notice a very handsome guy who looked like a younger version of JFK Jr. He was dining with an older woman. At first I wondered about a Mrs. Robinson scenario but quickly pushed that idea out of my head. They looked a little alike, so I decided that it had to be his mother. How sweet that, on a Saturday night, he was out to dinner with his mom instead of out carousing with his friends.

When their meal ended, our eyes met briefly as they gathered their things. They made their way out and I cursed myself for not having the nerve to walk up to him and say something.

Well, luck must have been on my side, because I realized that he left his credit card on the table. Before I could stop myself, I hailed the waitress as she picked it up and I told her that I knew the guy very well. If she wanted, I would run after him with his credit card. She shrugged and gave it to me. I wasn't sure what I was going to say if I caught them, but I knew I'd figure it out. I glanced at the name on the card, but it was his mom's. I ran out the door, looked to my left and then to my right. I wasn't sure which way they'd headed. Then I sprinted toward the corner, waving my arms as I saw them get into a taxi and pull away. Dejected, I walked back slowly to the restaurant with the card clutched in my hand. As I made my way to the table, my friend gave me a thumbs-up and a hopeful look, but I shook my head and gave the thumbs-down. The waitress smiled at me as I returned the card to her. She said it was nice of me to try running after them, that I was a good friend. I shrugged and decided to come clean. "I have a confession to make. I didn't really know that guy. I just thought he was handsome, and it seemed so sweet that he was with his mom. I was hoping to meet him." She looked at me in surprise.

Then I joked that I wished I had the nerve to leave him a note for when he came to retrieve the card. She started nodding enthusiastically and said, "Yes, yes, you should do it! I will make sure he gets it and put in a good word for you." She winked. You could tell that she was excited by the prospect of living vicariously through me. Maybe I was trying to get my mind off Jerkoff, or maybe I was just up for an adventure, but I took a piece of paper out of my handbag and scribbled a note. "Hi, I have never done this before but I couldn't help but noticing how sweet it was that you were out to dinner with your mom on a Saturday night. If you're single, I would love to have a drink sometime." I signed my name with my phone number. Then, as an afterthought, I added in the margin, "don't worry I am not crazy" and drew a little smiley face. I handed it to the waitress before I could change my mind and left the restaurant wondering if he would call. I figured if he was single, he probably would. I mean, wouldn't he'd be just a little curious about me?

BACK TO

Miss Interrupter

I need to pick men for her who will like her chatty personality. Or who at least won't be bothered if and when she interrupts, because it's inevitable that she will, even though I told her to try to resist. Thirty-five years of a habit can't be corrected overnight. I pulled up the NG (Nice Guy) file:

> What about Josh? He is quiet and would probably like a chatterbox. No, she'd find him boring. What about Bruce? Bruce's mom is very pushy, and he's probably used to a girl like Miss Interrupter. Maybe? Hmm, Craig the lawyer? Yes, Craig . . .

Craig is one of those truly bright guys who doesn't speak all the time, but when he does, people listen because they know he's going to say something intelligent. I gather he comes from a very nice Manhattan family. His parents are supposedly still happily married, and he is supposedly very close to his brother. I called him. He seemed excited and said he was game, but then he paused and asked an odd question. "Who pays for the drinks, me or the girl?" *Huh?* "The guy does, of course. You do." He quickly clarified, "Okay, I only asked because she paid for your service, so I wasn't sure if that meant she paid for the dates. I thought maybe that was your program." "It's not," I said with finality. I wondered if he was actually confused or just cheap. *I guess we shall see.*

Jerkoff Again

I went with him to his therapist today. He's been seeing her twice a week for the past three months. I was impressed. She seemed very caring. She knew who I was and thanked me for coming. She waved me toward a seat and asked me why I agreed to come. I looked over at Jerkoff and then told her that I agreed to come because he had asked and I figured it must have been difficult for him to ask. She got all *therapisty* and said she *applauded my generosity.* Then she asked me what I was hoping to get out of this session. Again I looked in Jerkoff's direction. I lied a little when I said, "I hadn't really thought about it. He asked me to come, his asking surprised me, and I've taught myself to have very low expectations when it comes to Jerkoff. So I decided to just come and see what unfolds." She nodded her head, pointed at me, and then at him and told me to ask Jerkoff why he had invited me. I laughed nervously and again looked toward him. "Okay, Jerkoff, why did you invite me here today?" My voice was shaking. He got tears in his eyes. "I want to be with you, but I don't know how. I feel so much pressure to be perfect for you and to be exactly what you fantasize that I should be, and I am scared that I will never live up to your fantasies, so sometimes I just don't even try."

I squinted at him and got a little defensive. "You are the one who puts all the pressure on yourself, not me. I just want to be with you, to spend time with you. If you think I am so difficult and if you can't handle me, then why not just walk away? You always come back just as I think I'm over you, and then you upset my apple cart and I am back a mess again. We know each other so well; we know everything there is to know about one another. So, for me, the choice is either to get married or to move on. But as soon as I even mention marriage, you retreat. Why do you do this to me? You know how I feel, you know what I want, just let me go." I started to cry. I didn't mean to but I did. I don't know why. His therapist looked compassionately my way and offered me the box of tissues. Then she asked me why I was crying. I looked at her square on and told her that I wasn't sure. "I guess I still love him, but it never gets any better. I never feel like he really loves me and you know what? I really just want to be loved." I was bawling now. *I want to be loved.* With that she ended the session and asked if I would be willing to come back to the session at the end of the week. I looked from her to Jerkoff and back to her again. I found myself saying yes. *Maybe I need this, too.*

BACK TO

The Hundred Thousand Dollar Man

He called this morning. He told me that things are moving along. He eliminated the Ph.D. woman, and so it was down to two, the big-boobed woman and my pick, the ethical girl. "I hope to be focused on just one woman by the end of the month, but in the meantime, I am having a lot of fun dating." Then he paused. "Do you think Mr. Bonus with the Pinkie Ring had as much fun with your women as I am having?" *Here we go again.* I pushed my hands against my temples. "No way, Hundred Thousand Dollar Man. His experience didn't even compare to yours!" He chuckled and said thanks; that was what he was hoping to hear. *Of course it was!*

BACK TO

Credit Card Guy

Five days have passed and I haven't heard from him. I guess he has a girlfriend or thought I was a freak. It doesn't really matter which because the end result is the same, he didn't call. I have to admit, I was daydreaming about our wedding announcement in the *New York Times* Style section and how charming our how-we-met story would be. I'm disappointed, but *c'est la vie,* I suppose.

BACK TO

The Troll

The Troll has been dating Victoria, the Southern girl who likes short men. I spoke to her a few times. She actually thinks it's cute that his nickname is The Troll, and she likes his quirkiness and intelligence. They've even taken an antiquing trip to the Berkshires together. *Go figure.* The Troll said that he doesn't know if she is the One, but he would like to take the time to get to know her better. He said she's different from any other woman he's dated in the past, but in a good way. "You seem to have a knack, Samantha." *Thanks, Troll.*

Mr. 46

I have been trying to stay busy and not obsess over the situation with Jerkoff, so I accepted a date for tonight. If someone had told me in advance that this guy was 46 and had never been married, I probably wouldn't have agreed to go. But I didn't know his age, so I found myself out with him. He was a nice-looking guy. I'm sure a lot of women like him. He was about six feet two, with sandy brown hair, green eyes, a cleft chin, and funny little ears that stuck out but didn't detract from his looks.

In my opinion, 46 is the cutoff age for guys being able to explain why they have never been married. A guy can come up with excuses, and people might buy them until he hits 45, but once he hits 46, that's it. Most people think he is a confirmed bachelor. *What excuse does he have left?* I don't believe that not one woman in his past thirty years of dating has interested him enough to make him take the plunge and get married. What could he possibly be looking for in a woman that he hasn't found in thirty years?

If you think about it, this guy has probably been dating since he was sixteen years old. If he went out on a date with a new woman every other month for the past thirty years, that's 180 dates with 180 different women. But I am guessing that there were some years in which there were many more dates than that, and maybe some years in which he was in a relationship, so there were fewer. But my guesstimate is probably pretty accurate. *This is a lot of women!* And you mean to tell me that not one of them has been good enough to marry?

I would much rather date a 46-year-old divorced guy. At least I know that he took the plunge once, and I have concrete evidence that he believes in the idea of marriage. Anyway, enough theorizing, back to my date. Of course we got into a conversation about why he wasn't married. He tried to turn it around on to me, but I wasn't going to be the subject of *that* conversation on this night. *His situation was more suspect than an unmarried Matchmaker, I am certain of it!* He got very defensive. "So what that I have never been married? I never really wanted to be married until recently. I have been having fun, but now I'm ready." I asked him whether he said that very sentence to all the women he dated in the past. He said that he always dated with no particular agenda, and he figured that when the right girl came along, he would marry her. That is his attitude right now. I rolled my eyes a bit.

"Are you very set in your ways?" I asked. He shrugged and said that he didn't know. Why did I ask? "Well, 46-year-old single men are usually very set in their ways, and I have found that it is very difficult to fit into someone's life when he is very set about everything." He leaned back in his seat and scowled. "I am not really interested in hearing *what you have found,*" he said. "I am supposed to be on a date with a woman, not a theorist. Why are you analyzing me?" *I really wasn't, or at least I didn't mean to. I guess I was in a mood.* I apologized, "You're right. I was going *all dating expert* on you, and I really try to keep my professional life out of my personal life. I guess sometimes it creeps in. I'm sorry. I guess I am just preoccupied and probably shouldn't have accepted a date." I started to feel the tears coming.

His face softened and he asked me if I wanted to talk about it.

Next thing I knew I was telling this complete stranger about Jerkoff and thereby breaking my number one dating rule. "I thought I was over my ex-boyfriend, but then he asked me to go to therapy with him and I said yes because I thought I should and now I am going to therapy with him and I have been sucked back in and I am starting to think that everything is all my fault and maybe I should be the one who is in the therapy, not him . . ." "Hey, it's okay, calm down, take a deep breath, you're shaking." He leaned over and rubbed my shoulder a bit. "It will be okay. Do you love him?" "What?" I looked at him funny. He repeated, "Do you love him? Do you want to be with him?" *When did it go from my analyzing him to his analyzing me?* I shrugged. "I don't know. I love him, but loving him is a challenge and so intense and scary. I don't know if I can be with him, although I want to be with him. I don't know." He chuckled and gave me a reassuring smile. "Look, Samantha, I don't know you at all, actually, but I would guess that all the things that have excited you in your life have been hard and scary, but that's why they have endured and remained a part of your life. Don't not be with him because it's challenging. People like us need challenging. We need highs and lows because otherwise our interest will evaporate in five minutes. You and me, we have waited a long time to take the plunge, so when it happens, it better be with someone who will hold our interest forever, even if he or she is a little challenging. Don't you think?" *His words were ringing true, but did I really dare even to start to imagine a life with Jerkoff?*

Miss 39 and Mr. Teeth

I woke up this morning to a message from Miss 39 that I needed to call her. *Please God, tell me that she just wants to say hello and that she is not calling to tell me that they broke up!* I called her back. "How's it going?" I asked, holding my breath until she answered. "Things are pretty good," she said. *Thank god!* "I am just feeling a little sad." *Oh no!* "Why? what's the matter?" I asked tentatively. She took a breath. "I like Mr. Teeth a lot, but I am starting to worry that I like him more than he likes me. I am always available for him, we get together whenever he wants, but I feel like he doesn't do the same for me. What do you think?" she asked expectantly. I sat back in my chair relieved. *This issue is workable.* "Hmm, I think that maybe your instincts are right. You might be too available to Mr. Teeth, which is why he isn't as available to you. Men need women to seem a little mysterious. They want you to be present and sexy and interesting when you're with them, but when you aren't, it's good to keep them off-kilter, make them wonder what you're doing and where you are." She sighed. "But isn't that game-playing? I am too old to play games, Samantha. I just want to get married." I laughed and shook my head. "I know, Miss 39, but I'm not suggesting games. I am just suggesting you play it a little smarter. Don't be available every time he suggests plans, even if your alternatives are just a quick dinner with a friend or a trip to the movies alone. Let him want you a little bit, let him miss you a little bit. Don't always answer the phone when he calls, and make him wait for your return call. Then getting that return call will bring a smile to his face." I wondered if she was paying attention. I continued, "Don't always tell him where you are when you aren't with him. Let him wonder, let him think that you are busy and fabulous and have lots of things to do whenever the two of you aren't together. Get it?" I asked hopefully.

"That sounds like games to me. I don't have so many friends or so many plans, and I like talking to him so I like answering when he calls. And I don't want him to think I'm out with other guys because I'm not, and if he thinks I am then he might feel the need to go out with other women, which I definitely don't want." I rolled my eyes and tried to state my case more emphatically. "I understand. I am not suggesting all that. I am simply saying that when he calls to make plans, instead of saying, 'Well, I can't do it Monday because I have a dinner with Suzy and I can't do it Tuesday because my dad is in town, and I can't do it Thursday because I am getting my legs waxed,' just say, 'I can do it on Wednesday.' Don't mention what's going on on the other nights. That way when you aren't with him he thinks you're doing something fabulous because he thinks you are fabulous and he doesn't know that it's just a leg wax or dinner with Suzy. Understand?" I pressed on with conviction. "Like I said, guys like women who seem interesting and fabulous and present when they are with them and a little mysterious when they're not with them. It can't hurt to try it." She chuckled in defeat. "Okay, you win, Samantha. I will try it." I smiled in relief as I hung up.

BACK TO

Miss Interrupter

She went out with Craig three times. I thought things were going pretty well. Then both of them called first thing this morning, separately. I called Miss Interrupter back first since she's the client. "I don't want to go out with him again. He's cheap," she said immediately. I squinted my eyes. "What does that mean? What's he done?" She huffed and said, "I offered him money on our first date, just to be polite, not because I wanted him to take it. And he didn't take it, thank god, or I wouldn't have ever gone out with him again, but he made a comment that I could get the check next time." Her voice rose. "Sure enough, next time he asked me out, he picked the place, but when the bill came he made no move to get it. A lot of time passed so eventually I just reached for it because it seemed like he was waiting for me to do so, and he only said thanks." She took a deep breath to continue her tirade. "Hey, hey, Miss Interrupter." I called out her name to grab her attention. "Calm down. It's going to be okay. If it's not this guy, there will be another one." "I guess, I am just annoyed," she huffed again. "Anyway, he asked me out for a third date, which was last night, and for some crazy reason I accepted because I wanted to make certain that I wasn't just deciding he was cheap when he really wasn't. This time he took me out with a group of his friends, and when the bill came, one of his female friends did the division and said it was $58 per person. I didn't even pay attention. I figured he would pay for both of us. I mean, how embarrassing if he didn't. But then fifteen minutes later the girl said, 'Wait, we are $58 short. Who didn't pay?' I looked up and said, 'Well, I didn't.' And I looked at him. But he didn't make eye contact with me, and I didn't know what to do, so I gave her my money. I barely spoke to him on the way home. Sam-man-tha, he's awful!" I started pushing on pressure points in my hand. "Okay, okay. I agree, if you don't want to see him again you don't have to. Or if you want me to try to salvage it or get to the bottom of it, I can ask him."

With her voice still at a feverish pitch, she said, "I don't care. Just find me a new guy, and don't make him cheap!"

I hung up the phone, wagging my head back and forth in disgust. *I don't get it.* But I was also a little intrigued. Why is Craig, now nicknamed Mr. Cheapskate, so cheap? He comes from a wealthy Manhattan family and makes a lot of money, at least I think he does. He's a lawyer at a big firm. I don't get it. I called a friend of mine who went to college with him and who was always good for some dirt. "Hey, what's the deal with that guy Craig?" I asked curiously. She lowered her voice conspiratorially, "Craig, the only thing I ever hear about him is how cheap he is." *Wow, a chronic cheapskate!* She started chuckling. "One of my friends went out with him and he told her that he loves to watch *The Sopranos* but doesn't have HBO. And when she asked why, he said that he could just go his parents' apartment to watch it, what does he need to have HBO for!" My eyes widened. "Then my friend told me that in the dead of winter he won't leave his heat on during the day, and sometimes he sleeps with a parka on because it's so cold in his apartment when he gets home!" I mouthed the word *what?* to myself. "The guy is weird." I scratched my head. "Wow, that's really odd. I guess I shouldn't set him up." My friend seemed to be on a roll. "Oh wait, I also heard from another girl that he's a really low tipper and sometimes tries not to tip at all. My friend felt like she was running behind him sprinkling money to people like the coat-check girl. He's really terrible!"

Confused, I hung up with my friend. Wow, Mr. Cheapskate is practically pathological. I had to call him back but I wasn't even going to try to salvage things. Miss Interrupter could do so much better. I got him on the phone. Immediately he launched in about Miss Interrupter, "She is driving me crazy. She talks way too much, and I can't take it anymore. I don't want to go out with her again." I immediately said no problem and started getting off the phone. Maybe he was expecting me to argue because he seemed stumped for a moment. Then he became conversational and tried to keep me on the phone. So I asked him if he wanted to hear what Miss Interrupter thought of him. He said, to my surprise, "Well, actually I think I would like to sit down with you and talk about hiring you to work with me. Maybe you can tell me that in person." *Uh-oh, Mr. Cheapskate as a client? Not so sure about that.* I wasn't sure how to handle this, so I started stammering, "Hmm. Um, you know my service is very expensive. It's $10,000, which includes a slew of services, but it is ten. Are you okay with that?" *I figured that telling him the price would solve my problem.* He became matter-of-fact and said he knew the cost and he wanted to have a meeting. I was intrigued, so I scheduled a consultation.

BACK TO

Looks Good from Afar Guy and Miss Excuse

They called me this morning, together. "Guess where we are?" they said in unison into the phone. *No clue.* "We are in bed together and we have been having sex all night!" I nearly dropped the phone. *Okay, too much information. It's only 10 A.M.* "That's great," I said. Miss Excuse grabbed the phone. "He's not gay, Samantha. Trust me, I know." Then I heard Looks Good from Afar Guy's voice. "She's great in bed, Samantha. I can't keep my hands off her, just like you said." "Thanks, Samantha," again in unison. *Wonder if I can convince her mom to pay me an advance on my bonus.*

BACK TO

Miss 39 and Mr. Teeth

She called again today. "Did you speak to Mr. Teeth? Has he noticed the difference? Am I more mysterious?" she asked hopefully. I apologized and said that I had not had time to call him but could call him later in the day. Her voice fell. "Oh, okay." Then she lingered on the phone. I asked if there everything else was okay and she said, "Well, I'm starting to feel like I'm not all that special to Mr. Teeth. I feel like he doesn't treat me any differently than he treats everyone else in his life, and call me crazy, but I think he should treat me differently. Don't you think so?"

I nodded. "I agree with you completely. A guy should make the woman he is dating feel different and more special than anyone else in his life. What happened specifically?" "He had a party at his house in Westchester and he put on the invitation that everyone should park on the street. I asked him if I could park in the driveway. After all, I am his girlfriend and I was going to be spending the night. He said no! *No one* gets to park in the driveway. It's a thing he has." She whined, "Samantha, I should not be *no one*. Not only should he have let me park there, but he should have offered. Don't you think?" I agreed with her, which fueled her desire to continue. "And then I needed some help moving some new furniture that I got at the flea market on Sunday, and I asked him if he could help me because he has a handyman with a pickup truck who works for him sometimes. Again, he said no, *no one* gets to use his people. He doesn't lend out the people who work for him to *anyone*." She started whining like a little girl, "Samantha, I don't want to be just *anyone*." "Miss 39, don't whine. This is fixable. I agree with you. He might not realize that he is making you feel that way." I made myself a note to say something to him. "When I check in with him this week, I will see if I can get into it with him in a roundabout way."

Mr. Bigger Better Deal

I introduced him to the perfect girl. She's perfect for him because she's Miss Bigger Better Deal. They're exactly alike. She chases parties, he chases parties, no guy is good enough for her and no girl is good enough for him. They are like cats chasing each other's tails, never quite able to catch the other. These two are focused intently on each other because they can never quite get the other to give 100 percent of their attention. It's pretty amusing actually. She calls me and complains that she thinks that she's more into him than he's into her, and he says the opposite. I told her that she needed to turn things around because it's always better to have the guy like you a little more than you like him. I told him the same thing. It's funny to watch them, but I think they are falling for each other.

Jerkoff Again

He's not very good at being patient. Even though we are in the throes of therapy, even though the therapist has said that it is too soon for us to start seeing each other, and even though he still doesn't seem to understand that he is the one who puts so much pressure on himself to be perfect, he showed up at my door with purple tulips. I was surprised to see him. I nervously pushed my hair out of my face and asked, "What are you doing here?" He looked at me with puppy-dog eyes and said, "I thought we could just hang out here and be close." He seemed so humble when he said that that I let him come in, but I told him it was just to talk. I moved out of the doorway, careful not to make contact with him or seem like I was initiating something that I had no intention of initiating. But of course, he wasn't even in my apartment for five minutes before we ended up in my bed. It's never just to talk between us—the sex is too intense. The sex felt different this time. Maybe I was imagining it, but I felt a different closeness, tenderness almost, a feeling of being home. He seemed more clingy, more connected. We talked a lot about us and our hopes and our childhoods, just stuff. I don't remember what exactly, but it felt right and different. In the morning he didn't seem to want to leave, but then he did and I didn't hear from him for two days. I was in a panic; I didn't know what had happened. *How could he just sleep with me and be so tender and then disappear?* I thought we had made progress with the therapist. *I can't do this anymore. I can't do this at all. I need to move on.* I left him an angry message: "I am finished with you. I can't do this again. I won't." Then, on a rampage, I called the therapist. I thought she would agree, but she insisted that I come to one more session. "For closure," she suggested. I wiped a tear from my eye and hesitantly agreed.

BACK TO

Miss 39 and Mr. Teeth

I had trouble concentrating on business with all that was going on with Jerkoff, but *the show must go on,* as they say in Hollywood, so I tried busying myself with the Desperados. I called Mr. Teeth mid-week. "Miss 39 is acting differently," he said, all confused. "Oh really? How so?" I started perking up. "Well, it's gotten more difficult to get her on the phone, and she doesn't seem as available as she has been in the past." *Oh really!* "Do you think she's dating someone else?" he asked cautiously. I answered reassuringly, "No, I don't think so. I think she just really likes you." (I remembered on their first date he needed to hear that she liked him, so I reminded him of that now to bolster his confidence.) "You think?" he asked hopefully. "Definitely. Maybe the problem is that you are not asking her for plans early enough in the week." I planted the seed. "Miss 39 is a very busy woman, and if you don't lock her in early, she might make other plans." He was thought-ful for a minute and said, "Hmm, I guess so. I guess I will have to or I won't get to see her, and I like seeing her." Then he confided, "The thing is, I guess I just assume that we can see each other whenever be-cause we are a couple." I smiled. "Have you had that conversation with her yet? Maybe if you told her that you see the two of you that way, it would be clearer how the plans will work." I pressed on. "Women need to have the state of your relationship all spelled out. We assume the worst until we know for certain. We are not as casual about things as you guys are." He sighed. "Oh, okay, I guess I didn't know that. I will try that."

I clapped my hands. "Good! And while I have you on the phone, I was talking to another client [not!] and I thought it might be helpful for me to point out what I talked about with him. Actually, I reminded him that women need to feel special, they need to be treated like they are someone special to the guy, someone who is different and more special than anyone else in his life." I paused to see if I had his attention. He urged me on. "The woman that my guy was dating was upset because the guy wouldn't let anyone use his personal bathroom in his house, and she felt like she wasn't just anyone. She should have been able use the bathroom even if no one else could." I waited to see what Mr. Teeth would say. Then on cue Mr. Teeth said slowly, "Hmm, I kind of did that to Miss 39, but I didn't mean to." "What did you do?" I asked, as if I didn't know the answer. "I had a party and we got into a fight because I wouldn't let anyone, including her, park in my drive-way. I have this weird, paranoid thing that if—God forbid—someone got hurt and an ambulance was needed, I would want them to be able to pull into the driveway without a problem." "Makes sense," I said, rolling my eyes. "Anyway, I wouldn't let anyone park in the driveway, including her. She got angry." "Mr. Teeth," I said patiently, "I'm not sure I blame her. It sucks to feel like *one of the masses* when you want to be *The One*." "I guess you are right. Maybe I will send her flowers." "Purple tulips always work," I said, but saying that made me think of Jerkoff, and I got a lump in my throat.

DESPERADO #30

Mr. Cheapskate

He came in for a meeting today. I decided in advance that I was going to level with him and tell him how he's perceived and see if he's open and able to make some changes. He surprised me again by saying immediately, "I already know what Miss Interrupter said to you about me. She said I was cheap, told you how I didn't pay for her at the dinner with my friends, right?" "Ummm . . . ?" I looked at him, wide-eyed. He interrupted me and continued, "Samantha, I get that a lot.

Women think that I'm cheap, but I am not. I'm just thrifty and a little cautious when it comes to money because my family is really wealthy, I mean big-time wealthy. I am not trying to impress you, I just want you to understand, my dad is probably worth several hundred million dollars." He paused to see my reaction, and I just continued nodding my head up and down in understanding. "I have a trust fund. I don't have any siblings, so . . . you get it. I have and will have a lot of money. Do you ever get clients like me?" *Maybe one or two or twenty!* I smiled compassionately and told him not to worry, many of my clients were very affluent and I knew just how to guard their privacy and make them feel comfortable. He looked relieved. Then he leaned in. "I test women a lot when I go on dates because I want to make sure that they are not after my money." *I knew it; I knew there was something "undiscovered" about this guy. So, why no HBO?*

I looked at him compassionately. "I understand, Mr. Cheapskate, I do. I can certainly understand your not wanting to be with a woman who only wants you for your money or who only cares about money. But I think you are sabotaging situations with women who could potentially be good for you." I paused to let this sink in. "I have to tell you, I do a lot of digging, and I know a lot of information about a lot of people. I had no idea that you were so wealthy, and neither did Miss Interrupter. And I know you didn't like her ultimately, so it doesn't matter. But if you had, you would have ruined it with your little tests." I looked at him intently, trying to figure out if he understood what I was saying. He took a sip of his iced tea and then, almost to himself, said, "I guess, but I don't know how to know who to test." I answered definitively, "Maybe you shouldn't *test* anybody and just let it unfold. You will be able to tell in due course her true intentions, trust me." I patted his hand on the table reassuringly, "And if we work together, I will be doing the testing for you, and since I now know that you are supersensitive about this issue, I will only pick women who are not after money or who come from their own money." He seemed happy with that answer. "I would prefer if they come from their own money. I think it's better for me. Then I will know that she likes me for me and not for my money."

"Got it." I wrote some notes on the margin of my questionnaire. "I need to ask one other thing." I paused. "What is this rumor I hear about your not having HBO because you can watch it at your parents' and about your not using heat? This makes you sound pathologically cheap." He laughed heartily. "You heard that? Oh god, I was dating this woman and I started thinking she was a major gold digger and I wanted to break up with her so I started telling her these really crazy things to scare her off." He laughed, lost in thought. "We were at her apartment and we were watching *Curb Your Enthusiasm*"—hearing him talk about *Curb Your Enthusiasm* made me think of Jerkoff. *Why does everything these days make me think of Jerkoff?*—"and I said that I was so excited to watch it at her house because I didn't have it at my house, but my mom had it, so I was lucky." He paused. When I didn't laugh, he pressed on, "Then one time I was away for the weekend and we walked into my apartment and she got all upset that I hadn't left the heat on." He smiled again as if proud of himself. "So I told her I never leave it on. I would rather sleep in a ski jacket than waste heat. Both of the comments were jokes. I was pulling her leg." Again he paused to see my reaction, and this time I shook my head in disapproval. "Mr. Cheapskate, the jokes are now *on you* because you have developed a reputation as a weirdo cheapskate. This is bad, so no more tests and no more jokes, okay? Promise me," I said emphatically. *Promise me. . . .*

Miss Interrupter

I had gotten so preoccupied with Mr. Cheapskate's antics that I forgot that he confirmed that Miss Interrupter is up to her old tricks. Then I ran into her at the gym and we started chitchatting. I said, "I am going to move on to another guy for you, but first we have to talk about how the dates went with Craig, even though you de——" She interrupted me immediately. "He's a total whack job, right? So cheap. Did you find out what his deal is? Did you yell at him?" "Miss Interrupter, you just interrupted me. What I was trying to say is that I don't want to talk about him. He is yesterday's news. I want to talk about you. He told me that he *also*"—I emphasized the word—"didn't want to go out with you again because you talked his ear off and interrupted him again and again and totally drove him crazy." She looked at me in surprise and started twirling a piece of her hair. "Oh, um, I did?" I nodded. "Yep. I warned you of this. You really need to work on it, and work on not talking so much, so incessantly, and on sharing the stage a bit. Let me ask you something. Why do you think you do this?" Her lip quivered. I looked around to see if anyone was looking at us. I didn't want Miss Interrupter to have an emotional breakdown in the middle of the Equinox gym. I took her arm and guided her toward the locker room. I figured it would be more private there. We sat down on a bench. I asked her again if she knew why she interrupted people. "I don't know. Ever since I was a little girl I have talked a lot. Everyone in my family did. It was hard to get a word in, actually." She looked at me to see if I was listening. *Hmm.* I was processing. "What number child are you, Miss Interrupter?" "The youngest." She sniffled. *We have made contact.* "Now I get it," I said. "I think you spent your life fighting for face time, talk time actually. Am I right? Did you feel like you didn't get enough attention?" Her eyes welled up. "Yes, I always felt like no one was listening to me, so I always had to yell to be heard." She was crying now and wiping her nose with the edge of her sleeve. I got up to get her a tissue. "It's good to cry," I said. *I have made a lot of progress on the letting-them-cry front!* I handed her a tissue and she blew her nose. I continued, "You are an adult now and you don't have to do that anymore because you are beautiful and interesting and people will listen to you and notice you just because they will. Can you understand that?" I asked patiently. She was thoughtful for a moment and then got a despairing expression on her face. "But let's say I can't change. I have been like this since I was probably six." I rubbed her shoulder gently. "We'll work on it together. And what do you think of going to a therapist? I have a few I recommend to clients."

BACK TO

Miss 39

She called me, all excited. She was out of breath. "Mr. Teeth sent me the most beautiful purple tulips today. They are gorgeous! And so unusual, I wonder what made him think to pick those." I could hear her smiling. "The card says, 'Just because.' So romantic." I grinned. "When I called to say thank you he was so sweet." She giggled. "He told me that he had spoken to you and that you made him realize that he should talk to me about his expectations about our situation." She chatted on, "We had a great conversation. We verbalized that we are boyfriend and girlfriend, and we talked about how making plans would work." *Wow, my Dating 101 couple is turning into experts!* She did an intake of breath and said nervously, "Samantha, I can't believe I am going to say this, but I think he might be the One." I smiled a great big smile at that comment.

BACK TO
Miss Interrupter

She started seeing the therapist I recommended. They decided, and I agreed, that she should put her membership with me on hold for a few months while she does some intensive work and then get back to dating in the fall.

Jerkoff Again

Tonight is the therapy session. I went back and forth a thousand times about whether to go. I don't owe this therapist anything—she isn't my therapist—and I don't owe Jerkoff anything. He is not my boyfriend and he is just a jerk. But finally I decided to go. I wanted to hear his explanation for not calling me back this time. I wanted to be able to end things in person and move on. I did my makeup carefully and spent an hour deciding what to wear. I wanted him to remember me looking gorgeous and to get a good look at what he was never going to have again. I brought his purple tulips with me, thinking that I would throw them at him for effect.

I walked down the hall to the therapist's office slowly. I was nervous and anxious and sad, but I was ready. It was time, really time, to cut my losses and move on. *How much can one person endure? Don't I deserve a normal, easy relationship?*

When I walked in the office, the lights were off. I reached for the switch and turned it on. And then I saw him, Jerkoff on his knee, surrounded by what must have been a thousand purple tulips, holding a ring box. I was in shock. *Oh my God, this is not happening. I am about to break up with him and he is about to propose with purple tulips and a ring.* I started to cry. I looked around for the therapist, but she was nowhere to be found. I looked at him kneeling there. I didn't know what to say or what to do, but I couldn't turn away. "Jerkoff, I—" He interrupted, "No, Samantha, I'm first. I left your apartment the other morning because my feelings for you were so overwhelming me that I couldn't handle it." He took several gulps of air. "And yes, I was planning on running away and retreating and not seeing you again. I didn't think I could deal with it. But then I kept thinking about you and our relationship, and I decided that the only way to try to make this work is to really go for it." A contented smile appeared on his face. "So, even though it's extreme, I went to Fred Leighton, got you the ring that I knew you wanted." He looked down at the box in his hand and continued, "And I called up the therapist and got her to play along." He looked at me for approval as I continued to stand there, rooted to my spot. "I know proposing in a therapist's office is not the most romantic place in the world, but I wanted to do it in a place where I promise truth and dedication to you, and that is here." He took several breaths again and started talking really fast. "So, will you marry me? I think it might be better for us to try to work on our issues while we're together so neither of us can walk away. Will you go through this crazy life with me, so we can be crazy and intense but most of all try to stay together forever and ever?"

I must have been staring off into space. *Oh my God, am I dreaming?* He interrupted my thoughts. "Samantha, are you here? Did you hear me? Say something, please." I was speechless. I wasn't sure what to say. He had stumped me. I never in my wildest dreams—*well, maybe in my wildest dreams*—imagined it like this, but it is *so* Jerkoff. *It's what I want, isn't it? It's what I have been waiting for since I was five years old.* I started to feel a little light-headed. I sat down on the edge of the therapist's couch and put my vase of tulips on the table. He was still on his knee. My mind was racing. *Is Jerkoff the guy for me, for better or for worse? Is he the guy I see myself walking down that street with in fifteen or twenty years, laughing at the same jokes and finding the same things annoying? Does what he is saying make sense: get engaged and married now, deal with our issues later? I wasn't so sure.*

I was about to throw caution to the wind, and then I thought about what had happened, and what he had just said, and all at once, things became crystal clear. *I can't go through my life worrying that he is going to freak and leave me. I need someone to love me always and forever without hesitation and without freak-outs. I don't know if Jerkoff can do that. I love him, but maybe he can't be My Guy.* I turned to him and, with more resolve than I felt, I said quietly, almost in a whisper, "I am so sorry, but I can't do this, not now." My voice started shaking. "It's too impetuous. I am not ready to believe that you can be there for me always. Maybe someday I'll believe it, but not today." I walked toward him and helped him to his feet. "Today I need to leave this office and go forward with my life and you need to go forward with your therapy and get better and figure things out so you won't run away every time conflict and difficulties arise." I held his one hand and I closed his other over the box as a gesture to signify putting it away. "I will always love you, but I don't think we should get married. I'm sorry." He dropped his hand from mine and shook his head in despair.

Before I could lose my resolve, I walked out the door. In the elevator, I almost pushed the emergency stop button. *What was I doing? He just proposed to me, I was just offered Jerkoff on a silver platter and I said no.* I held my hands tightly together. I got out of the elevator with a swirl of emotions enveloping me. I bumped into someone as I walked out, but so many tears were streaming down my face that I didn't even notice. I was sad and lonely but relieved and, more than anything else, hopeful—hopeful that I made the right decision and hopeful that My Guy, my *Right Guy* was out there somewhere. I just needed to be patient. I wandered down the street, lost in thought. My heart beat rapidly and I had knots in my stomach.

I called my voice mail to distract myself. I had one new message: "Hi, Samantha, this is Jonathan. *Who?* You left me a note on my mom's credit card in that restaurant on a Saturday almost a month ago." My jaw dropped. *Oh my god, Credit Card Guy!* "We just picked up the credit card last night because I was out of town and then too busy to swing by and get it. And yes, she was my mom and, yes, I would love to have a drink with you. I know it's been awhile since you left the note. I hope my timing is okay."

Yes, Credit Card Guy, your timing couldn't be better. I wiped my face and smiled a big hopeful smile as I dialed his number.

101 Dating Thoughts

1. There are no "supposed to's" in dating.
2. Excuses don't get you anywhere. If you want to meet someone, you need to be proactive and try to meet someone.
3. Let everyone in your life know that you are single and interested in getting set up. If you don't tell them, they won't think to do it.
4. You cannot wait ten days to call a woman back after the first time you have sex, no matter how rich you are.
5. Evaluate your friends and make sure they enhance, not detract from, your ability to meet people of the opposite sex. It is okay to have certain friends who you socialize with and other friends who you go to the movies or watch football with.
6. No pinkie rings, no matter what!
7. Men trade on their money and women trade on their looks. This is a fact of dating. If you got it, use it!
8. Just because you look good from afar does not mean that you will always get a second date. Work hard to be charming up close and personal as well.
9. If you date a workaholic, self-centered jerk who is not willing

to try to change, you will be married to a workaholic, self-centered jerk.

10. Initiating phone sex on a first date is highly inappropriate. No exceptions.

11. All single people suck at dating. You are not alone.

12. People judge people by the quality of their voice, even if they say they don't. If you think you have a problem, visit a speech therapist.

13. People create fantasies in their heads about who their dates are before they even meet them. These fantasies make reality very difficult to handle.

14. People do not like to be touched right away on first dates. Hold off until the appropriate time, which is no sooner than one hour into the date.

15. A woman can always say no to sex. No still means no.

16. In most instances, no good comes out of sex on a first date, except a little sexual pleasure (and that's what a vibrator is for). Don't do it.

17. Men will date women who remind them of a sibling or family member even if they are not their *usual type*.

18. Your best guy friend will become your acquaintance once he marries another woman, so if you are attracted to him, go for it, and don't worry about preserving the friendship.

19. Don't test your date on a date. This is not school.

20. Try to play nice. The best way to point out annoying traits is by teasing someone until they realize just how annoying the traits really are.

21. Do not suggest sitting French style (both of you on the same side of the table) at a restaurant unless and until you have *made out* at least once or unless or until you are out with a French person.

22. You cannot cultivate men in a petri dish. It doesn't work—I have tried it.

23. Bad teeth are bad teeth; whether you live in the United States or England, go to the orthodontist or buy Crest Whitestrips.

24. If you've met a lot of singles who weren't for you but were good people, become an amateur Matchmaker. What comes around could go around.

25. Endearments should be reserved for people who mean something to you and should be unique and special to that person. Otherwise, they really are sweet "nothings."

26. If you have big boobs, men are going to notice them. If that bothers you, get a breast reduction or learn to deal with the attention.

27. Sometimes people need to perceive interest before they feel comfortable expressing interest.

28. Don't be self-critical on your date. How is someone else going to like you if you don't seem to like yourself?

29. A little "spinning of the truth" on a date is fair play, and too much information on a date can be detrimental. Your date only needs to know what he/she *needs* to know.

30. Everyone's family is dysfunctional, but don't scare your date by making him/her think that yours should be institutionalized.

31. People gravitate to people who smile, have good posture, and don't cross their arms.

32. Indecision is a big turnoff. If you can't make decisions for one, how will you make decisions for a family?

33. Think about who *your* guy is. Make a list, then cross off the things that you can do without and circle the things you really need. Don't be greedy or you will be single forever.

34. Have an arsenal of backup dating conversation topics: an exotic vacation you took, funny childhood story, or your favorite new restaurant.

35. A man needs to know that a woman is willing to have children even though he doesn't want her to be desperate to have them immediately. This is a fine line; learn to walk it well.

36. People who use dating services are not desperate. They are busy and desirous of getting married.

37. Men like women who go out on a flirtatious limb, who unexpectedly send them an e-mail or take them out for an evening on the town.

38. Even beautiful, sexy women get nervous before dates.

39. Always wear a matching bra and panties—you never know who is going to see them.

40. It doesn't matter if a man can pick a great date place. At the end of the day, it's more important that he's willing to go to the places that a woman picks out. Once a couple gets married, the woman usually winds up making the social plans.

41. Men who come from picture-perfect families can have very high expectations for their own relationships. Keep this in mind as you date and try to get your man to live in the present instead of his childhood past.

42. Men who come from divorced families are not always dysfunc-

tional. A lot of times they want to have a better marriage than their parents had, and they will work harder for that.

43. Men like pretty, well-groomed women. This is a fact. You need to do the very best with what you have.

44. You get invited, you go; that's what my grandmother taught me.

45. Answering your cell phone several times during a date is inappropriate. If you know you will need to answer your phone, the polite thing to do is to tell your date up front so that he or she doesn't take it personally.

46. If you are in a bad mood, you are better off canceling the date.

47. If you are rude to waitstaff, your dates will think it's just a matter of time before you are equally rude to them.

48. If there's ever a lull in the conversation, go with a compliment. People love to be complimented.

49. Be wary of someone who immediately calls you their soul mate, who comes on like a bulldozer, who makes jokes about the two of you moving in together immediately, or who wants you to meet their mother before you have slept together. This is usually a recipe for a crash-and-burn situation.

50. Just because a guy is tall and gorgeous does not mean he has a large penis.

51. When a guy decides to stop seeing you, it is never because of one little thing that you did (it's never because the outfit that you were wearing made you look fatter than usual or because you had bad breath for an hour). It is because of something more substantial, something the guy has been thinking about for a while.

52. A makeover can do wonders for one's self-esteem.

53. Botox is not very painful, not all that expensive, and supposedly risk-free. If you have lots of wrinkles, try it. It will make you look much younger.

54. Contact lenses make a huge difference for a person who has always worn glasses.

55. Men who act weak, snivel, and don't work are not attractive to women.

56. Using a pretense to ask a woman out on a date is a turnoff. Be a man—just ask her out.

57. Height requirements might be stopping you from meeting your guy. What would be so bad if your Prince Charming was five feet seven?

58. Where a person grew up should be irrelevant as long the person does not insist that you live there or go there on a regular basis.

59. It is a mistake to commit to a time-consuming activity outside your hometown because that activity takes you away from the place where you should be meeting your mate.

60. If you spend all your time hanging out with married people, you are unlikely to find a person to marry yourself.

61. Do not let presents, trips, and empty sentiment lure you into a bad relationship. Actions speak louder than words.

62. Valentine's Day is a holiday full of expectations. If you expect less, you will get more.

63. Serial monogamists can be worse than players because they will lead you on by getting into a real relationship with you only to break up with you because they have a fear of commitment.

64. If you don't make changes in the way you live your life, nothing will change.

65. Try a boy toy. Everyone deserves a little sexual diversion.

66. Do not assume that the person you are dating has stopped seeing other people just because you have stopped seeing other people.

67. People who are in relationships spend the weekend together, or at least Saturday night together.

68. People who are in relationships introduce their mates to friends and family, and they introduce them as their girlfriend or boyfriend, not as their friend.

69. Men take longer than women do to want to become exclusive in a relationship.

70. It usually takes at least three seasons, sometimes four, to determine if a person is appropriate for you for the long term.

71. Vacation relationships do not always translate to real-world relationships.

72. Normal men want sex all the time and will never rebuke a naked woman.

73. Sometimes the more social you are, the more alone you feel.

74. If you find someone who has 85 percent of the things you want in a mate, run—don't walk—to the altar.

75. If you are always looking for the bigger, better deal, you might miss the person standing in front of you.

76. Women cannot have sex without feeling emotional attachment, no exceptions.

77. If the only reason you want to get married is to have a baby, consider going to a sperm bank.

78. If you are not good in social settings, think about alternative ways to meet people, such as using Matchmakers, doing online dating, or going on one-on-one blind dates.

79. You cannot be objective about a person you are romantically interested in.

80. You should buy trendy clothes only if the trends look good on you. Otherwise, you are doing yourself a disservice.

81. Never give up on love.

82. Women love to obsess over men. They love to call a half dozen friends and repeat the same story over and over to get different reads on the circumstance. They continue to do this until they hear an interpretation that they like.

83. Men like women who have something going on and who aren't waiting by the door when they walk in. It's good to be independent and let a guy know that you have your own life but that you also have room in that life for him.

84. Once you fall for someone, you will be surprised at how many of your "must-haves" will fall out the window.

85. Having the relationship talk, saying I love you, or crying during sex will cause a man to lose his erection.

86. As a woman, you should always let the guy be the first one to say I love you. If you say it first, it will probably freak him out.

87. Some men are attracted to high-maintenance women; however, *most* men are not.

88. If you don't respect yourself, a man will not respect you.

89. It is very rude to interrupt people when they are speaking. It makes you seem self-absorbed and ignorant.

90. There are certain people with whom you just click and other people with whom you don't. Don't try to fit a square peg into a round hole.

91. It is rude to stay out with someone for seven hours if you are not really interested in them.

92. It is very difficult to capture the attention of another person at a social event because there are so many distractions. If you have the opportunity, you should opt for a one-on-one date.

93. Women should seem interesting and interested when they are with a guy, but mysterious and aloof when they are not. It's good to let the guy wonder what fabulous things you do when you are not with him, even if you are just getting a leg wax.

94. Your significant other needs to feel like someone special to you and not just part of the group of "anyones" in your life.

95. Being cheap is bad form, no matter what.

96. Forty-six, single, and never married usually signifies a confirmed bachelor. If you are this guy, you better have a good explanation as to why none of the hundreds of women you have taken out during your thirty years of dating have intrigued you enough to marry. If you are dating this guy, you had better keep your options open.

97. If you are on the fence about whether you are sexually attracted to someone who appeals to you on all other levels, down a few cocktails and go in for the kill. You have nothing to lose, and you never know if that will put you over the hump.

98. If sex was intense with your ex, anytime you see him or her and you are single, invariably you will wind up having sex.

99. Women need relationship parameters spelled out.
100. Your special someone is the person you think you can imagine walking down the street with in fifteen or twenty years, laughing at the same things and finding the same things to be annoying.
101. Everyone just wants to be loved.

Acknowledgments

This book could never be complete without mentioning the many people who have supported me and who have given me the skills to make it all happen. First, I need to thank all my friends and clients, my exes and my good dates, my bad dates, my friends' bad dates and their friends' bad dates, for all the stories and all the memories. For those of you still in my life, I appreciate it and for those of you with whom I have lost touch, I miss you.

Now on to the specifics—First I want to thank my family for all their love, support, and teasing. My mother, Donna Daniels, you are with me always, making me be the woman that I am; there are no words that say enough. My father, Robert Daniels, who taught me what family means, how to never take no for an answer, how to be a kickass business woman, and how to stand up for what I believe in. My brother Sean for being my 24/7 business adviser, for giving me a shoulder to cry on more times than I can remember, and for being my L.A. compatriot. My brother Chris for being my press finder, my eyes and ears in pop culture, for admiring my creativity even when we were kids and I was drawing cartoon characters, and for his and Amy's critique of the first go-round of the book. My grandmother (who gets the dedication in the sequel), who always told me "you get invited, you go, because you never know who you will meet," and I have been doing that ever since. My grandfather (he gets the dedication in book three) for giving me makeup samples to sell in elementary school so I could be a businesswoman at a very young age. My Aunt Blanche, who calls everyone a doll, for chiming in for the seniors' contingent. My Uncle Richie, for sharing the responsibility and the love. Amy and Diane, the new ladies in the clan, for keeping my father and my brother Chris sane. Shari, Judy, Mindy, Sandy, for helping me remember. Marion, for moving to New York with me and helping me with all my hare-brained business schemes for years and years and for giving me invaluable best-friend advice.

To Mary, for sitting day after day with me in the Bu while I cranked this thing out, and for being a perfect partner in crime. To Beth, for always looking out for me and for inspiring me to open a Matchmaking service. To Jami, for all the brainstorming sessions. To Kenny, for reminding me to be confident even when I wasn't feeling all that confident. To John, for providing me with unbilled legal and relationship advice and a serious roller-coaster ride. To David, for teaching me that there are selfless guys out there. To Bob Dobrish, for giving me a chance in the matrimonial world. To Judge Saxe, for helping me get seven job offers. To Alan, for the quote even if it doesn't make it in and for making me think that the first few chapters were good enough to continue on even though they probably sucked. To Marnie, for being my L.A. constant. To Kendall, for helping me realize how to write this book the "right" way, and for being such a big fan, To Amy, for doing some "posing." To Alissa, for helping me recruit and for helping me figure out how to wear a hat as a skirt. To Marc, for having the forethought to believe in me all those years ago. To Ivy, for being my partner in charity party crime. To Lara, for motivating me to go the Hollywood route, even though you don't even know that you did that. To Hanna, the singer, for teaching me poker. To Nicole, for her press savvy. To Lisa, for the stories. To Kirsten, for our Emmy days. To Nathan, for listening to my obsessing. To Suzi, Cathy, Jim, Susan, Lori, Bret, Renee, Mimi, Judie, Lynn, Liz, well, you all know why.

To Miss Veneski, for making me the teacher's pet and convincing my parents to send me to private school. To Gary, for helping me navigate some pretty murky waters. To Jessica Zeive, for writing all my English papers and then teaching me how to do it. To Kenny Goodman, for having me come to see you on that very Monday on that snowy winter day. To Robbie Brenner, for putting all those chains in motion, and being the unsung hero. To Andrew S., even though I wouldn't call you my best best, I still remember what you did and I always give credit where credit is due. To Jeff Rake, for preserving my sanity and for so much more. To Jed Seidel, for somehow inspiring me to write this, as it is written, right there on the set of *Miss Match*. To my college freshman creative writing teacher, who gave me an A and said I had writing talent. To the Baldwin School for instilling leadership skills in me at a very early age. To Andrea, for giving me a place to stay and a savior when I desperately needed one. To Breck, for the silence. To Sunny, for helping me understand. To Marlene Kaufman, for helping me get through a very tough time. To Lisa Montalik, my dedicated assistant, for organizing me and taking care of me when I couldn't do it.

To Sarah Bernard, who just "got it" right away, to you I owe a ton.

To Jonathan, my lawyer, for giving me stabilizing answers to all my paranoid questions. To Glenn, my manager, for his hard work and endless energy on my behalf. To Kelly, for getting me the photograph that I desperately needed and for helping me to realize that if you have the right people on your team things get taken care of. To Annick Muller, for working 24/7 on my account and listening to a lot of crap. To Ina Trecokias, for rescuing me in the eleventh hour from the wrong publicists, getting me to work with the right ones, and always figuring out a way. To all the Simon & Schuster people, especially Tracey, Victoria, Annie, Mara, Kristen, Kai, and all the others who put all the pieces together.

And last, but certainly not least, to Dan Strone, and his assistant Hilary, for discovering my writing talents and helping me make this whole thing happen, and to Amanda Murray, for being an amazing editor, someone I respect and admire: "We did it and exactly on schedule!"

Xo
Samantha

Win a Dream Date
Through
Samantha's Table

Please go to my website
www.SamanthasTable.com
And click on the

To enter to win a Dream Date of a lifetime
With your very own Match!

About the Author

Samantha Daniels is the founder and president of Samantha's Table, *www.SamanthasTable.com*, one of the foremost Matchmaking services in the nation with offices in New York and Los Angeles. Prior to becoming a Matchmaker, Daniels was a practicing matrimonial attorney in Philadelphia and New York. Daniels is a modern-day Matchmaker who bases her Matchmaking strategy on the premise that many professionals have neither the time nor the inclination to go out on their own to search for their "Mr. or Mrs. Right" and would rather hire an expert to simplify the process. Her clients include CEOs, actors, models, lawyers, doctors, Hollywood producers, investment bankers, company executives, and entrepreneurs—people who have everything going for them in their lives except "The One" with whom to share it all; Daniels helps them find that special someone.

Daniels is a frequently relied upon and quoted dating and relationship expert. She has appeared on the *Today* show, CNBC, and CNN, among many others. She has been featured in the *New York Times*, *People* magazine, *Fortune* magazine, and many other publications. Daniels speaks often on a variety of dating and relationship topics and does dating coaching and makeovers for singles across the country.

Daniels was both the real-life inspiration and producer for the 2003/2004 hit NBC show *Miss Match,* starring Alicia Silverstone. Silverstone's character Kate Fox was inspired by Daniels's life, first as a divorce attorney, and then as a Matchmaker. At the moment, Daniels is working on a sequel to the book and on a relationship reality show that she will host and produce. Daniels is single and resides in Los Angeles and New York City.

For more information on the author or on Samantha's Table, please visit *www.SamanthasTable.com.*